Dire Emotions and Lethal Behaviors

D0220358

Dire Emotions and Lethal Behaviors explores the primary motivational system in human beings. Based on the work of C. G. Jung, James Hillman, Louis Stewart and Silvan Tomkins, Charles Stewart investigates the psychology of the innate affects, with a focus towards the emotional motivation of adolescents and young adults who have killed others, themselves, or both.

It is suggested that social isolation, dissociation of the personality, unbearable emotions, and possession by affects are necessary conditions for both homicide and suicide. Stewart argues that these conditions result from deep-seated emotional psychopathology which involves both the positive affects of the life instinct – Interest and Joy, and the crisis affects – Fear, Anguish, Anger, and Shame/Contempt.

Illustrated throughout with case studies of individuals who have committed homicide, suicide, or both, *Dire Emotions and Lethal Behaviors* aims to discover the emotional motivations for such behaviors so that through education and psychological treatment, such tragic outcomes can be prevented. This book will be of interest to professionals and students in the fields of mental health and criminal justice.

Charles T. Stewart is a Child Psychiatrist in private practice in Berkeley, California. He has spent 25 years working in community mental health where he directed programs, treated patients, and taught psychotherapy to trainees.

Dire Emotions and Lethal Behaviors

Eclipse of the life instinct

Charles T. Stewart

Routledge
Taylor & Francis Group

LONDON AND NEW YORK

First published 2008 by Routledge
27 Church Road, Hove, East Sussex BN3 2FA

Simultaneously published in the USA and Canada
by Routledge
270 Madison Ave, New York, NY 10016

*Routledge is an imprint of the Taylor & Francis Group,
an Informa business*

Typeset in Times by
RefineCatch Limited, Bungay, Suffolk
Printed and bound in Great Britain by
TJ International Ltd, Padstow, Cornwall
Paperback cover design by Lisa Dynan

British Library Cataloguing in Publication Data
A catalogue record for this book is available from the British Library

Library of Congress Cataloging-in-Publication Data
Stewart, Charles T.
    Dire emotions and lethal behaviors : eclipse of the life instinct /
Charles T. Stewart.
        p. ; cm.
    Includes bibliographical references and index.
    ISBN-13: 978-0-415-40877-6 (hardback)
    ISBN-10: 0-415-40877-6 (hardback)
    ISBN-13: 978-0-415-40878-3 (pbk.)
    ISBN-10: 0-415-40878-4 (pbk.)
    1. Emotions in adolescence. 2. Suicide – Psychology. 3. Teenagers –
Suicidal behavior. I. Title.
    [DNLM: 1. Suicide – psychology. 2. Adolescent. 3. Adult. 4. Affect.
5. Homicide – psychology. WM 165 S849d 2007]
    BF724.3.E5S7448 2007
    155.5'124 – dc22   2007004420

ISBN: 978-0-415-40877-6 (hbk)
ISBN: 978-0-415-40878-3 (pbk)

To Louis H. Stewart

Contents

Tables and plates

Tables

Plates

Foreword

John Beebe

It is not always apparent what psychotherapists do. The outset of my own career found me asking those who had been practicing psychotherapy a great deal longer than I what they thought their job as a therapist was supposed to consist of. Although each of the practitioners I approached seemed to find a different thing the most important aspect of their work, everyone agreed that listening had to be a major part of it. I wasn't satisfied. What, I wanted to know, were the therapists listening *to*? The best answer I got to this question came from a colleague who, though only slightly older than I, was much further along in his development as a therapist. Thomas Kirsch was the first Jungian analyst I had gotten to know personally, and it was he who told me, "We listen to emotion."

I have never forgotten this formulation of my life's work. Like most of my colleagues, I have gone on to study *theories* of what generates the affects we are expected to treat. I have long been trying to put together different perspectives into a unified theory of emotion. It's been like standing at the end of an assembly line, while off the conveyor belt arrive various fresh conceptualizations, each succeeding each other in a never-ending tide of clinical fashion: complexes, archetypes, projective and introjective identifications, primitive agonies, unmetabolized "beta" elements, specific configurations of object relations, narcissistic rage, toxic shame, the "dead mother," demonic defenses that serve as self-care systems to protect the spirit of the traumatized person. No matter how many theoretical pieces have come off this assembly line, I have never in my professional career seen a whole model of emotion satisfactorily assembled from them. After forty years of sitting with patients in their psychotherapies, during which in the words of R. D. Laing, "I make myself vulnerable and see what happens," I am usually able to find parts of my patients that fit these theoretical outlines. The parts, however, become significant only when they are seen to belong to a greater whole, which is the great machine of emotion itself, and for that I have never been privileged to see the blueprint. That is why the present book by Charles Stewart is so welcome, and why it has been a pleasure to help him get it together, because in these pages he has managed to establish the emotional ground of the work that a therapist is called to do.

Unlike most psychological writers, Dr Stewart doesn't presume emotion, he foregrounds it. For him, emotion is "first psychology." In the areas of human experience that he has chosen to focus upon throughout these turbulence-filled pages, which chronicle the inner events that lead to lethal outcomes, he is wise to maintain such fidelity to emotion. By casting the light of his empathy onto the passion-strewn roads that lead to a lethal episode, he establishes beyond dispute that every stone along those dark routes can be recognized as an affect-toned complex. His clarity about this affective ground enables us to make emotional sense of the path that leads to violent enactments. With Stewart as guide, a therapist like me can see just where the potentials for lethal breakout lie.

It may surprise some readers to discover that Stewart's is a Jungian book. Dr Stewart is certainly not alone among analytical psychotherapists in recognizing that for all its ability to construct symbolic images of situations to guide patient and therapist, Jungian theory has an even greater potential in enabling the working therapist to engage with the affects at the core of archetypes. He is rare among Jungian writers in being able to demonstrate how far a consistent engagement with affect can take psychological theory. Clinically, his many accounts of destructive outcomes in extreme cases make it clear that emotions are no respecters of pathology. They are equally present for the anxious person afraid of his feelings and the less inhibited individual who is sullenly brooding a vengeful enactment of what is going on inside. Stewart shows us that a working therapist must seek to attend to affect in both kinds of patients. Toward that end, he has produced a clear-sighted book that will enable his colleagues better to identify the emotions that are shaping their clinical responsibilities, and that can also make holding the same emotions a lot less hard for all of us to do.

Preface

On 20 April 1999, two seniors at Columbine High School in Littleton, Colorado, entered their school and shot and killed thirteen people, wounded twenty-three others, and then shot and killed themselves. Alarms went off across our nation – How? Why? – and one of those was mine. (One of the plans the two adolescents considered was to hijack an airplane, fly it to New York City, and crash it into one of its tall buildings!) I quickly learned that many school shootings had taken place before Columbine and others were to occur after it.

I began a research project focused on certain adolescents and young adults who had committed homicide, suicide, or both, because I wanted to find out what emotions motivated these lethal rampages. I believed that a deeper understanding of these tragic events would provide the groundwork for more effective preventive measures and therapeutic interventions.

In the course of my research, I formulated an original method for identifying the necessary conditions for these killings (Chapter 2), which is grounded in my longtime immersion in contemporary affect theory (Introduction and Chapter 1). This novel form of analysis is the most innovative aspect of my book. After formulating this explanatory procedure, I applied it to determine why certain individuals had barely avoided such lethal behaviors (Chapter 3) and why certain other individuals had not (Chapters 4–9).

I came to realize that prevention of these events needs to begin with the complete dismissal of a widely held and dangerous attitude, namely, "It can't happen here." As my study shows, it *does* happen here, because all human beings share a primary motivational system, the innate affects or emotions. This means that, given certain circumstances, these lethal behaviors can happen anytime, anywhere. I went on to assess how we might adapt our psychological treatment methods to meet the particular needs of this potential group of patients (Chapter 10).

Acknowledgements

I want to thank my editors at Routledge, Kate Hawes, Commissioning Editor, Claire Lipscomb, Jane Harris, and Tara Stebnicky, Senior Editorial Assistants, and Kathryn Russel, Senior Production Editor for their invaluable assistance in bringing my book to publication. Their thoughtful responses to each of my questions, from book proposal to book production, helped me move forward during each stage of the publishing process.

I want to thank my professional editor, the Jungian analyst and author, John E. Beebe, MD. For several years, we met regularly to review the manuscript and he consistently directed me toward greater clarity in expression of my ideas and to revisions in style which made the book more readable. He capped his support for my work by agreeing to write its Foreword. (I was not surprised to come across John's lead article, in *The Journal of Analytical Psychology*, 2006, 51(3), 329–56, "Editing as a psychological practice".)

I want to thank my wife Matilda, as well as my friends and colleagues Joan Chodorow, Renee Schwartz, Barbara Rosenkrantz and Nat Marshall, Millicent Dillon, Sylvia and Earl Shorris, Lise and Neal Blumenfeld, Jean Harasemovitch and Gary Truax, Mary Brady and Carey Cole, Robert Tyminski and Gady Heinic, Jill Fischer, Joan and Dick Barr, Wai Chung, and Shirley Armintrout and Moon Eng, whose lively interest in my research helped sustain me as I was writing this book.

Acknowledgements are due to the publishers of the following works for permission to quote extensively: From Jung, C. G., *The Collected Works of C. G. Jung* 1977 Princeton University Press. Reprinted by permission of Princeton University Press. From *Affect Imagery Consciousness* by Silvan S. Tomkins, Copyright 1963, Springer Publishing Company, Inc. Used with permission of Springer Publishing Company, Inc., New York 10036. From *Halfway Heaven: Diary of a Harvard Murder* by Melanie Thernstrom, copyright 1997 by Melanie Thernstrom. Used by permission of Doubleday, a division of Random House, Inc., US. From *Halfway Heaven: Diary of a Harvard Murder* by Melanie Thernstrom, copyright 1997, Doubleday. Used by permission of David Higham Associates Limited, UK. From *The Deadly Innocents*, by Muriel Gardiner, Yale University Press, copyright 1985. Used by permission of Yale University Press. From *Playing and Reality* by D. W. Winnicott, Copyright 1971, Routledge. Used by permission of Taylor & Francis Books UK. Photographic credit is due The Pierpont Morgan Library, New York, for reproduction rights for the William Blake illustrations to Milton's *L'Allegro*, Mirth, the Great Sun, and the Lark. I am, of course, solely responsible for the contents of my book.

Author's note

Sources in the text identifying quotations from the *Collected Works of C. G. Jung* as listed in the bibliography include year of publication by Princeton University Press followed by paragraph and page: (Jung 1968a: 63, 54).

Introduction

> The essential basis of our personality is affectivity. Thought and action are, as it were, only symptoms of affectivity.
>
> C. G. Jung, *The Psychogenesis of Mental Disease*

In this book, I am seeking to identify those conditions within human emotional psychology – one might better say, those *emotional* conditions – that motivate certain individuals to commit homicide, suicide, or both, and that govern the way these individuals express their feelings en route to such drastic choices. Beginning with the Preface and continuing through the Epilogue, readers will find themselves immersed in the psychology of the innate affects, which provide all human beings, both normal and disordered, with their primary motivations and the basis for all later differentiation of their emotions. As author, I have found it important to explain to readers this scaffolding from which the fresco delineating normal and pathological affects that I will be asking them to contemplate has been painted. Like my late elder brother, the Jungian analyst L. H. Stewart, with whom I was fortunate to collaborate for a number of decades, I have long worked on the problem of emotion, and learned from experience the importance of developing a notion of affect as having an archetypal substrate, innate in the human species.

The purpose of my interest in the innate emotions within this book is much more specific, however, than just another opportunity to set forth my particular version of a contemporary theory of affect. It has a more urgent source. The initial stimulus for this book was the occurrence on 20 April 1999 at Columbine High School in Littleton, Colorado, where two senior students, a few weeks shy of graduation, shot and killed thirteen people and wounded twenty-eight others before they killed themselves. The impact of this event was amplified by the fact that throughout the United States, school shootings had been occurring with some regularity and would continue to occur a number of times after this one. (Besides the United States, school attacks have been reported from Germany, France, Scotland, Russia, South Africa, and Yemen.) In the very same year as the event at Columbine the Surgeon

General of the United States published a report indicating that the incidence of suicide by adolescents and young adults was increasing and that it had now become the third leading cause of death in this age group. Unless we decide to write off these tragic occurrences as aberrations, we have to assume that some normal aspect of the emotional development of our young people has become, so to speak, regularly derailed, in ways it has become imperative for us to understand. The prevailing tendency, in trying to explain these events, has been a common-sense search for cause and effect in the psycho-social history of the individuals who have perpetrated these catastrophes, an approach that in my judgment is ill-suited to these types of cases unless it is expanded to address the actual emotions involved. To accommodate their presence at the heart of these tragic situations, I have formulated an explanatory method involving basic affective conditions for violent outcomes, which, I believe, provides us with a more effective instrument for analyzing how such shocking and lethal behaviors actually manage to emerge.

The goal of the present research is to attempt to understand such extreme events as murder and self-murder as arising out of disturbances in the normal development of emotional expression. In subsequent sections of this Introduction, I will acquaint the reader with a view of normal psychological development that focuses upon the innate emotions (specific affects, to which I will refer throughout this work with their first letters capitalized). I will also present in this study evidence for the pivotal significance of a particular dynamic between affects that I refer to as the life instinct. This I define as a dialectic between two key innate affects, Interest and Joy, which as their names imply, are essentially positive affects that set up exciting dynamisms around curiosity/exploration and fantasy/play, which are compelling motivators in all people. I have shown elsewhere that, whereas the more unpleasant to experience "crisis emotions" – Fear, Sadness, Anger, Shame/Contempt – are inevitable responses to the challenges of development, it is the happy dialectic of the life instinct between Interest in taking up the new and Joy in playing with it as it becomes familiar that is the driving force of development itself (C. T. Stewart 2001).

To me that means that when any of the crisis affects inevitably emerge as a consequence of any challenge to the present integrity of the individual, the outcome of such an event with regard to the disposition to go on developing and adapting to the new condition will depend to a considerable degree on the involvement of the creativity and energy of the person's life instinct. Because the life instinct, which is present at birth, directs development into different forms of conceptual and symbolic thought, and these new structures and modalities, once they emerge, become processes of the life instinct, we need to recognize that the life instinct itself is over time susceptible to vicissitudes and deformations in its functioning. And these traumatic and eventually psychopathological disturbances of the life instinct will have a profound effect on the individual's capacity to modulate and integrate the crisis emotions, which will then become too persistent and powerful, greatly hampering further development.

In the first section of this introduction, I will be emphasizing the healthy affective basis of the personality of which the life instinct is such a key part, drawing upon the ideas of C. G. Jung. In the second section, I will review the specific contributions of Jungian analyst Louis H. Stewart to a Jungian theory of emotion, presenting his model of the archetypal affect system. In the third section, I will reprise my own work on the special role played by symbols in channeling the innate affects to motivate the course of development. In the fourth section, I will take the reader beyond a consideration of the role of the affects of the life instinct in human development to consider the evolution of Interest and Joy in the mammalian species generally and contemplate the contributions that their characteristic dynamisms, curiosity/exploration and fantasy/play have made to the nature of the evolutionary process itself.

C. G. Jung: Affectivity as the basis of the personality

> In the long run no conscious will can ever replace the life instinct.
>
> C. G. Jung, *Memories, Dreams, Reflections*

In Late Thoughts, Chapter XII of *Memories, Dreams, Reflections*, C. G. Jung states that as a psychiatrist, a "doctor of the soul," he was always primarily interested in how he could help his patients recover the healthy basis of their personalities, which he found in their spontaneous emotions that for him were expressions of the life instinct. He writes:

> On this complicated base, the ego arises. Throughout life the ego is sustained by this [affective] base. When the base does not function, stasis ensues and then death. Its life and reality are of vital importance. Compared to it, even the external world is secondary, for what does the world matter if the endogenous impulse to grasp and manipulate it is lacking? In the long run no conscious will can ever replace the life instinct. This instinct comes to us from within, as a compulsion or will or command, and if – as has more or less been done since time immemorial – we give it the name of a personal daimon we are at least aptly expressing the psychological situation.
>
> (Jung 1961a: 348–9)

Elsewhere in his writings, Jung uses various terms to refer to this healthy basis of the psyche: among these terms (some of which are better than others at capturing the sense of deep individual purpose that is essential to Jung's notion of personality) are the "collective unconscious," the "ground plan," the "original mind," the "matrix mind," the "hereditary psyche," the "objective psyche", and the "self." Jungian analysts focusing on the development of the psyche in their patients have tended to prefer the "self."

In this view, the primordial self is complicated because it already contains the developmental anlage for the individual psychological life cycle in its totality. Jung said: "If we had complete knowledge of the ground plan lying dormant in an individual from the beginning, his fate would be in large measure predictable" (Jung 1969a: 498, 279). Jung understands the ego as arising when the original instinctual self is forced to negotiate its relations with the environment after birth. But Jung emphasizes that the ability of the ego to arise from the original mind is a consequence of the fact that the hereditary psyche already contains in virtual form the ego-nucleus, which provides the basis for all later unfolding of the higher functions that the ego will need to deploy as it strives to deal with outer and inner reality: the ego-nucleus, in other words, is part of the primordial self: "The self, like the unconscious, is an *a priori* existent out of which the ego evolves. It is, so to speak, an unconscious prefiguration of the ego" (Jung 1970d: 391, 259). This perspective, moreover, applies to the ongoing development and functioning of the adult ego through later differentiations of its consciousness just as much as it does to the child's ego development: "In the conscious life of the adult as well this unconscious, instinctive functioning is continually present and active" (Jung 1970b: 673, 349).

This is the healthy basis that sustains ego-consciousness throughout life; it is the ego's source of psychic energy: "It is the 'nourishing' influence of unconscious contents, which maintain the vitality of consciousness by a continual influx of energy; for consciousness does not produce its energy by itself" (Jung 1969a: 248, 142). The existential reality of Jung's formulation is expressed in the myth of the titan, Antaeus, who in Greek mythology was the son of the sea God Poseidon and Gaea, Mother Earth. Antaeus, a celebrated wrestler (a prototype of the ego), could only keep his giant strength through his contact with his mother, the earth, which we might reasonably interpret as the need of the ego nucleus to maintain a close relationship to the healthy affective basis of the personality. When wrestling Antaeus, the hero Heracles (an image of the more developed ego) recognized the source of his adversary's power and so "lifted him high into the air . . . and, despite the hollow groans of Mother Earth, held him aloft until he died" (Graves 1960: 147).

The paradox for Heracles and other heroic egos is that to move beyond the mother-bound condition of early cognitive and emotional development one must nevertheless stay in contact with her, because in a number of ways she remains the source of the ego's own standpoint. For example, the motivation to move past the mother and into the dangerous world as an independent personality bent upon mastering it originates in the affectivity of the life instinct, which only comes alive in the earliest mother–infant relationship.

Jung understood that "the essential basis of our personality is affectivity," (Jung 1960: 78, 38), which I take to mean that the primary motivational system in humans, the energy behind all agency, is to be found in the innate affects. But these archetypal mechanisms need a human container in which to unfold, and a human other through which they can be mirrored and responded to. That parent is the mother, and the world of affect that she supports is metaphorically, therefore, the mother world, even if a great deal of that world is structured by the Great Mother archetype within the child's own personality, which the actual mother serves to humanize. The ground the Great Mother provides to personality is emotion itself, which gives birth to all the other archetypes: "Emotions have a typical 'pattern' (fear, anger, sorrow, hatred, etc.); that is, they follow an inborn archetype which is universally human and arouses the same ideas and feelings in everyone. These 'patterns' appear as archetypal motifs chiefly in dreams" (Jung 1975: 537). In addition to this complement of innate emotional patternings, humans, like other mammals, carry innately an extremely sensitive mechanism for detecting positive and negative affects in others.

Axiomatic to our discussion of pathological cases in which things did not turn out well is our understanding that when the connection between an ego and its healthy base is severed, affects are no longer available to energize and nourish consciousness, and developmental arrest, stasis, and death can ensue. William James asks us to imagine what life would be without the emotions:

> Conceive yourself, if possible, suddenly stripped of all the emotion with which your world now inspires you, and try to imagine it *as it exists*, purely by itself, without your favorable or unfavorable, hopeful or apprehensive comment. It will be almost impossible for you to realize such a condition of negativity and deadness. No one portion of the universe would then have importance beyond another; and the whole collection of its things and series of its events would be without significance, character, expression, or perspective. Whatever of value, interest, or meaning our respective worlds may appear endued with are thus pure gifts of the spectator's mind.
>
> (James 1902:147)

He contrasts this bleak world with one that is filled with compelling emotions:

> The passion of love is the most familiar and extreme example . . . If it comes, it comes; if it does not come, no process of reasoning can force it. Yet it transforms the value of the creature loved as utterly as the sunrise transforms Mont Blanc from a corpse-like gray to a rosy enchantment; and it sets the whole world to a new tune for the lover and gives a new name to his life. So with fear, with indignation, jealousy, ambition, worship. If they are there, life changes. And whether they shall be there or not depends almost always upon non-logical, often on organic

conditions. And as the excited interest which these passions put into the world is our gift to the world, just so are the passions themselves gifts. Gifts to us, from sources sometimes low and sometimes high; but almost always nonlogical and beyond our control . . . Gifts, either of the flesh or of the spirit; and the spirit bloweth where it listeth; and the world's materials lend their surface passively to all the gifts alike, as the stage-setting receives indifferently whatever alternating colored lights may be shed upon it from the optical apparatus in the gallery.

(ibid.: 147–8)

Therapy, as Jung knew from his work with extremely depressed, dissociated, and psychotic patients, can often feel life-saving when it reconnects someone to the life instinct: "The revival of vital feeling, of this sense of streaming energy, is in general compared to a spring gushing from its source, to the melting of the iron-bound ice of winter in springtime, or the breaking of the long drought by rain" (Jung 1971: 351, 210). Jung quotes a passage from the Rig-Veda that has this theme: "The streams, imploring from afar the favour of the gods, have broken through the midst of the rock with their floods" (ibid.). The poignancy of this passage comes from its recognition that the damming up of libido impoverishes the very world of a person, until a fortunate intervention releases numinous affective energies so that the flow of life can continue.

Because of the developing psyche's propensity to personify the emotions, we often experience the life instinct as a spirit (or what Jung refers to as a daemon in both the ego-guiding and ego-undermining implications of the term):

At the pre-psychological stage, and also in poetic language, which owes its power to its vital primitivity, emotions and affects are often personified as daemons. To be in love is to be "struck by Cupid's arrow," or "Eris has thrown the apple of discord," and so on. When we are "beside ourselves with rage" we are obviously no longer identical with ourselves, but are possessed by a daemon or spirit.

(Jung 1970b: 627, 329)

In this sense the life instinct is a daemon, but for us it is also a dynamic. Modern psychological affect theory persuades us to believe that the life instinct that so energizes the ego is really a dialectical relation between two positive innate affects and their dynamisms. These affects are Interest and Joy. Students of Jung's psychology have already met them indirectly in Jung's writings, where they are discussed in relation to Logos and Eros, the masculine and feminine principles. It was L. H. Stewart who first recognized the importance of these intuitive concepts for an understanding of the life instinct.

Logos and Eros

Jung had considered the concepts Logos and Eros as referring to principles organizing the trend of psychological functioning. Logos was the principle guiding processes of separation and differentiation in the psyche, where Eros was the principle guiding its processes of linking and integration: "Logos is the principle of discrimination, in contrast to Eros, which is the principle of relatedness. Eros brings things together, establishes dynamic relations between things, while the relations which Logos brings about are perhaps analogies or logical conclusions" (Jung 1984: 700). He reiterates: "Eros is an interweaving; Logos is differentiating knowledge, clarifying light. Eros is relatedness, Logos is discrimination and detachment" (Jung 1968b: 60, 41).

L. H. Stewart, however, recognized that Logos is also a form of Interest, and so he often spoke of it as an "openness" that can be applied to any subject matter. Jung paved the way for this view of Logos as Interest when he wrote:

> The Logos element, being a principle of discrimination, not only allows one but forces one to give equal dignity to any object of thinking or observation. It enables a man to devote himself with almost religious concentration to the classification of lice, or to the different qualities of faeces, to put it quite drastically, as well as to counting the stars . . .
>
> (Jung 1984: 700)

Such openness is not only Logos/Interest however. For Joy/Eros also contributes to openness, as humans have and will again love any object in the world.

Jung also asserts that, for optimal functioning, these two principles need to blend with each other: "I may add here that the ideal Logos can only be when it *contains* the Eros; otherwise the Logos is not dynamic at all. A man with only Logos may have a very sharp intellect, but it is nothing but dry rationalism. And Eros without Logos inside never understands, there is nothing but blind relatedness" (ibid.: 701).

Logos and Eros, for Jung, are *forces* that motivate psychological development, and we can find them expressed through the different ego functions that appear in the course of personality maturation:

> Perhaps for the time being we could leave it with the statement that the functions are vehicles for the forces, or influences, or activities, which emanate from those two principles, those two gods, Logos and Eros. And perhaps you can also understand that if there were not principles outside of the functions, one could never hope to detach anything from the unconscious. There must be something which helps one to detach a function, some principle outside which allows one to tear it away from the original lump of the unconscious.
>
> (ibid.: 701)

L. H. Stewart's later view of the life instinct as a "dialectic" between Interest and Joy was clearly influenced by Jung's Logos–Eros theory, but Stewart's formulation found ground not just in an intuitive conception like Jung's, but in a practical understanding of the archetypal affect system, to which we will now turn.

Louis H. Stewart: the archetypal affect system and the life instinct

> Blessed indeed is the child who has playful and curious parents.
>
> Louis H. Stewart, *A Brief Report*

The archetypal affect system

In his theory of the archetypal affect system, L. H. Stewart has provided us with a specification of the structure and dynamics of the healthy emotional basis of the personality. He gave the following definition of his conception: "The archetypal affect system is an inherited regulatory system of the psyche which functions as an unconscious, energic, orienting and apprehension-response system which has evolved to replace an earlier system of programmed instinct" (L. H. Stewart 1987b: 135). Building on Jung's well known conception of an a priori self and Jung's less familiar, but not less seminal, statement that the very basis of psyche is affectivity, and linking these Jungian conceptions to the work of Silvan Tomkins on primary, innate, motivating affects, Stewart identified seven emotions as the archetypal affects of the primal self. He arrived at this pattern of innate affects in the following way. In *The Expression of the Emotions in Man and Animals*, Charles Darwin (1872) identified the following emotions as innate in human beings – Joy, Surprise, Fear, Sadness, Anger, Contempt, and Shame – and demonstrated that each of these affects is not only distinguishable from all the others, but also has a prototypical expressive behavior that is immediately recognized by humans everywhere. There has been but one major addition: Silvan Tomkins (1962, 1963), who views the innate affects as the primary motivational system in humans, identified an innate emotion that Darwin overlooked: Interest.

From the perspective gained through his work as a Jungian analyst, L. H. Stewart considered these affects to be archetypal – that is, emotional factors in the collective unconscious no less important for Jungian theory than the primordial images Jungians were trained to identify. Noting that cross-cultural studies have confirmed the universality of the innate emotions (Ekman 1994; Izard 1994), Stewart felt that it was time for Jungians to pay them at least a commensurate degree of attention, and also that the field of emotion and affect theory generally could benefit from the archetypal perspective, a view shared by Hillman (1992).

Lynd (1958), meanwhile, had demonstrated that contempt and shame are essentially the same emotion, directed, in the case of contempt, toward another and, in the case of shame, toward oneself (shame being, in effect, self-contempt). Stewart adopted these modifications to postulate seven archetypal affects in his system: Interest, Joy, Surprise, Fear, Sadness, Anger, and Shame/Contempt.

The Jungian term used by L. H. Stewart to refer to the evocation of the archetypal affect system is "constellation," which conveys, through the reference to a specific grouping of stars over someone's horizon, the symbolic overarching quality not just of some image of emotional experience, but of the experience itself. L. H. Stewart has described how an archetypal emotion is brought into play:

> The constellation of an archetypal affect occurs as follows. In response to a symbol, that is, the conjunction of a life experience, the stimulus, with an unconscious primal, innate image/idea (or the potential for such an innate image/idea), there ensues a rush of feelings of a specific quality which we label "the emotion." This is accompanied by a specific set of bodily innervations and a typical pattern of behavior.
>
> (L. H. Stewart 1987b: 138)

In our everyday lives, we are familiar with various emotions that move us through the day, but we are less cognizant of the images that accompany such emotions. We find that clinicians attempting to understand their patients' emotional lives have tended to focus more on emotions than on images, so that it still sometimes comes as a surprise to specify an event in the archetypal affect system in terms of the constellation of a primal image. Yet close attention to the phenomenology of how emotion is actually described by clients has led me to feel that Stewart is absolutely right to point to an archetypal image (Table I.1, Column 2) at the heart of any serious emotional event. Since the images are essential unconscious components of the same symbols through which the innate affects are triggered in the first place, they can hardly be left out of any description of the archetypal affect system.

Table I.1 Constellation of the archetypal affects

Life stimulus	Primal image	Innate affect
Novelty	Focused insight	Interest
The familiar	Diffuse illumination	Joy
The unknown	The abyss	Fear
Loss	The void	Sadness
Restriction	Chaos	Anger
Rejection	Alienation	Shame/Contempt
The unexpected	Disorientation	Surprise

The complexity of our relations to distressing archetypal affects is brought before us when we realize that dread emotional states: the Void of Anguish, the Abyss of Terror, the Chaos of Rage, and the Alienation of Shame/Contempt – all of which, when at too great an intensity, can bring us to our knees – function, when at optimal levels, to make a significant contribution to the development of the ego-complex. As L. H. Stewart originally suggested and I have gone on to verify (C. T. Stewart 2001), the patterns of behavior in the mind that are motivated by crisis affects contain the seeds of Jung's ego functions. The expressive dynamisms associated with these same affects create the basis of cultural attitudes (Henderson 1984). There is also an important contribution to ego development made by the affects of the life instinct.

The life instinct

The major components of the life instinct are two positive affects that newborn infants start to evince in the course of meeting the world, Interest and Joy. The stimulus to Interest is *novelty*, and familiarity is achieved through the exploration that follows. As *familiarity* is the life stimulus to Joy, and play creates novelty, the dialectical relation between Interest and Joy is immediately apparent. L. H. Stewart was the first psychologist to recognize this dialectic as the basic dynamic of the life instinct that is the motor of the individuation process:

> At a deeper level of the psyche . . . the motivation appears to arise from the instinct of life itself and its expression in the dialectical intertwining of the archetypal affects of Joy and Interest and their dynamisms Play/Imagination and Curiosity/Exploration. This is the source of psychic energy which can be invested in every aspect of the world and the self. It is the process which underlies individuation – becoming oneself.
> (L. H. Stewart 1990: unpublished manuscript)

Stewart's specific use here of the term "instinct of life" needs a bit of unpacking. All of the seven innate affects that constitute the healthy affective base of the personality sustain the ego-complex throughout life. And, in their motivational capacity, these innate emotions are all sources of psychic energy. Why then does he speak of the life instinct as mainly a product of the positive affects Interest and Joy? One answer is that the energies of the life instinct can be "invested in every aspect of the world and the self," while each of the crisis emotions has a narrower range of application. Another answer is that when Stewart viewed disturbances in psychic development and functioning from the standpoint of what was happening to the person's Interest and Joy, he was able to arrive at a novel formulation: "This suggests a more precise definition of psychopathology as the inability to move freely from play and imagination, on the one hand, to curiosity and constructive memory on the other; that is from the world of emprical reality, and back again" (L. H. Stewart 1987b: 155). Normal ego consciousness lives between the worlds of concept and symbol and moves freely back and forth between them.

L. H. Stewart has also related Interest and Joy, the affective components of the life instinct to terms from ancient philosophy, that served Jung so well as the first principles of all individuation, accounting to a great degree for how humans approach their transactions with the world:

> Play and curiosity are expressions of the instinct of life which make it certain that the young of the mammalian species will enter the world with joi de vivre and divine curiosity. Through these functions they are immediately engaged with life making it inevitable that . . . they will learn in active interaction with their world exactly the kinds of things they will need for a fully functioning adult life. It may be seen, moreover, that these two dynamic components of the instinct of life determine the basis for our human relatedness, Eros, and for our knowledge and understanding, Logos. The dialectic of their relationship must then provide the continual synthesis of relatedness and understanding which is essential for an integrated experience of life.
>
> (L. H. Stewart 1984: 1)

In an extension of this perspective, L. H. Stewart has correlated these two ways of experiencing life with Jung's description, in *Symbols of Transformation*, as "two ways of thinking," that is, directed or cognitive thinking (an elaboration of Interest–curiosity/exploration) and fantasy or symbolic thinking (a development of Joy–fantasy/play).

Complex family emotions

Although we will not be considering the dynamics of complex family emotions (L. H. Stewart 1988, 1992) in the cases we study in this work, it is important to acknowledge their significance:

> Of first importance is the natural division in the human emotions between the universal, innate affects of the collective unconscious, and the "complex family emotions" of the personal and cultural unconscious which are also universally known, yet are not innate. Jealousy and envy are prime examples of these complex family emotions. They assume such importance in the family because they are the shadow aspects of the two polar dynamics of the family; the *desire for love* and the *wish for power*.
>
> (L. H. Stewart 1988: 14)

Stewart indicates that it was Darwin who first made the distinction between innate and complex emotions:

In addition to these innate emotions, Darwin identified a number of other emotions that are well known to people all over the world, but lack a consistent or prototypical form of expression. In contrast to the fundamental, innate emotions, he called these "complex emotions." Complex emotions cannot be "read" by facial expression or bodily action alone, rather we are guided by our general or intuitive knowledge of the situation, the presence of other persons or tell-tale objects. Darwin's list of complex emotions includes jealousy, envy, avarice, revenge, suspicion, deceit, slyness, guilt, vanity, conceit, ambition, pride, humility, etc. (Darwin 1872: 261).

(ibid.: 14)

Stewart emphasizes the role of the family in the differentiation of the complex emotions:

By contrast, the complex emotions such as love, hate, jealousy, envy, greed, admiration, generosity and the like, are constellated simply, and solely, because there is a family. It is only through the relationships between children and parents, and siblings with each other that these complex emotions come into being. At bottom, of course, they must derive from the innate affects. But they ordinarily acquire their unique qualities through mixtures and modulations of the innate affects in relationships with mother, father, and siblings.

(ibid.: 15)

Stewart suggests that it is during infancy, through what I call dialogues with others and one's self framed by Interest and Joy, that the innate affects are transformed into the "archetypal complexes of the collective unconscious" (ibid.: 16).

Complex emotions are blends of the innate affects, jealousy, as well as envy, being prime examples:

Primal Jealousy is about love and suspected betrayal, it is the resultant of a three party relationship. It is constellated when we feel displaced in the affections of another: We are enraged when someone takes what, in our eyes, belongs to us, as witness Cain and Abel. But the emotion is not simply rage, because we are also aware of the fact that we have loved the one who now betrays our love. Classic situations in the family which can lead to a jealousy complex are the birth of a sibling, and the rivalry of a boy with the father over the mother, or the girl's rivalry with the mother over the father, the famous Oedipus and Electra complexes.

(ibid.: 18)

Stewart compares this pattern of Jealousy with that of its polar emotion, Envy:

> But what about envy? In a sense envy is the mirror image of jealousy; it is the emotion we experience when we desire the power that someone else has. It is a two party relationship and has to do with power . . . Envy is about power denied; jealousy about love betrayed. The classic family situation which leads to an envy complex is the relationship of a younger sibling to a older one, as in the famous tales of Hermes and Apollo, of Jacob and Esau, or, the relationship of the son or daughter to the father or mother.
>
> (ibid.: 18)

Stewart goes on to point out that the prominence of jealousy and envy in our lives should not blind us to the existence of the many other complex emotions, as Darwin suggested:

> There are, of course, a myriad number of family emotions as human experience and the pages of a thesaurus show. The many terms express finer and finer differentiations of the basic inherited emotions. The complexity and subtlety of the human emotional capacity is extraordinary. The number of distinct emotions that are traceable to the dynamic relationships of family life however, is also limited. This limited number may have many fine degrees of expression. Most of the emotions we experience are in fact varying degrees of intensity of the innate affects, as well as their many co-minglings.
>
> (L. H. Stewart 1992: 99)

The importance of symbols in bridging the relation between consciousness and the healthy affective basis of the psyche will be our focus in the next section.

Symbols and the healthy affective basis of the personality

> The unconscious can be reached and expressed only by symbols and for this reason the process of individuation can never do without the symbol.
>
> C. G. Jung, *Alchemical Studies*

In the last section, I pointed out that what generates an archetypal affect, what Hillman would call its "efficient cause," is a symbol. The relation between the terms *symbol* and *archetype*, however, requires further clarification.

Jung defines archetypes, which he understands to be essential contents or organizing principles of the collective unconscious, in the following way:

"Archetypes are systems of readiness for action, and at the same time images and emotions" (Jung 1970c: 53, 31). In this definition, Jung does not distinguish between archetypal-image and archetype-as-such. Strictly speaking, as a content of the original mind before experience has had the chance to make its impact upon the psyche, the archetype-as-such is not directly knowable and only reaches consciousness in the form of a symbol or image that seems to carry the stamp of an a priori archetypal pattern that has contributed to its construction. Jolande Jacobi has explained the significance of this distinction between archetypal-image and archetype-as-such for our understanding of the symbol's relation to the archetype it comes to symbolize:

> When the archetype manifests itself in the here and now . . . it can be perceived . . . by the conscious mind. Then we speak of a symbol. This means that every symbol is . . . determined by a nonperceptible "archetype per se." In order to appear as a symbol it must, in other words, have "an archetypal ground plan." But an archetype is not necessarily identical with a symbol. As a structure of indefinable content, as a "system of readiness," "an invisible center of energy," . . . it is . . . a potential symbol, and whenever a general psychic constellation, a suitable situation of consciousness, is present, its "dynamic nucleus" is *ready to actualize itself and manifest itself as a symbol.*
>
> (Jacobi 1959: 74)

Jacobi emphasizes how important it is to use these concepts, archetype and symbol, precisely: "In order to distinguish as sharply as possible between the archetype as such, the quiescent, non-actualized, and hence nonperceptible archetype, and the archetype which has already made its appearance in the area of consciousness . . . concretized [and] transposed into an archetypal image . . . the term 'symbol' will be used . . ." (ibid.: 76, n. 4) I have attempted to follow her usage of these terms archetype, archetypal-image, and symbol. I understand the healthy base of the personality to have both a virtual, innate form – the archetype-as-such – and a realized and actual form – the archetypal-image or symbol.

In dealing with symbols, it is important to remember that their essential characteristic is that they are affect-laden. In dreams, affect-toned complexes are remolded into symbolic forms: "Instead of observable details with clearly discernible features, it is life itself that wells up in emotions and symbolic ideas. In many cases emotion and symbol are actually one and the same thing. There is no intellectual formula capable of representing such a complex phenomenon in a satisfactory way" (Jung 1977: 570, 249). The emotional components of these symbols are the innate affects of the primordial self that we identified in the last section.

Nevertheless, we cannot reduce symbol to affect, because a key aspect of any symbol is a specific image. As Jung tells us, "The symbolic process is an experience *in images and of images . . .*" (Jung 1969a: 82, 38). As I have demonstrated in my previous book, *The Symbolic Impetus*, the developing mind is awash in symbolic images, and an ability to resonate to these images is particularly important when an individual attempts to integrate the innate affects to achieve a more conscious emotional standpoint. Again Jung pointed the way with his own inner work with the images that presented themselves to him in the course of his 1913–17 experiment with direct exploration of the unconscious, as recounted in *Memories, Dreams, Reflections*:

> To the extent that I managed to translate the emotions into images – that is to say, to find the images which were concealed in the emotions – I was inwardly calmed and reassured. Had I left those images hidden in the emotions, I might have been torn to pieces by them. There is a chance that I might have succeeded in splitting them off; but in that case I would inexorably have fallen into a neurosis and so been ultimately destroyed by them anyhow. As a result of my experiment I learned how helpful it can be, from the therapeutic point of view, to find the particular images which lie behind emotions.
>
> (Jung 1961a: 177)

One reason that what Jung says is true is that emotions impel actions, and their primal images give developmental direction to these actions:

> The primordial image is thus a condensation of the living process. It gives a co-ordinating and coherent meaning both to sensuous and to inner perceptions, which at first appear without order or connection, and in this way frees psychic energy from its bondage to sheer uncomprehended perception. At the same time, it links the energies released by the perception of stimuli to a definite meaning, which then guides action along paths corresponding to this meaning. It releases unavailable, dammed-up energy by leading the mind back to nature and canalizing sheer instinct by mental forms.
>
> (Jung 1971: 749, 445)

We need to keep in mind, as we read this passage, that the primal images that most contribute to the sort of affect constellation that Jung is postulating here are quite often uncanny ones, the Unknown, the Void, Chaos, Alienation. We further need to recognize that the states of mind with which they are associated will require imaginative differentiation during development if they are to be truly integrated and not just tolerated.

We are thus justified, I believe, in applying Jung's definition of archetypes to symbols so that they too are "systems of readiness for action, and at the same time images and emotions." Archetypal-image and symbol may be used interchangeably when we are clear about our level of discourse and their common groundedness in affect.

In *The Symbolic Impetus*, I have shown that the symbolic process itself undergoes development, as does the conceptual process, in successive stages, from Infancy through Adolescence. The motor of these developments is the dialectic between Interest and Joy, the twin affects of the life instinct. Returning to Jung's view that the innate ground plan of the personality "can be reached and expressed only by symbols and for this reason the process of individuation can never do without the symbol," I have urged therapists to recognize failures in symbolic development, since these will sooner or later contribute to an inability of ego-consciousness to remain in touch with the healthy affective basis of the personality. When these failures are overcome through symbolic advances, it is often felt in practice to be a "recovery." As Jung said, "The symbol-producing function . . . is an attempt to bring our original mind back to consciousness" (Jung 1977: 591, 257–8). When symbolic development lags, there will also be a lessening of the ability of ego-consciousness to discover the images behind its affects and this will eventually create a split in experience and a serious dissociation of personality. For our understanding of the case studies in this book, in some of which the ego is literally "torn into pieces," we need to be cognizant that when symbolic development is severely compromised such normal components of fantasy as killing of others, oneself, or both may too easily turn into *actual* lethal behaviors.

Our analysis in the next section of the evolutionary roots of emotional response will enable us better to grasp the depth, primacy, and universality of the innate affect system.

The life instinct at play in evolution

> The urge to indulge in rough-and-tumble play is the birthright of the mammalian species . . .
>
> Jaak Panksepp, *Current Directions in Psychological Science* (1998)

Late in his career, when he was summing up his theory of the development of the mind, Jean Piaget (1971) used the term "bursting of instinct" to refer to a revolution that he felt must have taken place as mammals evolved into higher primates. According to his view, the cognitive organization found in lower primates and the non-primate mammals that did not participate in this revolution is based on species-specific programmed relations between expectable stimuli and predictable neuro-psychological responses. Cognition of animals at this evolutionary level occurs without a great deal of mediating activity on the part of the organism: theirs is largely an instinctive response to the environment. The higher primates, on the other hand, have so to speak "burst" this instinctive way of reacting and substituted a set of responses that are highly influenced by stimulus-independent, "autonomous" psychological activities. This means that the higher mammals were capable of evolving a very flexible set of self-regulations. At best, this means that higher mammals have a lot of choice in how they react; at worst, it makes them like Hamlet, a higher primate with four acts between his first perception of a stimulus and his ultimate response to it. But even in the worst case, it is clear that a new kind of cognition has evolved (Piaget 1971: 367). Further, this cognition has its own developmental line.

Although I agree with the main outlines of Piaget's argument, I believe that there is in the evolutionary history of the animals we have become an even earlier "bursting of instinct," which occurred at the time of the first appearance of mammals. The dramatic development then was the emergence of a much more flexible motivational system than the simple stimulus-response arcs that had always governed the lower animals. This new capability was self-motivation, which one can identify even in lower mammals, and consisted of a set of primal affects or emotions that could literally move the animal to respond in new and more complicated ways. This set of primal affects, appearing for the first time within the mammalian species, we refer to in this book as the archetypal affect system. As L. H. Stewart puts it:

> Everything in the evolution of the emotions points to the central position they hold in the development of the most valued human capacities . . . Play, curiosity, consciousness and the symbolic function are all part and parcel of the "flexibility complex" which distinguishes the mammalian species from earlier species. Moreover, all of these functions are directly dependent upon the emotions for their energic and expressive aspects.
>
> (L. H. Stewart 1984: 5)

"Bursting of instinct," then, can be understood in two ways – one is as the rupture of the simple stimulus response arc that governs lower animal behavior, the other is as the dynamic release of the life instinct and crisis affects in startling and unpredictable ways from their containment within previously prescribed patterns.

Paul D. MacLean

The case for this evolutionary advance has been made by Paul D. MacLean, Chief from 1971–1985 of the NIMH Laboratory of Brain Evolution and Behavior, in his conceptualization of the *triune brain*. The triune brain includes an ancient, reptilian brain (known to neuroanatomists as the striatal structure); a more recent, paleomammalian brain (neuroanatomically, the limbic system); and the most recent, neomammalian brain (the neocortex). MacLean links the emergence of affects to the appearance of the limbic system in the evolution of mammals. As he puts it, the key recognition that informed him and other affective neuroscientists was that "factors related to the evolutionary development of the forebrain of early mammals (the paleomammalian brain or so-called 'limbic system') were responsible for the emotional feelings that guide behavior required for self-preservation and the procreation of the species" (MacLean 1993: 67)

Seeking to understand how humans, along with other higher mammals, have managed to evolve emotional expression, MacLean compares the reptilian brain with the paleomammalian brain in terms of several behaviors that characterize the more recently evolved species: "There are three cardinal forms of behavior that characterize the evolutionary transition from reptiles to mammals: (1) nursing, in conjunction with maternal care; (2) audiovocal communication for maintaining maternal-offspring contact [the separation cry]; and (3) play" (ibid.: 74).

It is not hard to see the affective issues of attachment and loss, so critical to many higher species, in the first two behaviors. But the appearance of play requires special emphasis. It implies *motivation* by the positive affect of Joy, which suggests, once again, the presence of a life instinct that, as we have defined it, tends to be an innate motivational force in mammals.

Jaak Panksepp

It is my belief that the contemporary affective neuroscientist Panksepp has encountered in his neuroanatomical studies of the emotional systems the key components of the life instinct, Interest–curiosity/exploration and Joy–fantasy/play. Summing up his conclusions after years of research in which he was able to demonstrate in a variety of animals that emotional and motivational impulses are elaborated by neural networks that course through the limbic system, Panksepp (whose epigraph on play being the birthright of the mammalian species leads off this section) has said "The underlying assumption here is that basic emotional values are homologously organized in all mammalian species" (Panksepp 2000: 37). He further considers it likely that "our basic emotions are still intimately entwined with the generation of distinct and powerful forms of action readiness" (ibid.: 31).

In other words, mammals emote to be motivated to react in certain situations, and both their emotions and their patterns of behavior have an a priori neural substrate, as does, in all probability their ability to recognize situations that call for emotion and action. The parallel to Jung's idea of the archetype being an emotion, pattern of behavior, and image of a situation could not be greater and is part of why I speak in this book of an archetypal affect system. Among the basic emotional systems Panksepp has identified, along with their key brain areas and key neuromodulators, are Seeking/Expectancy and Play/Joy (Panksepp 2002). In these designations, I believe, we can recognize the emotional components of the life instinct.

Frederick Snyder

There was a third emergence, in addition to emotions and play, accompanying the mammalian explosion. That was the appearance of a novel sleep pattern, the REM state. In his evolutionary theory of dreaming, Frederick Snyder, sleep physiologist at NIMH, conceives of the REM State as "a third state of earthly existence ... which is at least as different from sleeping and waking as each is from the other ..." (Snyder 1966: 121). He states that whether the REM state exists at the reptilian level is problematic, but there is no doubt REM sleep is a phenomenon that occurs in all mammals and birds. As Snyder points out, "... the fact ... that this third organismic state is shared by at least the entire class of mammals raises [the] issue ... of the biological or evolutionary origin of dreaming" (ibid.: 122).

Although dreaming is not identical with playing, their content has much in common, and we might infer that the capacity to experience, modulate, and express archetypal fantasy is one of the key system capacities that seems to appear with REM sleep, at the time of the emergence of mammals and birds. L. H. Stewart (1981) has postulated an essential relation between dreams and play in his paper, "The play-dream continuum and the categories of the imagination".

Adolf Portmann

Emotions, play, and dreaming all move mammalian species to develop subjectivity. The Swiss zoologist, Adolf Portmann, for instance, has indicated that play contributes to what biologists designate as "inwardness": "What we call inwardness is the specific mode of existence of living beings. We know it best from our own experience, but find evidence of it in other organisms, though decreasingly as we move farther away from man" (Portmann 1954: 345).

In fact, for Portmann, it is only with mammalian play that the evidence for interiority first becomes compelling: "In the play of the higher animals, we observe a particular variety of the inwardness that we count among the most important characteristics of our own species" (ibid.: 349).

Konrad Lorenz

Konrad Lorenz, on the other hand, emphasizes the importance of the curiosity that accompanies play when he contrasts *specialists*, those organisms with "the wonderfully differentiated patterns of a specially adapted organism," with *non-specialists* who only "possess a few instinctive motor patterns with a small degree of differentiation" (Lorenz 1976: 85). The adaptive capability of the former, more "cosmopolitan" group of animals is manifested in their *versatility*, which includes a certain independence from food-seeking behavior in their exploration and play. As Lorenz says:

This very *independence* of the exploratory learning process from momentary *requirements*, in other words from the *motive of appetite*, is extremely important. Bally (1945) regards it as the major characteristic of *play* that behaviour patterns really belonging in the area of appetitive behaviour are performed "in a field released from tension." As we have seen, the field released from tension – a *sine qua non* for all curiosity behavior just as for play – is an extremely important common feature of the two kinds of behaviour!

(ibid.: 88)

When we turn our attention to the evolutionary theories of Jean Piaget and Stephen J. Gould, exploration and play occupy predominant positions, quite as if they were basic behaviors in their own right.

Jean Piaget

In the Introduction to one of his lesser known works, *Behavior and Evolution*, Jean Piaget (1978) identifies two mechanisms for evolutionary advance. The first is mutation and natural selection. The second involves transformation of the genome through its assimilation of adaptations that have occurred within the phenotype and been referred back through a feedback loop of some kind to the genome itself. (Such modifications of the genome during the life of an organism, when they occur, can be passed down to later organisms, but organisms, still, so far as we know, do not pass down in a Lamarckian way most characteristics that the phenotype has acquired separately from the genome.) Piaget's interest is not so much in updating evolutionary genetics as in taking up the role of an organism's *behavior* in shaping the direction of evolution.

As a broad evolutionary context for his analysis of such phenomena, Piaget draws upon the phenomenon of paedogenesis, which allows an evolutionary line of descent to proceed, counter-intuitively, from immature stages of ancestral organisms: "This shows first of all that juvenile initiatives may be richer than those of static or regressive later stages (a fact which might help to explain why the child so often seems more creative and intelligent than the average adult; the regression, alas, being sometimes already apparent in student years)" (Piaget 1980: 43–4).

Another lesson is to be drawn from paedogenesis:

It effectively shows us that the mainspring of new adaptive variations . . . is not to be found right off in mutant modifications of the genome . . . evolutionary innovations are due not to direct environmental influences, but to the organism's active variation in relation to its environment, and thus to action exerted *on* rather than *by* this environment.

(ibid.: 44)

Piaget argues that a certain amount of behavioral initiative in relation to the environment, accompanied by a measure of feedback to the genome, greatly reduces the necessity of the organism's evolution having to be put on hold pending the appearance of improbable factors of chance. Rather, the successful initiatives incorporated into the genome increase the number of sustainable adaptations:

> Such adaptations embody a "savoir-faire" presupposing a work of accommodation on the part of the organism itself, and not merely an automatic sorting procedure effected from without on the basis of what does or does not foster survival. We are forced to conclude that the ultimate aim of behavior is nothing less than the expansion of the habitable – and, later, of the knowable – environment. This expansion begins as "*exploration*" in animals of various degrees of complexity, but it extends far beyond the needs of immediate utility, and of precautions, until we find it operating on levels where a part is played by simple *curiosity* about objects or events, as well as by the subject's pursuit of every possible activity. There exists, therefore, a practical and cognitive adaptation far more general in nature than adaptation-survival, an adaptation that calls not only for selection's mechanisms of acceptance and rejection but also for structuring of the environment by the organism itself.
>
> (Piaget 1978: xix–xx, emphasis added)

Piaget points out that every animal that has been studied from the beginning of its life is effectively engaged in constructive conduct, meaning that its adaptation is also changing the environment to which it must adapt. Then, he makes the following statement: "In more advanced species, the importance of *play and exploratory* activities proper to childhood is well enough appreciated . . . And such patterns of behavior have their beginnings at least as early as birth" (Piaget 1980: 114–15, emphasis added). From my perspective, Piaget in this passage identifies as behavioral motors of human evolutionary advance, the twin dynamisms of the life instinct: curiosity/exploration and fantasy/play.

Stephen J. Gould

Stephen J. Gould believes that the key to human evolution lies in the continuation of childhood behaviors into juvenile and adult states along with a corollary delay in somatic development. Going even further than Piaget, Gould identifies *flexibility* as the "hallmark of human evolution," a theme he repeats often throughout his meditations on the way organisms evolve. His thesis lends itself to the position that exploration and play contribute immeasurably to evolutionary development. Before Gould, Piaget had used the term "paedogenesis" to account for the way immature forms can contribute to the development of a species, and he intended, in using this word, to suggest that they do so as long as they have the childlike capacity to explore and to play. Gould uses the term "neotony" for the same phenomenon: "Neotony provides evolutionary flexibility as a moderately common pathway to adaptation . . . its occurrence is promoted by the common developmental correlation of delayed maturation with retarded somatic development" (Gould 1977: 345); "A neotonic hypothesis of human origins has been available for some time, but it has been widely ridiculed and ignored. Nonetheless, I believe it is fundamentally correct and that the framework I have established may help to vindicate it" (ibid.: 351).

He elaborates on the basis for his belief:

> Flexibility is the hallmark of human evolution. If humans evolved, as I believe, by neotony . . . then we are, in more than a metaphorical sense, permanent children. (In neotony, rates of development slow down and juvenile stages of ancestors become the adult features of descendants.) Many central features of our anatomy link us with fetal and juvenile stages of primates . . . *In other mammals, exploration, play, and flexibility of behavior are qualities of juveniles, only rarely of adults. We retain not only the anatomical stamp of childhood, but its mental flexibility as well.* The idea that natural selection should have worked for flexibility in human evolution is not an ad hoc notion born in hope, but an implication of neotony as a fundamental process in our evolution. Humans are learning animals.
>
> (Gould 1981: 333, emphasis added)

I would add to this only that humans are not only *learning* animals but *naturally developmental* ones. Both adaptive learning and natural individuation however, draw upon the same dialectic of the twin affects of the life instinct, Interest–exploration and Joy–play, to advance human capacities.

Silvan Tomkins

Silvan Tomkins, the dean of modern theorists of affect and emotion, liked to point out that, in comparison to the drive system, the affect system – because it comes into play across a generality of times, has a marked freedom with respect to the objects toward which it is deployed, and displays a spectrum of intensity – is a much more flexible motivational system than the drives. Tomkins also suggested that natural selection has shaped the human being in such a way as to heighten three distinct classes of affects – affects for the preservation of life, affects for people, and affects for novelty:

> [The human being] is endowed with specific affects to specific releasors so, for example, he fears threats to his life, is excited by new information

and smiles with joy at the smile of one of his own species . . . The human being is equipped with innate affective responses which bias him to want to remain alive and to resist death, to want sexual experiences, to want to experience novelty and to resist boredom, to want to communicate, to be close and in contact with others of his species and to resist the experience of head and face lowered in shame.

(Tomkins 1962: 27)

Tomkins assigns specific primary affects to the elaboration of each of these emotional dispositions. For instance, he identifies Joy, one of his two "positive" affects, with "the affects for people," and Interest, the other positive affect, with the affects that enable us to "embrace novelty." In the same way, he assigns various of the primary crisis affects (e.g. Fear, Anger, Shame/ Contempt) to the solution of other common human affective problems.

Peter C. Reynolds

Peter C. Reynolds, a contemporary anthropologist, believes that the history of human beings as an evolving species within the larger history of evolution consists largely of a progressive elaboration of a *flexibility complex* and identifies play as an intrinsic element in this complex. Conversely:

Play cannot be considered in isolation but must be viewed as part of an adaptive complex involving ontogenetic plasticity in behaviour, infantile dependency, a capacity for learning from previous action, and parental care. I refer to them as the *flexibility complex*. Like other behavioural complexes, such as the advent of terrestrialism [by this term he means the movement that stirred organisms adapted to living in the sea to come up onto the land], it gave to living matter a whole new range of evolutionary options.

(Reynolds 1976: 622)

Thus, flexibility, and its corollary openness, have become watchwords across several disciplines to refer to the fact that the most emotionally differentiated, curious, and playful species we know, humans, owe these very characteristics to the new freedom in evolutionary development that began with the mammalian explosion.

We can conclude this section with the conviction that the innate affective basis of our human personality, the archetypal affect system, out of which emerges the life instinct that so deeply defines our species, profoundly influences both our individual histories and the development of our species.

Chapter I

How the innate affects work

> Emotion, incidentally, is not an activity of the individual but something that happens to him.
>
> C. G. Jung, *Aion*

The neonate is gifted with an innate, organized, adaptive system of emotions which is already differentiated at birth. This system includes the life-enhancing affects, Interest and Joy; the existential affects, Fear, Sadness, Anger, Shame/Contempt, and the reflexive affect, Surprise. Although experience will develop and shape them, these innate affects are the essential basis of all later emotional expression and motivation in humans. It is important, therefore, to understand how these affects are brought into play, how they are structured into complexes, and the ways in which their intensities are registered and gauged. In this way, we will provide a perspective for our examination in subsequent chapters of pathological emotional complexes that have motivated individuals to kill others, themselves, or both.

Constellation of an innate affect

There are three ways that an innate affect can be activated: (a) by contagion from the emotions of others; (b) in response to a life stimulus and primal image working in tandem to become an efficient symbol keyed to evoke the affect; and (c) through continuous constellation of an affect-toned complex already constructed in the course of development.

Contagion from innate affects of others

Contagion is that involuntary process whereby emotion is transmitted from one person to another. Nothing is as infectious as affects: "When you are in a crowd which is moved by an emotion, you cannot fail to be roused by that same emotion ... somebody makes a joke and people laugh, then you laugh too in an idiotic way, simply because you can't refrain from laughing"

(Jung 1977: 318, 138). As realized, contagion is a fundamental consequence of affectivity itself:

> All affects, with the exception of startle, are specific activators of them-selves – the principle of *contagion*. This is true whether the affect is initially a response of the self, or the response of another. By this we mean that the experience of fear is frightening, the experience of distress is distressing, the experience of anger is angering, the experience of shame is shaming, the experience of disgust is disgusting, the experience of joy is joying, the experience of excitement is exciting.
>
> (Tomkins 1962: 296)

It is understandable, then, that Tomkins would accept the perception of someone else's emotional state to be a primary experience for all of us and that he would therefore consider emotional contagion as a fundamental process in the shaping of our social being:

> The characteristic of contagion is critical for the social responsiveness of any organism. It is only when joy of the other activates joy in the self, fear of the other activates fear within, distress of the other activates distress within, anger of the other activates anger within, excitement of the other activates one's own excitement that we may speak of an animal as a social animal.
>
> (ibid.: 296–7)

During a discussion of the therapeutic process, James Hillman arrived at a like conclusion:

> The primary contact with the soul of another person is emotion ... In short, emotion is wholeness and the affective contact is the first level of healing, of making whole. Therefore the patient continually provokes the emotion of the therapist, involving him in anger, in love and desire, in hope and anxiety, in order to get a whole reaction. It is only this wholeness perhaps which works a cure.
>
> (Hillman 1992: 275)

Empirical studies by developmental psychologists have shown that mater-nal expressions of Joy, Anger, and Sadness induce these same affects in their 10-week-old infants, and vice versa (Haviland and Lelwica 1987; Malatesta 1985; Malatesta and Haviland 1982). One factor that affects the individual's susceptibility to contagion is that person's level of ego-consciousness.

The susceptibility to affect contagion is maximal at birth, and may even occur prenatally (Mastropieri and Turkewitz 1999), because the infant's rela-tion to the world is one of "adualism" (Piaget), "primary unitary reality"

(Neumann), or "unconscious identity" (Jung). Each of these terms refers to the fact that at birth the infant does not differentiate between subject and object or inner and outer reality:

> Differentiation is the essence, the *sine qua non* of consciousness. Everything unconscious is undifferentiated, and everything that happens unconsciously proceeds on the basis of non-differentiation – that is to say, there is no determining whether it belongs or does not belong to oneself. It cannot be established *a priori* whether it concerns me, or another, or both. Nor does feeling give us any clues in this respect.
>
> (Jung 1972: 329, 206)

Jung pioneered the exploration of what affective life is like when there is no differentiation of subject and object:

> Unconsciousness means non-differentiation. There is as yet no clearly differentiated ego, only events which may belong to me or to another. It is sufficient that *somebody* should be affected by them. The extraordinary infectiousness of emotional reactions then makes it certain that everybody in the vicinity will involuntarily be affected.
>
> (Jung 1954: 83, 41)

Susceptibility to contagion on the basis of non-differentiation of self and other persists throughout life, although progressive development of the ego-complex enables the individual at least to determine, with ever increasing clarity, the origin of affective events:

> The weaker ego-consciousness is, the less it matters who is affected, and the less the individual is able to guard against it. He could only do that if he could say: you are excited or angry, but I am not, for I am not you. The child is in exactly the same position in the family: he is affected to the same degree and in the same way as the whole group.
>
> (ibid.: 83, 41)

Although later in life contagious affects can be traced to many sources in an individual's social milieu, it is the parents who are the primary source of contagion during early development. Emotional contagion from the parents may be optimal and foster normal development or it may be pathological, that is, fall above or below optimal intensity, and thus hinder emotional development. We need to remember, however, that conscious affects are usually not the primary source of pathogenic contagion: "For all lovers of theory, the essential fact behind all this is that the things that have the most powerful effect upon children do not come from the

conscious state of the parents but from their unconscious background . . ."
(ibid.: 84, 41).

The most general determinants of the effects of experiences of affect contagion include the frequency, intensity, and duration of contagious episodes
as well the effectiveness of parents and infants in modulating and integrating
potentially pathogenic affects into developmental channels.

Affect contagion between patient and therapist is a constant process during
psychological treatment: "The emotions of patients are always slightly contagious, and they are very contagious when the contents which the patient
projects into the analyst are identical with the analyst's own unconscious
contents. Then they both fall into the same dark hole of unconsciousness,
and get into the condition of participation" (Jung 1977: 322, 140).

Constellation in oneself of innate affects

From the perspective of Jungian affect theory, the efficient cause of emotion
is a symbol, which is composed of a conscious component – some life stimulus – and an unconscious prototype for perceiving and reacting to that stimulus in a particular way – an innate primal image (see Introduction, Table I.1,
Rows 1 and 2). In response to the symbol, moreover, there ensues a rush of
feelings of a specific quality, which we label as "the emotion." L. H. Stewart
has described this process as the "constellation" of the emotion:

> This is accompanied by a specific set of bodily innervations and a
> typical pattern of behavior. The consequence is an *abaissement du niveau
> mental* which both heightens and narrows the conscious field to focus
> primarily on the stimulus situation. This is a total reaction which for a
> varying period of time transforms the ego. It leads to a heightened
> awareness within a narrowly focussed consciousness, along with a rapid
> mobilization of energy which takes the form of a stereotyped behavior
> pattern accompanied by typical vocalizations, facial expressions and
> body tensions.
>
> (L. H. Stewart 1987b: 138)

Although activation of the innate affects recurs throughout life, it is those
constellations that occur during infancy that provide the first evidence of the
healthy affective base of the personality:

> The first year of life sees the constellation of all the innate affects in
> the infant's daily experience, no matter how attentive and nurturing the
> mother and father may be. But it is the empathic responsiveness of the
> "good enough" parent that provides the modulating effects which make
> these eruptions of the innate affects bearable and containable. Through
> the infant's own play and curiosity, mirrored by the parent's responsive

playfulness and attentive interest, the innate affects are continually modulated and transformed. These transformed affects make up the "archetypal complexes" of the collective unconscious.

(L. H. Stewart 1988: 15–16)

I have shown that, beginning in infancy, constellation of the innate affects occurs not only in social but also in individual contexts, that is, when the infant is exploring and playing alone (C. T. Stewart 2001).

As in the case of contagion, it is the frequency, intensity, and duration of emotion constellations, as well the effectiveness of parents and infants in modulating and integrating them, that determines whether activated affects contribute to development or distort it.

Constellation in oneself of affect-toned complexes

Another source of the individual's experience of emotion is the activation of already structured affect-toned complexes. (In the next section of this chapter, I will discuss how during development the innate emotions are structuralized into such complexes.) If the size of the affect-toned complex is small, then it will be activated only occasionally at low intensities. If the affect-toned complex is of sufficient magnitude, however, it may become *autonomous* and *continuously* activated: "The persistence of a feeling-toned complex naturally has the same constellating effect on the rest of the psyche as an acute affect" (Jung 1960: 90, 43). Even if an affect-toned complex is of such an intensity that it is continuously activated, in the total psychic economy it may be either normal or pathological. If the former, it can contribute to a robust and creative emotional life. In subsequent chapters, we will give examples of the severe, even lethal consequences that can follow the constellation of structuralized, pathological affect-toned complexes, which are already in a continuous state of excitation.

Structuralization of innate affects

Jung's discovery of the feeling-toned complex ranks as one of the seminal events in modern psychology (see Beebe, Cambray, and Kirsch 2001). The subsequent differentiation and specification of the innate affects by Tomkins, L. H. Stewart, as well as by Carroll Izard, Paul Ekman, Virginia Demos, and other contemporary affect theorists, has only deepened our appreciation of the significant roles affect-toned complexes play in normal developmental and in clinical contexts.

My understanding of how the healthy affective base of the personality is transformed and restructured during life into a system of sometimes pathological complexes is drawn in part from the insights of both C. G. Jung and Silvan Tomkins. Because their views of affect structuralization have not, in my experience, managed to reach the offices of many clinicians, I will review them here.

Jung on affect structuralization

The following statement regarding the process by which primal affects are transformed into affect-toned complexes holds true whether the emotion that follows arises as a consequence of contagion or constellation:

> *Every affective event becomes a complex.* If it does not encounter a related and already existing complex . . . it gradually sinks with decreasing feeling-tone into the latent mass of memories, where it remains until a related impression reproduces it again. But if it encounters an already existing complex, it reinforces it and helps it to gain the upper hand for a while.
>
> (Jung 1960: 140, 67)

The comprehensive reach of this principle makes it clear why the frequency, intensity, and duration of *every* affective event, as well as the success or failure of *each* attempt at modulation and integration of these emotional experiences, are so important in determining the ongoing structuring of any particular affect-toned complex.

As we have said, the frequency of emotion constellation is an important factor in the formation of complexes. Carol Malatesta and Jeannette Haviland (1982) observed mothers in face-to-face play interactions with their 3-month-old infants and found that the expressions of emotions by the babies changed every seven to nine seconds! (Mothers, trying to keep up with their babies, were found to change their facial expressions at an average rate of 8.05 changes per minute.) The *pace* of complex formation is obviously quite rapid.

In addition to their emotional characteristics, affect-toned complexes generate unreflected, involuntary fantasy images: "[Complexes] have a dynamic and formal aspect. Their formal aspect expresses itself, among other things, in fantasy images that are surprisingly alike and can be found practically everywhere at all epochs, as might have been expected" (Jung 1977: 1257, 533). If they are proportionate, such fantasies can contribute to differentiation of the ego; but if they extend beyond these limits they become static and stunt development: "Excessive fantasy activity is always a sign of faulty application of libido to reality. Instead of being used for the best possible adaptation to the actual circumstances, it gets stuck in fantastic applications" (Jung 1961b: 303, 133).

At the center of an affect-toned complex is its nuclear element: "The nuclear element consists of two components: first, a factor determined by experience and causally related to the environment; second, a factor innate in the individual's character and determined by his disposition" (Jung 1970b:

18, 11). This concise definition needs a bit of unpacking to make room for Jung's view of archetypal factors in the construction of personal complexes. The nucleus of a complex is composed of four elements: (1) the individual's apprehension of an environmental life stimulus; (2) the primal image which is unconsciously selected to symbolize the significance of the environmental stimulus; (3) the innate affect that is evoked by the efficient symbol (stimulus + primal image); and (4) the fantasy elaboration of the meaning of the affect through the further activity of the "archetypal imagination" (L. H. Stewart 1992), or what Jung would call creative fantasy. In Jung's association experiments, the environmental components were various stimulus-words. Writing of one such subject whose associations were altered by a crisis affect that the test elicited, he wrote:

> These varying stimulus-words conjured up a certain scene, a particular picture from the mass of memories. The memory consists of a large number of single images; we therefore refer to it as a *complex-image*. The complex of these images is held together by a particular *emotional tone*, that is, by the *affect of terror*, the vibrations of which can continue gently for weeks or months and keep the image of terror fresh and vivid for that length of time.
>
> (Jung 1973a: 891, 418)

In L. H. Stewart's archetypal affect system, the environmental elements are the life stimuli for each of the innate emotions.

The increase in size of an affect-toned complex has two aspects, one qualitative, the other quantitative:

> The nuclear element has a constellating power corresponding to its energic value. It produces a specific constellation of psychic contents, thus giving rise to the complex, which is a constellation of psychic contents dynamically conditioned by the energic value. The resultant constellation, however, is not just an irradiation of the psychic stimulus, but a selection of the stimulated psychic contents which is conditioned by the *quality* of the nuclear element. This selection cannot, of course, be explained in terms of energy, because the energic explanation is quantitative and not qualitative. For a qualitative explanation we must have recourse to the causal view.
>
> (Jung 1970b: 19, 12)

The qualitative element of a complex is a specific nuclear emotion, the "glue" that holds all of its associations together. The number of associations in a complex, which vary greatly from complex to complex, are a quantitative measure of its energic intensity.

Tomkins on affect structuralization

Tomkins (1963) has used the term *affect theory* to refer to his model of the differing organizations of affective experiences, that is, their structuralization:

> At a moment in time an affect theory may exemplify the monopolistic model, the intrusion model, the competition model or the integration model. Across time monopolism has the analog of the snowball model, intrusion has the analog of the iceberg model, competition has the analog of the co-existence model, and integration had the analog of the late bloomer model. These relationships hold for any type of affect theory, whatever the specific affect.
>
> (Tomkins 1963: 302)

Tomkins's choice of the term monopolistic for one model is particularly apt, in my opinion, because it allows us to make both qualitative and quantitative inferences. From a qualitative perspective, a monopolistic model indicates that one particular affect, usually a crisis affect, has attained major dominance over the other emotions. From a quantitative perspective, this monopolistic model indicates that one particular affect has cornered the market, so to speak, of psychic energy.

Monopolistic affect-toned complexes

It is the snowball–monopolistic model which will command our attention as we discuss the emotional life of those individuals discussed in Chapters 4–8: "In the monopolistic theory, shame or self-contempt [or any other crisis affect] dominates the affective life of the individual. Its developmental analog, the snowball model, is the case in which early experience, whether monopolistic or not, continues to snowball and more and more dominates the personality" (ibid.: 302). In this way, the magnitude of an affect-toned complex increases as development proceeds.

Tomkins found that a "monopolistic, snowball theory of humiliation is common only among those human beings whom we ordinarily consider severely neurotic or psychotic" (ibid.: 349). Once a monopolistic complex composed of an innate affect has reached a certain level of magnitude and intensity, it is capable of generating its own further expansion. Tomkins has described this process in the case of humiliation theory:

> The occasion of the critical initiation of a monopolistic humiliation theory may be any event, no matter how trivial, if it occurs when a series of humiliation experiences has been suddenly accelerated to have reached a critical density. Given this critical density, the wildfire of humiliation may be ignited through spontaneous combustion or through any trivial

event which inflames the imagination. This critical density may have been produced either by a massed series of humiliations, by a massed series of memories of past humiliations, or both. In such a case the individual may suddenly encounter humiliation much more often than he can readily assimilate. These in turn act as names for long-forgotten similar experiences which now increase the density of the total set of such experiences until a critical density is reached which is either self-igniting or requires only the slightest discouragement to accelerate into monopolistic humiliation theory.

(ibid.: 404)

This same spontaneous snowballing can apply to any of the crisis affects. Jung has taken a look back from the moment when consciousness is invaded by a complex and discerned its period of incubation (in Tomkins's terms, its snowballing):

The moment of irruption can, however, be very sudden, so that consciousness is instantaneously flooded with extremely strange and apparently quite unsuspected contents ... In reality, the irruption has been preparing for many years, often for half a lifetime, and already in childhood all sorts remarkable signs could have been detected which, in more or less symbolic fashion, hinted at abnormal future developments.

(Jung 1972: 270, 175–6)

Socialization of innate affects

Tomkins considers the way parents socialize their children's innate affectivity as the primary developmental origin of emotional organizations. In "The socialization of affect and the resultant ideo-affective postures which evoke resonance to the ideological polarity" (1995a), Tomkins has presented his general views on the behaviors through which parents socialize in their children excitement, enjoyment, distress, shame and contempt, fear, and anger. In another work, he has also offered a detailed discussion of the punitive socialization of Shame/Contempt (Tomkins 1963: Chapter 21). He wrote: "In order for humiliation to play a monopolistic role in the life of the child, and later to snowball into the life of the adult, the socialization of these affects must amplify and maximize them" (Tomkins 1963: 350). In Chapter 22, "The structure of monopolistic humiliation theory, including the paranoid posture and paranoid schizophrenia", Tomkins builds on the previous chapter: "We are now in a position to examine the nature of a monopolistic, snowball model of humiliation theory, and to examine the over-interpretation and over-avoidance strategies which comprise it ..." (ibid.: 421). This approach will be applied in subsequent chapters to analyze the affect-toned complexes of individuals enacting lethal behaviors.

In L. H. Stewart's formulation of the archetypal affect system, we can discern another model for assessing parental socialization of the innate affects. It is in his formulation of the life stimuli for each of the innate emotions (Table I.1, Column 1) that he has provided us with this guide. For if we assimilate parental actions to the life stimuli for emotion activation, then we have a way of observing how parents are evoking innate affects, with varying frequency, intensity, and duration, in their children. In Chapter 1 of *The Symbolic Impetus*, I applied this method to show that mothers of securely attached infants are best defined by the robustness of their life instinct, that is, their capacity for social exploration and play with their babies. When I turned my attention to mothers of insecurely attached infants, I demonstrated (a) that a correlation could be made between the each of the four main types of insecure attachment and the predominance in the infant of one of the four crisis affects, and (b) that maternal behaviors correlated with the life stimulus for the constellation of the crisis affect for that particular type of insecure attachment. (In these mothers, the life instinct was less active.) In the cases that we will discuss in Chapters 4–8 of this work, we do not at present have the developmental data necessary for making a factual determination of the nature of the socialization of emotion in each of these individuals. Therefore, my comments in this work on socialization of affects in these individuals are to be understood as opinions, speculations, and conjectures.

In the next section, I will take up what ways we have to measure affect-toned complexes quantitatively.

Quantification of innate affects

My discussion of assessment of the quantitative aspects of affect-toned complexes will draw upon the insights of both C. G. Jung and Silvan Tomkins, which I will now review.

Jung on affect quantification

Jung indicated that the applicability of the energic viewpoint to psychology depends exclusively on the question whether a quantitative measurement of psychic energy is possible or not. Here was his answer to this question: "This question can be met with an unconditional affirmative, since our psyche actually possesses an extraordinarily well-developed evaluating system, namely the *system of psychological values*. Values are quantitative estimates of energy" (Jung 1970b: 14, 9).

He focuses first on the question of the subjective value system, the subjective estimates of the single individual. Although their measurement is not absolute and objective, we "can weigh our subjective evaluations against one another and determine their relative strength" (ibid.: 15, 9):

In the case of subjective evaluation, feeling and insight come to our aid immediately, because these are functions which have been developing over long periods of time and have become very finely differentiated. Even the child practices very early the differentiation of his scale of values; he weighs up whether he likes his father or mother better; who comes in second and third place, who is most hated, etc.

(Jung 1970b: 17, 10)

When he turns to the possibility of objective estimates of quantity, Jung considers the feeling-toned complex from this perspective: "The nuclear element is characterized by its feeling-tone, the emphasis resulting from the intensity of affect. This emphasis, expressed in terms of energy, is a value quantity" (ibid.: 19, 11). When the nuclear element is unconscious, as is frequently the case, then an indirect method of evaluation must be used. Jung suggests as an objective estimate of psychological value intensities, the following proposition: "*the constellating power of the nuclear element corresponds to its value intensity, i.e., its energy*" (ibid.: 19, 12). He believes that we can estimate the energic value of this constellating power "(1) from the relative number of constellations effected by the nuclear element; (2) from the relative frequency and intensity of the reactions indicating a disturbance or complex; and (3) from the intensity of the accompanying affects" (ibid.: 20, 12).

Jung also used the phenomenon of *numinosity* to assist him in making quantitative estimates of psychic intensities. This notion was taken from the studies of Rudolf Otto (1923) who referred to the dynamic manifestations of the holy which were not caused by an arbitrary act of will as the *numinosum*. Numinous psychic contents grip, fascinate, seize, and thrill us, as well as impelling us to action. A corollary of the numinosity of a content is its *autonomy*:

It is important to remember that my concept of the archetypes has been frequently misunderstood as denoting inherited ideas or as a kind of philosophical speculation. In reality they belong to the realm of instinctual activity and in that sense they represent inherited patterns of psychic behavior. As such they are invested with certain dynamic qualities which, psychologically speaking, are characterized as "autonomy" and "numinosity."

(Jung 1977: 1273, 541)

In Jung's writings, the autonomy and numinosity of psychic contents is usually linked with the activity of archetypes. As Jung defines archetypes as "systems of readiness for action, and at the same time images and emotions" (Jung 1970c: 53, 31), we are, I believe, fully justified in considering both numinosity and autonomy as attributes of the innate affects and quantitative measures of their energic charge. (In his book, *Emotion*, Hillman (1992) devoted Chapter VII, "Emotion as quantity" to a review of those theories that explain affect by means of quantitative concepts.)

Tomkins on the ratio of positive to negative affects

The ratio of the affects of the life instinct to the crisis affects is a quantitative factor which, as this book will show, is of major importance for our understanding of both optimal and pathological psychological development. At present, we do not have a method for the precise measurement of this ratio, but we can estimate it. Piaget's studies, for instance, of the development of his three children provide observations of how the individual's capacity for robust curiosity/exploration and fantasy/play, the dynamisms of the life instinct, in conjunction with optimal constellation of the crisis affects, contributes to constructive patterns of psychological development (Piaget 1952, 1954, 1962). (See also C. T. Stewart, *The Symbolic Impetus*.)

In his writings on personality theory, which he refers to as script theory, Silvan Tomkins has emphasized the importance of the ratio of positive to negative affects. The key elements in this theory are scenes and scripts:

> The basic units of analysis are *scenes* (What's happening?) and *scripts* (What does this mean? What to do about it?). Scenes are affect-laden episodes, intrapsychic experiences as well as objectively observable events; scripts are developed by co-assembling a "family" of related scenes, a process of "psychological magnification" that depends on our capacities for differentiation and generalization.
>
> (Carlson 1995: 296)

Are scripts, formed by the co-assembly of related scenes, similar to our notion of complexes? Scenes appear to be what, from our perspective, are constellations of the various innate emotions:

> It is extraordinarily improbable that *any* human being will emerge from his/her earliest years innocent of having enacted *exciting scenes*, responded to rapidly and with increased tonus; *enjoyment scenes*, responded to with equally rapid but relaxed responses, with decreased tonus; *surprise scenes*, responded to with the most rapid increase of startle; *terrifying scenes*, responded to with very rapid increased tonus in escape or avoidance; *distressing scenes*, responded to with increased level of tonus; *enraging scenes*, with an even more increased level of tonus; *disgusting scenes*, responded to with literal or analogous distaste responses and expulsion; *dissmelling scenes*, responded to with literal or analogous removing the nose from the offending bad-smelling source; and finally, *shaming (and/or guilt-inducing) scenes* . . .
>
> (Tomkins 1995b: 314)

Tomkins refers to the scripts that predominate when the ratio of positive to negative affects is positive, as affluent scripts: "When the ratio of the density of positive affect over the density of negative affect is very high, the major scripts are scripts of affluence, of positive scenes as ends in themselves" (Tomkins 1991: 195). Scripts of affluence may be contrasted with antitoxic scripts which predominate when a negative ratio indicates an excess of negative affects over positive ones:

> Next are scripts of toxicity, which address scenes of sufficient negative affect density and threat that they must be opposed, or excluded, attenuated, escaped, or avoided, or confronted or defeated, but which by virtue of their density and the disadvantage of a stable ratio of negative over positive affect limit the ability of the individual to permanently rid herself of experienced threat or of experienced negative affect. This is the mirror image of scripts of affluence.
>
> (Tomkins 1995b: 352)

Tomkins elaborates on the challenge faced by the individual in developing an optimal level of positive emotions (Interest and Joy) when experiencing an inverted ratio dominated by negative emotions:

> It would be very difficult to lead a life of predominantly positive affect were one forced to confront massive daily scenes of shame, distress, disgust, terror, dissmell, or rage, no matter how effective the individual was in reducing them daily, only to confront more of the same every day.
>
> (Tomkins 1991: 195)

In Chapter 2, we will discuss the ways in which the life instinct and the crisis affects condition both optimal and pathological psychic development.

Optimal vs. violent expression of affect: a new way to understand the emergence of each of these outcomes

In this chapter we will develop a method of taking emotional conditioning into account as a way to help us answer why certain individuals kill others, themselves, or both, and why most people, even when severely stressed, are able to stop short of enacting such lethal behaviors. We will be using this method in subsequent chapters, so it is important to ask for some forbearance on the part of the reader. Discussions of method are notoriously tedious. Understanding the method of analysis I am proposing is essential, however, for following the interesting cases that will be presented in Chapters 3–9, as well as my proposals for psychological treatment in Chapter 10. The present chapter also forms a vital link in the chain of this book's main argument, that lethal behaviors are not random accidents attendant upon the shadow side of being human, but can be demonstrated to result from long-incubated disturbances in the normal emotional development of the individual.

Conditionalism

The method of accounting for such developments that will be presented here derives from Max Verworn's *conditionalism*. I first encountered "the conditional approach" in the writings of Jung and the Jungian analysts, Jolande Jacobi and James Hillman. In the theoretical introduction that Jung provides to his seminar on the analysis of children's dreams, Jung explicitly turns to conditionalism to account for the psychological phenomena that emerge. He distinguishes this method from the more simple causal method that would be used to explain an outcome in physics:

> In every instance where the phenomena can be isolated for the experiment – i.e., demonstrated – where the same conditions can be presented in other words, strict coordination between cause and effect can be observed. In the case of biological phenomena on the contrary, we are hardly in the position to establish any natural tendency from which certain effects would necessarily result. For here we have to do with such complex material, with such manifold and far-reaching conditions, that a

causal connection could not be said to be the only one. Here the concept of *conditionalism* is far more in place; that is, under conditions which are constituted in such and such a way, such and such consequences can follow. This is an attempt to dissolve strict causality through the interactive effects of the conditions, to widen the one meaning of cause and effect through the multiple meanings of the connection of effects. The causal explanation is not discarded, it is only adapted to the many aspects of the living material.

(Jung 1938–9: 3)

The key idea here is the complexity of biological and psychological systems. Jung pointed out in another place that even the etiological conception favored by modern medicine is no longer a causalism for the illness that emerges but rather a conditionalism, and (somewhat drolly) he agrees with those who have "urged that the word *causality* or *cause* should be expunged from the medical vocabulary and replaced by the term 'conditionalism' " (Jung 1960: 533, 245).

Jung explained the relevance of the conditionalist method to the analysis of dreams as follows: "The dream is a natural psychic phenomenon which is not brought about by a conscious act of will. The method of explanation cannot be a causal one but only a conditional one. The causal explanation is therefore eliminated because we cannot determine a circumstance from which the dream must of necessity arise" (Jung 1936–7: 4).

Later on, in a letter to Medard Boss, Jung referred to archetypes as conditions, again contrasting these with causes: "Archetypes have never been for me pure *causae*, but conditions [*Bedingungen*] . . . It is a condition . . . and as such has a certain *efficacitas causalis*, for only that which has effects has reality . . . On the contrary it has many modalities, expressed in a variety of symbols . . ." (Jung 1975: xl–xli).

In her introductory book, *The Psychology of C. G. Jung*, Jolande Jacobi gives Verworn's own summary of the logic that informs his conditionalist method:

A state or process is determined by the totality of its conditions: (1) similar states or processes are always the expression of similar conditions; dissimilar conditions find their expressions in dissimilar states and processes; (2) a state or process is identical with the totality of its conditions. From this it follows that a state or process is fully known to science if the totality of its conditions is established.

(Jacobi 1973: 83, n. 2)

From this description, Jacobi concluded, in agreement with Jung, that conditionalism is an expanded form of causality. She emphasized the importance given to the individual context by this explanatory method:

The crucial factor is always the situation of the moment with its actual conditions. In the conditionalist view, the same problems, the same causes, have different meanings according to the context; one can no longer ignore situation and circumstances and say that a phenomenon always has the same meaning.

(ibid.: 84)

In a pioneering monograph, James Hillman (1992) analyzed the major theories of emotion in existence up to 1960 using a method that is, at one and the same time, phenomenological, amplificatory, and historical. To arrive at his own integrated perspective on the nature of emotion, Hillman draws upon Aristotle's notion of the Four Causes that can be seen to govern the coming to be of any phenomenon – Material, Efficient, Formal, and Final – and postulates that all of the "causes" come together in creating the conditions for the emergence of emotion.

> . . . the four causes offer the model for a complete theory because they satisfy the demands for *necessary and sufficient* explanation. By being an irreducible number of categories and yet still covering all the possibilities within the field, they provide a special method of types for ordering the various explanatory hypotheses which have been put forward to answer the "why" of emotion.
>
> (Hillman 1992: 20, emphasis added)

He adds that Aristotle's idea has a modern ring: "One is reminded of Verworn's concept of 'conditionalism': 'A state or process is identical with the totality of its conditions' " (ibid.: 20).

Perhaps when we turn to applications of emotion theory to the explanation of such specific behavioral outcomes of affective development as homicide and suicide, we should be cautious about postulating any set of conditions as *sufficient* for the emergence of violence. But in the next section of this chapter, I will present a series of four conditions that I consider *necessary* for emotional development and differentiation, whether normal or pathological.

The necessary conditions for optimal affective adaptation or, conversely, for killing oneself, others, or both

As the title of this section suggests, there is an eerily neutral similarity between the way optimal affective expression develops and the way dysfunctional violent emotional expression comes into being. Both normal and lethal emotions develop out of a series of conditions that makes that emergence possible, and after a certain point, the quality of what emerges is quite predictable as, if not the inevitable, at least the likely consequence of a set of conditions. The explanatory method that I have constructed for my study of the emergence of violent behaviors involves a continuum of developmental possibilities (see Table 2.1) that is intended to encompass both normal (Column 1) and pathological (Column 2) development. The continuum comprises four conditions (Rows 1, 2, 3, 4). All of these conditions, as their descriptions within the table are intended to make us remember, are grounded in the innate affectivity of the psyche.

Jung's term for optimal psychological development at its most complex was individuation. He noted that there are two main arenas for this: "Individuation has two principal aspects: in the first place it is an internal and subjective process of integration, and in the second it is an equally indispensable process of objective relationship. Neither can exist without the other, although sometimes the one and sometimes the other predominates" (Jung 1966: 448, 234).

From my present understanding of the fundamental dynamic of the life instinct, I formulated the first necessary condition for optimal emotional development in my continuum by referring to what Jung had called "objective relationship" as "Emotional Dialogues with Others Framed by Interest and Joy." I named the pathological form as "Social Isolation." I was then able to establish, as a second necessary condition, an analogue to Jung's

Table 2.1 Continuum of necessary conditions

Necessary conditions for normal emotional development and the expected adaptive outcomes	Necessary conditions for killing others, oneself, or both and their maladaptive outcomes
1 Optimal frequency, intensity, and duration of the constellation of positive affects of the life instinct within enabling social contexts. Emotional dialogues with others framed by Interest and Joy	1 Critical decrease, in disordered interpersonal contexts, of frequency, intensity, and duration of constellation of the positive affects of the life instinct: Social isolation
2 Within the individual, optimal frequency, intensity, and duration of constellation of positive affects of the life instinct. Emotional dialogues with one's self framed by Interest and Joy	2 Critical decrease, within the individual, in frequency, intensity, and duration of constellation of the positive affects of the life instinct: Dissociation of the personality
3 Optimal social and individual frequency, intensity, and duration of constellation of crisis affects. Normal suffering	3 Critical social and individual increase in the frequency, intensity, and duration of constellation of crisis affects: Unbearable affect
4 The ability to perceive that an emotional state of consciousness may be problematic. Consciousness of affects	4 The inability to see that there is a problem with an emotionally charged state of consciousness: Possession by affects

"subjective integration," which I called "Emotional Dialogues with One's Self Framed by Interest and Joy." The pathological form of this we named "Dissociation of the Personality."

My selection of "Normal Suffering" as my third necessary condition for optimal development brought the crisis affects into our continuum. The word "normal" acknowledges the central contribution of painful affects in the construction of the ego-complex, and I refer to their pathological potential when we speak of "Unbearable Affect."

Our designation of "Consciousness of Affect" as my fourth necessary condition for optimal development acknowledges the importance of ego-consciousness in regulating all of the innate affects. The alternative to consciousness would be the contrasting pathological state that I refer to as "Possession by Affect."

Necessary conditions for optimum development

It is reasonable to postulate that the innate affects are elements of a whole, in accord with the pioneering work of C. G. Jung on the innate matrix of personality and L. H. Stewart on the archetypal affect system. It follows that the developmental transformations that then occur as the archetypal base is made more human – Jungians speak of these emotional transformations as constellation, structuralization, and differentiation – will be reciprocal processes, in which outer objects, acculturation, and education will affect us as well as be affected by the innate archetypal system. From this perspective, the four necessary conditions for emotional development within the continuum we have been tracing will also form a whole, that is, will undergo developmental transformations and have reciprocal relations with each other as the affect system matures. The form of this developmental reciprocity between the developing emotional self and the conditions affecting its development is perhaps best visualized as an expanding spiral. Even as we examine each of the necessary conditions as a separate process, which it can be, it will be important to keep in mind the whole made by all the conditions and their intrinsic reciprocality.

Emotional dialogues with others framed by Interest and Joy

The novelist Philip Roth has given a vivid picture of how such a spiral of development can continue to proceed throughout a life with his description of the dialogues that his senior peer, Saul Bellow, born in 1915, was having, in his ninth decade, with a small group of friends and colleagues.

> The four of us tried to get up to Vermont for three or four days every summer because Saul demonstrably enjoyed our visits, and we had a good time together staying at a nearby inn. The conversation was sharp

and excited, lots of lucid talk directed mostly at Saul – *whose curiosity was all-embracing and for whom listening was a serious matter* – and much hilarity about the wonders of human mischief, particularly as we evoked them around the dinner table at the Bellows' favorite local restaurant, where *Saul would throw back his head and laugh like a man blissfully delighted with everything.* The older Saul got – and in '98 he was eighty-three and growing frail – the more our annual pilgrimage resembled an act of religious devotion.

(Roth 2005: 72: emphasis added)

In this delightful example, we can certainly experience how the reciprocity of interaction with others is framed by the archetypal affects of Interest and Joy.

The great developmental psychologist Jean Piaget was quite attuned to the role of the interesting and enjoyable in motivating emotional development because he had observed it in his own daughter. Jacqueline Piaget was born in 1925 and, when she was in the seventh month of her first decade, her father recorded the following observation:

At 0;6 (25) J. invented a new sound by putting her tongue between her teeth. It was something like *pfs.* Her mother then made the same sound. J. was delighted and laughed as she repeated it in her turn. Then came a long period of mutual imitation. J. said *pfs,* her mother imitated her, and J., watched her without moving her lips. Then when her mother stopped, J. began again, and so it went on. Later on, after remaining silent for some time, I myself said *pfs.* J. laughed and at once imitated me. There was the same reaction the next day, beginning in the morning (before she had herself spontaneously made the sound in question) and lasting throughout the day.

(Piaget 1962: 19)

Piaget suggests that Jacqueline is using *pfs as a device "to make interesting things last,"* which is correct as far as it goes. *Pfs* is also the content of a charming *tête-à-tête* that Jacqueline is having with her parents, framed by Interest and Joy, which is contagious: all three seem to be enjoying it to the fullest, and furthering the differentiation of these emotions with their reciprocal interest and delight in them. Although the content is naturally at a different level, there is not so great a difference as one might think in the process of using Interest and Joy to foster emotional differentiation, language development, and cultural sophistication in a Nobel-prize winner at 83 and a psychologist's daughter at 6 months. Both the baby in her family and the novelist among colleagues and friends are engaged in emotional dialogues with others framed by Interest and Joy.

One difference, however, is significant, and that is time of life. Jacqueline's conversation with her parents occurred toward the end of a period that

Daniel Stern has studied with great interest. His focus was on caregiver–infant social interactions from three to six months. What he observed and sought to understand were "moments that are almost purely social in nature" (Stern 1977: 2):

> The immediate goal of a face-to-face play interaction is to have fun, to interest and delight and be with one another. During these stretches of purely social play between mother and infant, there are no tasks to be accomplished, no feeding or changing or bathing on the immediate agenda. There is nothing even that has to be taught. In fact, if the task is to teach the infant something, he won't be able to learn what the play experience might hold for him. We are dealing with a human happening, conducted solely with interpersonal "moves," with no other end in mind than to be with and enjoy someone else.
>
> (ibid.: 71)

Once again, we find empirical evidence that exploration and play are basic dynamisms in the development of emotionally significant relationships. Stern describes the specific affective components of such relationship-building moments:

> Beside the gratification of feeding and warmth, these involve the mutual creation of shared pleasure, joy, interest, curiosity, thrills, awe, fright, boredom, laughter, surprise, delight, peaceful moments, silences resolving distress, and many other such elusive phenomena and experiences that make up the stuff of friendship and love.
>
> (ibid.: 71)

This observation confirms our view that social interaction directed by the twin affects of the life instinct, Interest and Joy, is likely to play the strings of all of the other innate affects. Directing his reader's attention to the immediate goal of the interaction, Stern introduced the notion of "optimal range": "The mother tends to adjust the stimulus level of her behavior within the optimal range appropriate for the infant. They both thus tend toward the same goal of maintaining a set of optimal ranges, which correspond to the experiences of mutual interest and delight, of following one another in the dance pattern" (ibid.: 73).

Jung's colleague Erich Neumann also emphasized the lifelong significance of the primal relation between mother and infant: "A child's later personal relationship to its mother, as the basis for every subsequent love relationship and indeed of every human relationship, stands or falls on the primal relationship" (Neumann 1990: 41).

Emotional dialogues with one's self framed by Interest and Joy

There is, however, another dialogue that we need to come to terms with, and that is the dialogue with oneself as another. To see this, we might compare the behavior of Saul Bellow in his ninth decade with that of another of Piaget's children, Laurent, in his third month of life. The observation Philip Roth made of Bellow ". . . Saul would throw back his head and laugh like a man blissfully delighted with everything" (Roth 2005: 72) is typical of the full development of the innate capacity for Interest and Joy. It is the delighted expression of a man who, in psychological terminology, is "subjectively inte-grated," at one with himself and therefore also the world. But it is just as true to say that in this state of self he is fully and objectively interested in what is around him.

In the following observations, made of Laurent Piaget by his father, Laurent is just beginning a "process of subjective integration" that will lead to this kind of interested objectivity. Yet no less than Bellow, he is tuning his affective system by attending to the world: "At 0;2 (21), in the morning, Laurent spontaneously bends his head backward and surveys the end of his bassinet from this position" (Piaget 1952: 70). The fact that Laurent has recognized his ability to look at the world upside down as part of who he is and what he does is expressed by a joyful smile: "Then he smiles, returns to his normal position and then begins again" (ibid.: 70). We can expect, now that Joy has been evoked, that Laurent will now be motivated by this affect too, in addition to just Interest, and begin to play with "self-motion" because it's fun: "As soon as Laurent awakens after the short naps to which he is accustomed, he resumes this activity. At four o'clock in the afternoon after a long sleep he has barely awakened before he bends his head backward and bursts out laughing" (ibid.: 70). These observations of Laurent in his third month, taken as a whole, exemplify, I believe, what Jung means by his "process of subjective integration." I prefer to designate it as an "Emotional Dialogue with One's Self Framed by Interest and Joy." It's precisely such a dialogue that informs Saul Bellow's long project as a novelist.

In 1998, Philip Roth proposed to Bellow that they "do an extensive written interview about his life's work" (Roth 2005: 72). Over the next two and a half years, Bellow sporadically wrote and sent Roth some pages, but not the extended, concentrated work that Roth had contemplated. Roth has now published these pages without any editorial correction or alteration and though the result may lack some of the shape of a finished interview, it is fascinating for a psychologist of affect to survey. In one of his letters to Roth, Bellow describes what I believe is a numinous moment of creative dialogue with himself.

He was in his early thirties and had traveled to Paris in 1948, not so long after its liberation. He was working at that time on a new novel, which was about two men in a hospital room, and the story was stifling him. He was "deep in the dumps" (ibid.: 74). He arrived in Paris in the fall, and it was on a morning in the following spring that "Augie March" was born. It was on his usual walk from his home to his studio when he "made the odd discovery that the streets of Paris were offering [him] some kind of relief" (ibid.: 74): "Parisian gutters are flushed every morning by municipal employees who open the hydrants a bit and let water run along the curbs . . . Well, there was a touch of sun in the water that strangely cheered me . . . But it wasn't so much the water flow as the sunny iridescence" (ibid.: 74).

Then he began a dialogue with himself that started with a question: "Well, why not take a short break and have at least as much freedom of movement as the running water" (ibid.: 74). The first thought that followed was that he must get rid of the hospital novel for it was poisoning his life. It was manifesting a too ready acceptance of his bitterness and misery ("the dumps"), which suggested that in some way he had allowed himself to be bottled up. Then he remembered an early playmate: "I seemed to have gone back to childhood in my thoughts and remembered a pal of mine whose surname was August – a handsome, breezy, freewheeling kid who used to yell out when we were playing checkers, 'I've got a scheme!' " (ibid.: 74). This was the model for Augie March, the character who brought Saul Bellow out of his creative slump. He says to Roth that the decision to write about Augie and his family came on "in a tremendous jump . . . subject and language appeared at the same moment. The language was immediately present – I can't say how it happened, but I was suddenly enriched with words and phrases. The gloom went out of me and I found myself with magical suddenness writing a first paragraph" (ibid.: 75). (He is describing, I believe, a numinous moment of subjective integration and transformation.)

Although he was "too busy and happy to make any diagnoses or look for causes and effects," Bellow did confide that "In writing 'Augie March,' I was trying to do justice to my imagination of things" (ibid.: 75).

After he began to compose "Augie," Bellow noted a newfound relationship to language: "It was enormously exhilarating to take liberties with language. I said what I pleased and I didn't hesitate to generalize wildly and to evoke and dismiss epochs and worlds. For the first time I felt that language was mine to do with as I wished" (ibid.: 75).

Some babies seem to behave just like a novelist who has had a creative breakthrough. When Laurent Piaget was in his third month, his father documented that he became extremely free with his newly-established vocal repertoire: "At 0;2 (7) Laurent babbles in the twilight [says goodbye to the day and hello to the night] and at 0;2 (16) he does this on awakening early in the morning [says goodbye to the night and hello to the day] often for half an hour at a time" (Piaget 1952: 79). Three weeks later, Laurent went even further and began to experiment with intonations to create an expressive or symbolic world of pure sound: "At 0;3 [Laurent] played with his voice, not only through interest in the sound, but for 'functional pleasure,' laughing at his own power" (Piaget 1962: 91).

This is how the capacity for what I refer to as an Emotional Dialogue with One's Self Framed by Interest (02; (7) and 0; 2 (16) and Joy (0;3) really begins. When Laurent joyfully plays with the vocal-auditory schemes he has constructed, he is facilitating the integration of his developing vocal skills into the self, or as we say in common speech, "making them his own." Laurent's laughter marks his self-reflective awareness of this new level of ego-competence. In and through his playful babbling, Laurent is also discovering the *expressive intonations* of each babble. These intonations convey his emotion through the vocal channel. As researchers have observed, "The infant's musical rhythm seems to be closer to folk music and jazz improvization than to the classical Western music" (Papousek and Papousek 1981: 192). Here, too, the affects of Interest and Joy take the lead.

Normal suffering

When we turn our attention from exuberant self assertion through the affects of the life instinct to the emotional basis of human suffering, we come up against the "crisis affects" – Fear, Sadness, Anger, and Shame/Contempt. It is obvious that human suffering is unavoidable, though why this is so is not always so clear. Jung suggested that "Life demands for its completion and fulfilment a balance of joy and sorrow" (Jung 1966: 185, 81). At the very least, it is possible to show that normal suffering is a *necessary condition* for optimal development. L. H. Stewart postulated that the crisis affects actually motivate the development of the various functions of the ego that Jung identified – Intuition, Sensation, Thinking, and Feeling – as well as the traditional cultural attitudes that Joseph Henderson has called attention to – the Religious, the Aesthetic, the Philosophical, and the Social. The relation of specific affects to these orienting parts of the ego complex are shown in Table 2.2.

In *The Symbolic Impetus*, I presented empirical evidence in support of L. H. Stewart's hypothesis by demonstrating the relations, evident in the course of development, between Anger and the ego function Thinking, Shame/Contempt and the ego function Feeling, between Fear and the ego function Intuition and that function's further development in the cultural sphere, the

Table 2.2 Crisis affects, ego functions, and cultural attitudes

1 Innate affect	Fear	Sadness	Anger	Shame/contempt
2 Ego function	Intuition	Sensation	Thinking	Feeling
3 Cultural attitude (highest value)	Religious (the holy)	Aesthetic (the sublime)	Philosophic (the true)	Social (the good)

Religious cultural attitude. L. H. Stewart and I had already analyzed the way in which Piaget's oldest child Jacqueline constructed an aesthetic cultural attitude during the last quarter of her infancy (L. H. Stewart and C. T. Stewart 1981). All these demonstrations indicate that normal suffering, defined as an activation of the crisis affects at an optimal level of intensity, duration, and frequency is necessary for the differentiation of the ego-complex.

This idea helps us make sense of another comment of Saul Bellow's about his creative process. Just before the emergence of "Augie," probably his greatest creative breakthrough, Bellow told Roth his mood was "depressed, downcast, gloomy, in the dumps." After his literary epiphany, the "gloom" went out of him. Commenting, almost half a century later, on the dramatic transformation of his mood, the novelist wrote: "Perhaps I should also add that it has been a lifelong pattern with me to come back to strength from a position of extreme weakness. I had almost been suffocated and then found that I was breathing more deeply than ever" (Roth 2005: 75). I wish to suggest that this lifelong pattern marks a creative process wherein the innate affect Sadness–Anguish, expressed by Bellow in his crisis affect-driven moods, provides the force and energy for the development of the artist's aesthetic cultural attitude, which became the organizing principle of his literary creativity.

The relation of the crisis affects to the development of anyone's ego-complex cannot be understood, however, without reference to the relation between the crisis affects and the affects of the life instinct. In *The Symbolic Impetus*, I demonstrated that the dialectic between these latter affects, Interest–curiosity/exploration and Joy–fantasy/play is the humming motor of development and that, as a consequence of this fact, modulation and integration of the crisis affects is conditioned by this happy dynamic of the life instinct. The life instinct, in other words, provides the motivating dynamic context within which the energies of the crisis affects can be channeled by the ego nucleus to differentiate its characteristic individual functions and attitudes and develop a sense of identity. Within this context, it is, as Tomkins (1995a) has suggested, the *ratio* of the constellation of the affects of the life instinct to that of the crisis affects that is determinative. A considerable density of the crisis affects, in other words what most would consider a stormy, difficult emotional life, can be integrated if the activity of the life instinct is robust. (This is part of what psychotherapists try to ensure in their patients even when there is little prospect of changing their difficult life circumstances.) If the constellation of the life instinct is significantly decreased, however, it may be difficult or impossible for even a lesser density of crisis affects to be channeled into any kind of developmental process. The various ratios between life instinct and crisis affects are, I believe, points on a continuum, and perhaps one day there will be a system for their calculation that enables us to present their consequences. At present, our only method is the study of individual lives.

A level of consciousness in which affects can be objectified

It is an achievement for a person to attain a level of consciousness at which he or she can be aware of powerful emotions without becoming them. During the first year of life, when the innate affects are being constellated for the first time, infants are normally one with their emotions – and they expect everyone and everything else to be one with them too: "Thus, most likely, when a baby is happy or sad, he colors his whole universe with his joy or grief . . ." (Piaget 1927: 200). The effect of this is that the baby perceives affect as something he participates in as part of his primary unity with the world. This level of our first important experiences of affect has implications for the development of human culture as well. Ernst Cassirer, for instance, in his classic four-volume work, *The Philosophy of Symbolic Forms*, holds that mythical consciousness takes origin in the assumption that affective expression is to be found in a fully, particularly animated world that surrounds us:

> Where the "meaning" of the world is still taken as that of pure expression, every phenomenon discloses a definite "character," which is not merely deduced or inferred from it but which belongs to it immediately. It is in itself gloomy or joyful, agitating or soothing, pacifying or terrifying. These determinations are expressive values and factors adhering to the phenomena themselves; they are not merely derived from them indirectly by way of the subjects which we regard as standing behind the phenomenon.
>
> (Cassirer 1957: 72)

Why are the Terrible Twos so terrible? It is because most of the time a now mobile child is still subjectively identified with his or her affective states. To be sure, there are now periods when ego-consciousness has differentiated itself sufficiently from emotion to be able to engage in the process of self-regulation. It is still, however, the parents, as they had been during infancy, who are expected to provide the toddler with affective integration through *their* ability to be conscious of their emotions and those of their child, and to retain their objectivity toward both!

Later, during the preschool period, the child's ego development includes a significant measure of interiorization, so that structures experienced as belonging to the self, such as the ego-ideal and shadow, appear. During this period, much progress is made in the child's ability to self-regulate the emotions. And by the beginning of middle childhood, family and school both can reasonably expect children to be able to modulate their affects at a high level of efficiency. Peer relations now become the arena for the ongoing development of consciousness, and they help considerably with control of affect, for participation in just about any game with other children requires continuous self-regulation. Moral feelings emerge at this stage, and a not unimportant concomitant is the development of the child's will, which also occurs during this period: "Thus, affectivity from seven to twelve years is characterized by the appearance of new moral feelings and, above all, by an organization of will, which culminates in a better integration of the self and a more effective regulation of affective life" (Piaget 1967: 55).

It remains only for the child to collect all these developments and recognize them as a coherent identity. This happens in adolescence. Under optimal circumstances, in spite of its turmoil, the period of adolescence and the consolidation of one's ego-identity will further strengthen the capacity for a more effective regulation of affective life.

By this point, one's affects are also experienced differently: they become objects requiring our attention, not just different faces of our own subjectivity. The next step in development, which occurs often only in the second half of life, is to objectify the affects themselves. Jung was preoccupied throughout most of his career with the problem of how to find an objective standpoint toward the emotions. In the following citation, he vividly contrasts immersion in emotion with its objectivation at a higher level of consciousness:

> What, on a lower level, had led to the wildest conflicts and to panicky outbursts of emotion, from the higher level of personality now looked like a storm in the valley seen from a mountain top. This does not mean that the storm is robbed of its reality, but instead of being in it one is above it. But since, in a psychic sense, we are both valley and mountain, it might seem a vain illusion to deem oneself beyond what is human. One certainly does feel the affect and is shaken and tormented by it, yet at the same time one is aware of a higher consciousness looking on which prevents one from becoming identical with the affect, a consciousness which regards the affect as an object, and can say, "I *know* that I suffer."
>
> (Jung 1968b: 17, 15)

Necessary conditions for killing others, oneself, or both

In this section, we will encounter the urgency of all we have been learning about optimal development, by describing situations in which the very same factors that theorists of emotion have taught us to recognize within normal individuation can be seen to play their roles in creating dysfunctional and potentially lethal personality patterns. I will discuss the necessary conditions for certain individuals to commit homicide, suicide, or both (Table 2.1, Column 2). Each of these conditions identifies a critical divergence from the necessary conditions for optimal emotional development and adaptation (Table 2.1, Column 1). Even as we track this divergence, our focus will continue to be on the vicissitudes of the life instinct, the fate of the crisis affects, and the state of ego-consciousness in the new condition. An overarching fact is that pathological complexes with unusually strong emotional charges fetter the whole individual.

Social isolation

The divergent condition we call *social isolation* refers not so much to a literal physical condition of being isolated in time and space from other people, but a psychic one, that is, feeling isolated even in the presence of others. This is not to be confused with Winnicott's notion of the healthy capacity to play alone in the presence of another. Social isolation in the sense we are using the term here frequently begins with parents' inability to generate a robust mutual activation of the life instinct, specifically exploration and play, when the child is being related to. The capacity for dialogic emotional interaction is, therefore, one that parents normally foster through their interactions with their children. If this capacity is not nurtured, the child's social development cannot proceed normally. Virginia Demos has observed a wide range of mothers' attitudes toward dialoguing with their infants during the first year of life:

> We saw many variations within our sample cases, all the way from one mother placing her baby outside in a carriage so she would not be tempted to play with him; to other mothers who could become playfully engaged when the mood suited them, but otherwise seemed unaware of the infant's readiness to play; to mothers' who thoroughly enjoyed playing with their infants.
>
> (Demos 1989a: 295)

FAILURE TO THRIVE

Five-month-old Billy's isolation from his mother, 17 years old, and his father, 21 years old, began soon after his birth. By the time he was 5 months old he was on the verge of starving to death because of the condition known as nonorganic failure to thrive. When the family was first seen, there "appeared to be no connection between the young parents and their baby" (Shapiro, Fraiberg, and Adelson 1980: 197). Billy was a tense, morose, somber baby who looked "like a little old man." When his therapist visited the family at their home, she found the parents treating Billy "like a newly arrived stranger whom they had to approach cautiously and from a distance" (ibid.: 199). There was no social play or exploration, although Billy was capable of solitary play with his toys: "There were few signs of human attachment. Even though he could creep, Billy rarely approached his mother. He rarely made eye contact with her. He rarely smiled unless mother used gross tactile play. When he fussed, his mother put him to bed with a pacifier and honey" (ibid.: 200). Billy's mother reported with evident sadness that Billy did not enjoy cuddling. It is not hard to see why: Billy's life had been marked from its beginning by a relative absence of "Emotional Dialogues with Others Framed by Interest and Joy." By modeling social exploration and play while the mother watched, the therapist was able to evoke the mother's capacity for such dialogues with her baby and the infant soon began to thrive.

ANACLITIC DEPRESSION

In the course of a longitudinal study of 123 infants who lived in a nursery for the first 12 to 18 months of their lives, Rene Spitz encountered a striking syndrome in 19 of the subjects beginning when they were 6 months old, which he named anaclitic depression. Infants who developed this condition had all been cared for by their mothers up to the time of the onset of the disorder, which always developed according to the following sequence of emotional events:

> *First Month:* The children become weepy, demanding, and tend to cling to the observer when he succeeds in making contact with them.
> *Second Month:* The weeping often changes into wails. Weight loss sets in. There is an arrest of the developmental quotient.
> *Third Month:* The children refuse contact. They lie prone in their cots most of the time, a pathognomonic sign ... Insomnia sets in; loss of weight continues. There is a tendency to contract intercurrent diseases; motor retardation becomes generalized. Inception of facial rigidity ...
> (Spitz 1965: 270–1)

There was one significant factor present in the history all the infants studied that developed the syndrome: "In all of them the mother was removed from the child somewhere between the sixth and eight month for a practically unbroken period of three months, during which the child did not see its mother at all, or at best once a week. This removal took place for unavoidable external reasons" (Spitz 1946b: 319).

The life of the 19 children studied had been, for the first six months, enriched by "Emotional Dialogues with Others Framed by Interest and Joy." When these dialogues were abruptly discontinued, however, each of the infants rapidly developed an anaclitic depression. When their mothers returned within a few months, the infants quickly resumed joyful play and excited exploration.

HOSPITALISM (MARASMUS)

In a separate study of the emotional deficiency diseases of infancy, Spitz conducted a longitudinal study of 91 children in a foundling home. During the first three to four months of their lives, these children were cared for by their mothers and reached normal developmental levels. After three to four months, they were separated from their mothers. Subsequently, they were adequately cared for in every bodily respect, "but as one nurse had to care for eight children officially, and actually up to twelve, they were emotionally starved" (Spitz 1951: 271).

Spitz noted that after separation from their mothers, these children went rapidly through the stages of anaclitic depression. Then, their behavior worsened dramatically:

> Motor retardation became fully evident; the children became completely passive; they lay supine in their cots. They did not achieve the stage of motor control necessary to turn into the prone position. The face became vacuous, eye coordination defective, the expression often imbecile. When motility reappeared after a while, it took the form of spasmus nutans in some of the children; others showed bizarre finger movements reminiscent of decerebrate or athetotic movements.
>
> (Spitz 1965: 278)

These children were not capable of individual exploration or play and typically reacted in the way of this child to social invitations from others:

> When approached she did not lift her shoulders, barely her head, to look at the observer with an expression of profound suffering sometimes seen in sick animals. As soon as the observer started to speak to her or to touch her, she began to weep. This was unlike the usual crying of babies, which is accompanied by a certain amount of unpleasure vocalization, and sometimes screaming. Instead she wept soundlessly, tears running down her face. Speaking to her in soft comforting tones only resulted in more intense weeping, intermingled with moans and sobs, shaking her whole body.
>
> (Ibid.: 270)

(From a therapeutic standpoint, I believe this type of interaction is of great value, for, with the support of the observer, the infant is beginning to integrate the innate affect Anguish–Agony which is at the root of her marasmic condition.) Spitz was able to conduct a follow-up study of these children when the youngest was 2 and the oldest 4 years old. When these children were 15 months old, they had been placed on another ward which had a much more favorable social environment. Psychosocial testing when the children were 2 to 4 was uniformly negative:

> Notwithstanding this improvement in environmental conditions, the process of deterioration had proved to be progressive. It would seem that the developmental imbalance caused by the unfavorable environmental

conditions during the child's first year produces a psychosomatic damage that cannot be repaired by normal measures. Whether or not it can be repaired by therapeutic measures remains to be investigated.

(Spitz 1946a: 115–16).

The earlier, the more severe, and the longer lasting the deficit in "Emotional Dialogues with Others Framed by Interest and Joy," the greater the developmental psychopathology will be.

SOCIAL ISOLATION IN SCHIZOID PATIENTS

As a specialist in therapeutic work with adult patients suffering from schizoid disturbances, Harry Guntrip has repeatedly observed people who experience severe forms of social isolation:

As I have watched the analysis of such patients go deeper and deeper, I have become ever more impressed with their narrowing concentration on one unvarying central feature of their inner experience. Somewhere deep within them they come upon the feeling of being absolutely and utterly alone, or of being about to fall into such a condition. This is not just a feeling of loneliness, of being detached and solitary, of wishing they could make friends more easily and so on. It is something *sui generis*, final, absolute, and when felt in extreme form is accompanied by a sense of horror. Thus a woman of forty reported that for a week she had been vividly seeing an image of herself as a baby sitting in a high chair, with nothing to do [no individual exploration or play], no one to talk to and no one to talk to her [no social exploration or play], in an empty room, and she was just sitting there immobile except that she was slowly shaking her head from side to side.

(Guntrip 1969: 218)

Jung commented on the relation between social isolation and states of terror: "Only when the individual realizes that he cannot help himself in his difficulties, and that nobody else will help him, is he seized by panic, which arouses in him a chaos of emotions and strange thoughts" (Jung 1960: 480, 219).

One of Guntrip's patients revealed the developmental background for her schizoid condition: " 'I'm always dissatisfied. As a child I would cry with boredom at the silly games the children played. It got worse in my teens, terrible boredom, futility, lack of interest. I would look at people and see them interested in things I thought silly. I felt I was different and had more brains. I was thinking deeply about the purpose of life' " (Guntrip 1969: 43). Another patient of Guntrip's described the family atmosphere within which such a "serious" attitude develops: "[Guntrip had suggested] It was as if her mother was always saying, 'Stop laughing or you'll be crying in a minute.' She replied, 'That is exactly what they were always saying to me,' and in fact she rarely laughed and felt it was wrong to enjoy oneself" (ibid.: 169).

It is evident in these observations that such exclusively sober states of mind preclude the warmth of shared expressions of the life instinct: One patient said: "I've no real emotional relations with people. I can help people, but when they stop suffering I'm finished. I can't enter into folks' joys and laughter . . ." (ibid.: 38). Guntrip concluded: "One cannot easily get in touch with the heart of the schizoid person [who] is usually aware of the fact that he does not have the capacity to feel with emotional warmth and liveness of interest that other people show" (ibid.: 90). In his patients, the most common lethal behaviors Guntrip encountered were suicidal thoughts or attempts: "Schizoid suicide is not really a wish for death as such, except in cases where the patient has utterly lost all hope of being understood and helped. Even then there is a deep unconscious secret wish that death should prove to be a pathway to rebirth" (ibid.: 217).

Jung wrote a colleague regarding the importance of relationships for psychological advancement: "The formulation that individuation takes place . . . by way of introspection and meditation, is a bit too positive. To avoid misunderstanding, one would immediately have to add that a responsible relationship of whatever kind is essential, otherwise that particular side of the individual remains undeveloped" (Jung 1973b: 544). I would add that for emotional development to occur within it, the responsible relationship needs to be framed by the innate affects of the life instinct, Interest and Joy.

Dissociation of the personality

The fact that the psyche has a natural tendency to split, which means that "parts of the psyche detach themselves from consciousness to such an extent that they not only appear foreign but lead an autonomous life of their own" (Jung 1970b: 253, 121), has both favorable and unfavorable consequences. On the positive side, psychic splitting means the possibility of change and differentiation: "It allows certain parts of the psychic structure to be singled out so that, by concentration of the will, they can be trained and brought to their maximum development" (ibid.: 255, 122). On the negative side, splitting may progress to such a degree that the normal reciprocal assimilation between psychic structures is interrupted, and then we must speak of dissociation of the personality.

Dissociation, lack of connection and communication between parts of the psyche, occurs in several forms: (a) dissociation between parts of the ego-complex, which results in one-sidedness; (b) dissociation between ego-consciousness and the personal unconscious, which results in neurosis; (c) dissociation between ego-consciousness and the cultural unconscious, which results in writer's block; and (d) dissociation between ego-consciousness and the healthy affective basis of the personality, which is a necessary condition for certain individuals to kill others, themselves, or both. In this section, our focus will be on dissociation (d).

The primary reason for dissociation between consciousness and its healthy affective base in the archetypes of the collective unconscious is the development of pathological, monopolistic complexes, composed of any one of the crisis affects at high intensities – Panic, Agony, Fury, Humiliation/Loathing. A pathological complex acts like a dam, which blocks the transmission of any of the positive affects, such as Interest and Joy, into the ego-complex. The initial effects of such a blockage are a decrease in the quality of life and a diminished capacity to modulate and integrate the crisis affects, which discharge frequently yet seem to be incapable of eliciting more than symptomatic relief for the problem they are signaling. The long term effect is a developmental arrest, assimilation of the ego-complex, and all the deleterious consequences of such a major pathological condition: "As the unconscious contains not only the sources of instinct . . . but also . . . the creative seeds of the future and the roots of all constructive fantasies a separation from the unconscious . . . means nothing less than a separation from the source of life" (Jung 1961b: 761, 330–1).

When dissociation reaches a critical level, the compensatory symbols produced by the unconscious, which are meant to restore the broken bridge, do not reach consciousness. When the compensatory function of innate affects is blocked, the emotions themselves become destructive in character and may be realized literally and concretely. For instance, someone who dreams or even thinks of killing someone may have trouble distinguishing the thought, with all its rich symbolic meanings, from the act, which can only have one literal aim. This tendency of emotion to erupt into narrowly focused violent action is particularly common in situations where the affective charge has become unbearable and the symbolic capacity of the individual is severely impaired.

Dissociation of Interest and Joy may begin early in life when parents meet the child's play and excitement by evoking negative affects. For instance, the child's individual play is seen by adult caretakers as an aberration that needs to be overcome: "The child's play and playfulness are not valued per se. Play may for some time be regarded as neutral in value but eventually it is derogated as childish in contrast to adult norms, which are always to be favored over childish play. In an atmosphere of pervasive gloom or hostility, play may wither for no particular ideological reasons" (Tomkins 1995: 172–3).

The child's individual exploration and excitement may be responded to in a similar fashion.

> There is no unwillingness in many families to inhibit the child's excitement. The motives for such inhibition are varied, and many of them are independent of ideological considerations. Children may be believed to

be primitives or animals who need to have their animal spirits curbed if they are to be admitted to the human race. The belief that children should be seen and not heard is another basis for the inhibition of excitement since excitement in children is so often vocal and loud. Excitement is often curbed out of motives of convenience, since the child's excitement may interfere with the parent's excitement or enjoyment . . . Excitement may be inhibited because the child's loudness and visibility arouse shame in the parent at the reaction of others, or because others may be disturbed by the child's noisy excitement.

(Ibid.: 174)

It is not hard to understand why, subjectively, a child feels crushed and angry and will be reluctant to manifest the life instinct in such family atmospheres.

We know from clinical experience that affects of pathological intensity – for instance the affects aroused by *traumatic overstimulation* – also contribute to psychic dissociation:

As we have already explained at some length, affects have a dissociating (distracting) effect on consciousness, probably because they put a one-sided and excessive emphasis on a particular idea, so that too little attention is left over for investment in other conscious psychic activities. In this way all the more mechanical, more automatic processes are liberated and gradually attain to independence at the cost of consciousness . . .

(Jung 1970a: 339, 181)

The alternative to dissociation might be called "subjective integration," which is the happy result of an open relation between the ego-complex and the collective unconscious, one that is stable enough to allow for the integration of whatever emotions come up and flexible enough to deal with the unexpected.

GABRIELLE

After Gabrielle (Winnicott's patient in *The Piggle*) enters the second year of life, she experiences a brief dissociation of her personality. It turns out that a terrifying "black mummy" has been constellated in her psyche because of anxieties in her mother around the birth of a second child. Gabrielle suffers from the fear that her mother's new ambivalence about being a mother has stirred up, and the fear is located for her in the image of "black mummy," i. e., a depressed, angry mother who might want to kill her children. This black witch has become an inner persecutor who makes Gabrielle fear emotion itself and so cuts her off from the healthy base of her psyche and the life instinct. If she plays at all, she will encounter the horrifying image, and so symbolic experience is no longer safe for her to enter into. As a consequence, she experiences a *curiosity disruption*: "She becomes easily bored and depressed which was not evident before, and is suddenly very conscious of her relationships and especially of her identity" (Winnicott 1977: 6). She also displays a *play disruption*: "She used to play all the time, but since the change occurred she tended to lie in her cot and suck her thumb without playing" (ibid.: 14). Following the very first consultation with Winnicott, however, the dissociation is overcome, i.e., she begins to explore and play again, although Gabrielle's treatment continued for several years, eventually clarifying the anxiety in Gabrielle's mother that had resulted in the constellation of the terrible mother image within Gabrielle's own psyche.

C. G. JUNG

Jung has described the characteristics of a dissociative state, and its cure, in the form of a Renaissance allegory: "You are sterile because, without your knowledge, something like an evil spirit [a complex] has stopped up the source of your fantasy, the fountain of your soul" (Jung 1970e: 191, 161). Jung elaborates on the psychopathology of this condition and points the path to its cure:

> If you will contemplate your lack of fantasy, inspiration and inner aliveness, which you feel as sheer stagnation and a barren wilderness, and impregnate it with *interest* born of alarm at your inner death, then something can take shape in you, for your inner emptiness conceals just as great a fulness if only you will allow it to penetrate into you. If you prove receptive to this "call of the wild," the longing for fulfilment will quicken the sterile wilderness of your soul as rain quickens the dry earth.
>
> (ibid.: 190, 160–1: emphasis added)

He warns of the danger inherent in rejecting the hoped-for response from the depths: "Unless the content given you by the unconscious is acknowledged, its compensatory effect is not only nullified, but actually changes into its opposite, as it then tries to realize itself literally and concretely" (ibid.: 192, 162). Once again we sense the relation between personality dissociation and lethal enactments: the capacity to hold feelings symbolically is lost. With this loss, there is also an affective consequence: Joy and Interest, the affects of the life instinct, are dulled, so that the acting out has a grim, dutiful quality, devoid of real satisfaction. If the unconscious content is acknowledged, however, and its symbolic significance can be realized, the flow of the life instinct will resume: "If attention is directed to the unconscious, the unconscious will yield up its contents, and these in turn will fructify the conscious like a fountain of living water" (ibid.: 193, 163).

Unbearable affect

It is the same pathological complexes that contribute to social isolation and dissociation that act to flood consciousness with crisis affects of great intensity:

> Every emotional state produces an alteration of consciousness which Janet called *abaissement du niveau mental*; that is to say there is a certain narrowing of consciousness and a corresponding strengthening of the unconscious which, particularly in the case of strong affects, is noticeable even to the layman. The tone of the unconscious is heightened, thereby creating a gradient for the unconscious to flow towards the conscious. The conscious then comes under the influence of unconscious instinctual impulses [crisis affects] and contents.
>
> (Jung 1970b: 856, 446)

It is in discussions of unbearable affect that we regularly find a linkage between a state of mind and suicide or homicide. This was the correlation emphasized by the ancient Greek tragedians. In the *Ajax* of Sophocles (440 BC), the protagonist is driven to suicide by intolerable and unremitting Humiliation. Two thousand years later, in *The Anatomy of Melancholy*, Robert Burton (1621) noted that suicide, homicide, and psychosis are all conditioned by unbearable affect. Of the melancholic's turn to suicide, he wrote: "In such sort doth the torture and extremity of his misery torment him, that he can take no pleasure in his life, but is in a manner enforced to offer violence unto himself, to be freed from his present insufferable pains" (Burton 1621: 368). He notes that the burden of insufferable affect may lead as well to either homicide or psychosis, because long-term intolerable suffering puts judgment itself at risk:

> This only led me to add that in some cases those hard censures of such as offer violence to their own persons, or in some desperate fit to others, which sometimes they do, by stabbing, slashing, & c. are to be mitigated, as in such as are mad, beside themselves for the time, or found to have been long melancholy, and that in extremity; they know not what they do, deprived of reason, judgement, all, as a ship that is void of a pilot must needs impinge upon the next rock or sands, and suffer shipwreck.
>
> (Burton 1621: 373)

On the basis of his psychotherapy experiences with psychotic patients, Elvin Semrad concluded, 300 years after Burton's book was published, that unbearable, intensified affect was the ultimate and *sufficient* condition behind the emergence of lethal behaviors even when other conditions, such as psychosis, seemed to be present:

Ego decompensations, regression, and clinical psychosis occur in periods of *intensification of affect*. Unpleasure increases and re-evokes the impossible pain of early relationship. The burden is intensified by the liberation of previously unbearable affects. Once integration with reality crumbles and our patient enters a disorganized and exhausting state of psychophysiological pain which he never could bear, other solutions are demanded. All that is open to the vulnerable ego at this point is *suicide, murder, or psychosis*. Suicide or murder are the extreme expressions of affect (principally rage) translated into action; psychosis is the partially rationalized containment of the affect, the sacrifice of reality to preserve life.

(Semrad 1969: 23, emphasis added)

Even though many observers, including myself, would probably say that unbearable affect is only one of the necessary conditions for a lethal outcome, it must be noted that many others who have looked into the psychodynamic origins of extreme behavior have come to similar conclusions as Semrad's.

Building upon Federn's statement that psychopathic behavior may be a defense against psychosis, Suzanne Reichard and Carl Tillman have formulated the way unbearable affect is managed by pathological expression ". . . the common factor in murder and suicide, on the one hand, and schizophrenia on the other, is that they represent alternative manifestations of unassuagable anger; hence discharge of rage through any *one* of these channels may lessen or obviate the likelihood of its expression through the others" (Reichard and Tillman 1950: 150). In support of this observation, these authors present not only their own clinical experiences but also those of other psychiatrists.

After years of the psychological study of suicide, Edwin Shneidman concluded, with stark simplicity, that mental pain, or what he called "psychache," was the final common pathway for every variety of this lethal behavior:

Suicide is caused by psychache . . . Psychache refers to the hurt, anguish, soreness, aching, psychological *pain* in the psyche, the mind. It is intrinsically psychological – the pain of excessively felt shame, or guilt, or humiliation, or loneliness, or fear, or angst, or dread of growing old or of dying badly, or whatever. When it occurs, its reality is introspectively undeniable. Suicide occurs when the psychache is deemed by that person to be unbearable. This means that suicide also has to do with different individual *thresholds* for enduring psychological pain . . .

(Shneidman 1993: 51)

The self-psychologist Heinz Kohut pointed, more specifically, to unbearable humiliation as the prime motive for suicide, particularly in mature individuals, who feel they cannot any longer rationalize, on the basis of inexperience, the catastrophes that have marred their adaptation: "The suicides of this period [late middle age] are not the expression of a punitive superego, but [represent] a remedial act – the wish to wipe out the unbearable sense of mortification and nameless shame imposed by the ultimate recognition of a failure of all-encompassing magnitude" (Kohut 1977: 241).

A link between unbearable affect, whether shame or other kinds of psychic pain, and homicide has also been postulated by Hurvich, Beveniste, Howard, and Coonerty (1993), Heide (1993), Crimmins (1993), and Williams (1995). The connections between unbearable affect and suicide have been elaborated by Hussain and Vandiver (1984), Slaby and Garfinkel (1994), Kienhorst, De Wilde, Diekstra, and Wolters (1995), Williams (1995), Lester (1997), Fowler, Hilsenroth, and Piers (2001), and Maltsberger (2004), and between unbearable affect and psychosis by Garfield (1995), Williams (1995), and Armstrong-Perman (1995).

JUSTIN

Justin was 4 years old when he attempted to hang himself. He was described as having experienced significant distress for the past two years, the underlying factor being the marital discord of his parents. Just before he attempted to hang himself, Justin's pain had become so unbearable that he said he wanted to "go away." For weeks before his attempt, he said again and again, "I am going to see God" (Leenaars, Lester, and Heim 1996: 146).

JOHNNY

Focusing on the unusual problem of children's suicide, Donald McGuire once recounted a case presented to him by Eileen McGrath, Director of Shell Hope, Brooklyn, New York. Johnny was the sixth of eight children and by the time he was 5 years old he felt alienated from his family: "Every time he wanted to say something he was hushed up or told 'go out and play', or 'do the dishes', or 'set the table', or 'help do the dishes' " (McGuire 1982: 15). One day when he was sitting alone and doodling, a brother heard him say to himself: "Nobody wants me around here, I'm going to kill myself . . . I know what I'll do, I'll wait on the corner, and when the car goes by real fast, I'll run in front of it . . . nobody will miss me anyway" (ibid.: 15). About three weeks later he did run in front of a truck which struck him head on: "And everybody was saying, 'What a terrible accident' " (ibid.: 16). Although Johnny died four days after he was hit by the truck, he was conscious long enough to have a conversation with Ms McGrath that she recaps as follows:

> So, when I was called to speak with him, he said – he could just about speak, but he said very softly – he couldn't move, he looked around to see if anybody was around, and he said, "It wasn't an accident." I said,

"What are you telling me, John? Did you really want to kill yourself? Did you really want to get hurt that bad and die?" He said, "I figured, if I died, it wouldn't hurt as much as if I lived."

(ibid.: 16)

This account tells us that this child's emotional life had become unbearable by the time he was 5 years old.

LEONARD

Leonard was 9 years old when he was admitted to a child psychiatry inpatient unit after he had jumped out of a second-floor window at a residential treatment center. He had been at the center nearly two months before this lethal behavior emerged, but he had had difficulty in adjusting there, and had run away on several occasions:

> Leonard's mother noticed that he had been withdrawn and depressed since he entered the residential center. She said, "He phones me saying he is going crazy. He told me that he does not belong. He wishes he were not born and wants to die. He told me he often thinks about killing himself and will do it unless he is returned home. He told me that he is not afraid to die."
>
> (Pfeffer 1986: 6–7)

Leonard's leap from the window had occurred after he got into a fight with two boys at the center and was sent to his room to calm down: instead, "he was so enraged, unhappy, and confused that he decided to kill himself by jumping out the second floor window" (ibid.: 7). This example underscores the need for affect management in the potential suicide.

THE VOID

A. Wilson described a troubled adolescent patient who found it necessary to organize her entire life so as to avoid her particular experience of insufferable agony: "[This] suicidal borderline adolescent patient lived in dread of an emotional state [that] she called 'the awful nothing.' Her suicidal gestures were often preceded by its onset, and she choreographed her daily life in order to avoid this feeling" (Wilson 1986: 237–8).

Is the "awful nothing" an expression of the primal image, the Void?

CESARE PAVESE

Cesare Pavese, the internationally known Italian novelist, was born in 1908 and died in 1950, when he committed suicide. Shneidman studied his life and devoted considerable energy to an analysis of his diary. In his article on Pavese, Shneidman noted an entry from 30 October 1940, *ten years* before the novelist's death:

> Suffering is a fierce, bestial thing, commonplace, uncalled for, natural as air. It is intangible; no one can grasp it or fight against it; it dwells in time – is the same thing as time; if it comes in fits and starts, that is only to leave the sufferer more defenseless during the moments that follow, those long moments when one relives the last bout of torture and waits for the next . . . The moment comes when he screams needlessly, just to break the flow of time, to feel that *something* is happening, that the endless spell of bestial suffering is for an instant broken, even though that makes it worse.
>
> (Shneidman 1993: 125–6)

It is important to recognize, however, that a state of unbearable emotion is frequently accompanied by a partial eclipse of ego-consciousness, which Jung, adopting a term first used by Pierre Janet, liked to refer to as *abaissement du niveau mental* (lowering of the mental level):

> *Abaissement du niveau mental* can be the result of physical and mental fatigue, bodily illness, violent emotions, and shock, of which the last has a particularly deleterious effect on one's self-assurance. The *abaissement* always has a restrictive influence on the personality as a whole. It reduces one's self-confidence and the spirit of enterprise, and, as a result of increasing egocentricity, narrows the mental horizon. In the end it may lead to the development of an essentially negative personality, which means that a falsification of the original personality has supervened.
>
> (Jung 1969a: 214, 120)

Although such a lowering of the level of consciousness may have a positive outcome, for instance giving spontaneous cerebration, such as a dream image, a chance to emerge, under negative conditions, the *abaissement* merely prepares the way for an invasion from the unconscious, which usually causes a decrease in the adaptive capacity of the ego and a diminution of affective resilience, and thus gives rise to inadequate emotional reactions. From this perspective, the *abaissement* is simply the prelude to full-blown *possession* by an affect-toned complex.

Possession by affect

Possession may be defined as the capture of the ego-personality by an affect-toned complex. Jung was preoccupied throughout most of his career with this phenomenon, which led him to seek an objective standpoint toward the emotions. In his paper, "Psychological Types," (Jung 1971: 883–914, 510–23), Jung discusses what he refers to as problematic and unproblematic states of consciousness, seeking an explanation for the difference in the attitude toward the affects involved. A problematic state of consciousness develops "when a doubt arises as to whether affects – including our own affects – offer a satisfactory basis for psychological judgments" (ibid.: 886, 511):

> For this purpose the primitive, unpsychological man, who regards affects in himself and others as the only essential criterion, must develop a problematical state of consciousness in which other factors besides affects are recognized as valid. In this problematical state a paradoxical judgment can be formed: "I am this affect" and "this affect is not me." This antithesis expresses a splitting of the ego, or rather, a splitting of the psychic material that constitutes the ego. By recognizing myself as much in my affect as in something else that is not my affect, I differentiate an affective factor from other psychic factors, and in so doing I bring the affect down from its original heights of unlimited power into its proper place in the hierarchy of psychic functions. Only when a man has performed this operation on himself, and has distinguished between the various psychic factors in himself, is he in a position to look around for other criteria in his psychological judgment of others, instead of merely falling back on affect. Only in this way is a really objective psychological judgment possible.
>
> (ibid.: 887, 512)

Jung found an ideal model of the kind of objectifation of the affect that he was talking about here in the system of Kundalini yoga. This system portrays a progressive movement of consciousness, conceived as a serpent – the Kundalini – rising and bringing its energy out of "lower" centers of drive and affect up into "higher" centers of emotional objectivity, to release the capacity for reflection and compassion that is the mature potential of the human affective apparatus. In the system of Kundalini, the potential to objectify one's affects and therefore not become so possessed by them is symbolized as the move of the Kundalini serpent from the *manipura* chakra (just at the level of the diaphragm) up to the *anahata* chakra (at the level of the heart):

> But mandala psychology begins when one succeeds in forming the magic circle against the fires of passion; then one is in *anahata*. When you are able to say, "I am in a state of passion," you create the magic circle that saves you from the destructive effects of identifying with your emotion. For being merely emotional, without realizing what kind of condition you are in, destroys you as human being, you simply function as an animal.
>
> (Jung 1976: 349)

He also contrasts the *anahata* and *manipura* states, which he considers, respectively, as problematic and unproblematic:

> In *manipura* one has an entirely emotional psychology, with no idea of objectivity, one has not disposition of one's emotions, one is the emotion. In *anahata* one can say, I am in a bad mood, but in *manipura* one *is* a bad mood, nothing but a bad mood, so that one cannot even admit it. If one says to a person in that condition, You are in a bad mood, he replies, No, I am *not!* But in *anahata* he says, By jove, you are right, and that is the higher condition, that is the difference between *manipura* and *anahata*.
>
> (ibid.: 406)

The fact that the transition from an unproblematic (*manipura*) to a problematic (*anahata*) state of consciousness is a developmental process provides us with a normal context for our consideration of possession by affect.

The overwhelming of ego-consciousness by a monopolistic affect-toned complex is both a process and an event:

> The moment of irruption can, however, be very sudden, so that consciousness is instantaneously flooded with extremely strange and apparently quite unsuspected contents . . . In reality, the irruption has been preparing for many years, often for half a lifetime, and already in childhood all sorts remarkable signs could have been detected which, in more or less symbolic fashion, hinted at abnormal future developments.
>
> (Jung 1972: 270, 175–6)

Possession as a process, its preparation over many years, consists of: (a) a gradual increase in the magnitude of a pathological complex due to the presence of a toxic environment that constellates the emotion in question continuously; (b) a progressive decrease in the individual's capacity for affect modulation and integration; and (c) the individual's increasing complex-sensitivity, so that minor stimuli have an exaggerated constellating effect.

As the complex grows in intensity and autonomy, it begins to affect the functioning of the ego-complex:

> As a rule there is a marked unconsciousness of any complexes, and this naturally guarantees them all the more freedom. In such cases their powers of assimilation become especially pronounced, since unconsciousness helps the complex to assimilate even the ego, the result being a momentary and unconscious alteration of personality known as identification with the complex. In the Middle Ages it went by another name: it

was called possession . . . When someone is in the throes of a violent emotion we exclaim: "What's got into him today?"

(Jung 1970b: 204, 98)

Experience of assimilation of the ego is one of the more unpleasant events in an individual's life:

It is understandable that people should get panicky, or that they eventu-ally become demoralized under a chronic strain, or despair of their hopes and expectations. It is also understandable that their will-power weakens and their self-control becomes slack and begins to lose its grip upon circumstances, moods, and thoughts. It is quite consistent with such a state of mind if some particularly unruly parts of the patient's psyche then acquire a certain degree of autonomy.

(Jung 1960: 521, 240)

Jung's description of assimilation of the ego of a 42-year-old psychotic patient shows the ultimate power of the monopolistic complex: "We can conclude that . . . she [a dressmaker] is under the sway of the complex, she speaks, acts, and dreams nothing but what the complex suggests to her" (ibid.: 208, 109).

Jung's notion of arrested development helps explain the relation between the process of preparing for possession and the moment of possession itself:

I seriously consider the possibility of so-called "arrested development," in which a more than normal amount of primitive psychology remains intact and does not become adapted to modern conditions. It is natural that under such conditions a considerable part of the psyche should not catch up with the normal progress of consciousness. In the course of years the distance between the unconscious and the conscious mind increases and produces a conflict – latent at first. But when a special effort at adaptation is needed, and when consciousness should draw upon its unconscious instinctive resources, the conflict becomes manifest; the hitherto latent primitive mind suddenly bursts forth with contents that are too incomprehensible and too strange for assimilation to be possible. Indeed, such a moment marks the beginning of the psychosis in a great number of cases.

(ibid.: 529, 244)

The actual moment of possession is often experienced by the individual as a tremendous invasion from the unconscious:

You experience sometimes what you call "pathological" emotions, and there you observe most peculiar contents coming through an emotion:

thoughts you have never thought before, sometimes terrible thoughts and fantasies . . . Those are invading fragments of the unconscious, and if you take a fully developed pathological emotion it is really a state of *eclipse* of consciousness when people are raving mad for a while and do perfectly crazy things. That is an invasion.

(Jung 1977: 65, 32)

It is often not only possible to identify the moment possession takes over the individual but also a precipitating event just before this occurrence, the "last straw," the "drop that falls into a vessel already full," or the "spark that ignites the powder." Not infrequently, it is an adaptive challenge that the person cannot meet that "breaks the camels back": ". . . the moment of the outbreak of neurosis is not just a matter of chance; as a rule it is most critical. It is usually *the moment when a new psychological adjustment, that is, a new adaptation, is demanded*" (Jung 1961b: 563, 246).

After having formulated this continuum, I came across the following statement by Jung in which, I believe, he has identified three of the above necessary conditions at levels somewhere between those in Table 2.1, Columns 1 and 2:

The prime situation of distress consists either in a withdrawal of the favourable gods [a critical decrease in positive affects] and the emergence of harmful ones [a critical increase in crisis affects], or the alienation of the gods [critical decrease in subjective integration] by man's negligence, folly, or sacrilege . . .

(Jung 1970e: 604, 419)

The emotional development of two children during infancy

To illustrate how both optimum and compromised development emerge from different socialization experiences operating upon the same basic affective system, we will now review the early emotional individuation of two different infants, Donna and Teddy, whose histories have been detailed in the literature. Donna demonstrates how optimum development proceeds, while Teddy show how severely compromised development emerges. We have organized the information collected about their emotional development according to what degree various necessary conditions for either functional or dysfunctional outcomes were actually present in each infant's history.

Social exploration and play are robust for Donna and beyond the scope of Teddy's agency (see Table 2.3).

Individual exploration and play are rich and varied for Donna and virtually non-existent for Teddy (see Table 2.4).

Table 2.3 Emotional dialogues with others framed by Interest and Joy vs. Social isolation

Donna	Donna's family seemed to maximize opportunities for experiencing intense, prolonged positive affects in both "I" and "we" contexts, and to facilitate an easy and smooth flow between these contexts (Demos and Kaplan 1986: 216). Throughout her 4th, 5th, and 6th months, Donna and her mother "enjoyed prolonged social exchanges, with a range of intensities of the affect interest and enjoyment . . ." (ibid.: 199)
Teddy	He became less active in his approaches to people and was not responsive to them (Provence and Lipton 1962: 131). The usually playful responses of social games such as peek-a-boo, pat-a-cake, so-big, etc. . . . were not seen (ibid.: 134)

Table 2.4 Emotional dialogues with one's self framed by Interest and Joy vs. Dissociation of the personality

Donna	By the end of the first year Donna is full of enthusiasm and zest and is the initiator of complex plans which she carries out with persistence and flexibility (Demos and Kaplan 1986: 216). [When] Donna was 10½ to 12 months old, we note her intense excitement and joy at the out door baby pool. She is able to generate novelty and play happily for as long as 15 minutes (ibid.: 200)
Teddy	His investment in toys diminished markedly and he had little or no interest in solving the problems appropriate to babies of his age. He was lacking in playfulness, and the impoverishment of his affective expressions was increasingly apparent. He lacked animation and had an energyless look (Provence and Lipton 1962: 131). The light in Teddy has gone out: "If you crank his motor, you can get him to go a little; he can't start on his own" (ibid.: 135)

Table 2.5 Normal suffering vs. Unbearable affect

Donna	By the end of the first year, Donna's distress, anger, and fear were decreasing in intensity and duration, thereby allowing her to remain in distressing, and frustrating, or frightening situations and to develop new solutions (Demos and Kaplan 1986: 214–15)
Teddy	He was solemn-faced, unsmiling, and miserable looking (Provence and Lipton 1962: 131). Outstanding were his soberness and his forlorn appearance . . . (ibid.: 134)

Crisis affects are modulated and integrated by Donna and are approaching the unbearable for Teddy (see Table 2.5).

Donna is able to deploy her affects for her own development, while Teddy chronically appears to be in the grip of negative affects (see Table 2.6).

Table 2.6 Consciousness of affect vs. possession by affect

Donna	Donna's mother was able to tolerate Donna's expressions of moderately intense negative affects and saw her role primarily as a facilitator of Donna's efforts to cope with her own affects and their causes, intervening only when Donna was unable to manage the situation. This stance by the mother and the family in general allowed Donna to develop her affective competence by exercising and strengthening her capacities to modulate her negative affective states and to communicate her needs with affective signals (Demos and Kaplan 1986: 215)
Teddy	When he was unhappy he now had a cry that sounded neither demanding nor angry – just miserable – and it was usually accompanied by his beginning to rock (Provence and Lipton 1962: 134)

We conclude with an observation of Donna, at 54 weeks, in which she rides an upsurge in the life instinct to reach new physical and emotional high points:

As Donna plays with blocks, etc. [her sister] Maggie climbs up and down the ladder chair. Donna crawls over, fusses when Maggie refuses to relinquish the ladder chair, but then joins her brother as they pound on the peg bench. She quickly resumes her interest in the ladder chair, crawls over with vocalized protest noises, and mother intervenes by offering her a box of toys. She sings as she takes out each car from this box and plays contentedly for several minutes as mother is engaged with her in this activity. She eventually crawls back to the ladder chair when Maggie leaves – only to find her sister quickly running back to claim possession. Mother intervenes and tells Maggie that the baby wants to climb. Donna tries to mount the stairs but is simply unable to master the task. Mother helps her and Donna looks triumphant when she reaches the top. She climbs down again with mother's help. In an apparent effort to make the task easier, mother puts the chair on its side. Donna protests immediately and vigorously. Mother quickly perceives that Donna has a clearly defined goal, is being persistent, and assertive, and returns the chair to its original position. Donna now persists as she works very hard – and successfully – to get up the first step. She vocalizes happily as she then continues her climb to the top. This process is now repeated over and over again – and each time she gets to the top, she "sings" her song of victory. She is now completely absorbed in the climbing. Mother retreats into the background so that she remains immediately available if Donna should be in any danger – but is not restrictive or intrusive. Donna's interest remains high as she learns how to manage her legs and she becomes an adept climber. Her joy at her success is palpable and is

demonstrated by her happy smiles and her singing. She gradually introduces variations on the theme of climbing as she ascends from the opposite side.

(Demos and Kaplan 1986: 200–1)

In this affectively telling vignette, Donna's mother has made four key
interventions. The first time Donna finds her access to the ladder chair
blocked by her sister, she becomes mildly angry, that is she "fusses," but then
adapts to the situation by joining her brother in his play. When she makes a
second effort to take the ladder chair, her mother intervenes for the first time,
to minimize her daughter's frustration, by encouraging Donna's engagement
in individual play and offering herself as a participant observer. When her
sister leaves the chair ladder, but quickly returns when Donna tries to take
possession, their mother intervenes a second time. She firmly tells Maggie
that it is now Donna's turn. When Donna's first attempt to climb the stairs is
unsuccessful, mother intervenes for the third time, but this time she errs.
Donna objects to her attempt to make the task easier and mother quickly
corrects her mistake. Mother now makes her fourth intervention, which is to
retreat into the background and provide Donna with the opportunity to
explore and play alone "in the presence of another." This is an opportunity
that Donna exploits to the fullest!

Caveat

In Chapters 4–9, I will present case studies of individuals who have killed
others, themselves, or both, which will show that at the time of these killings
each of the them was experiencing the four conditions that I have postulated
in this chapter are necessary determinants of such lethal enactments. I will
also offer my conjectures about (a) the presence in these individuals of
unconscious, pathological affect-toned complexes and (b) how these structuralized complexes contributed to the development of the four necessary
conditions in each of the subjects. Although these conclusions are based on
incomplete evidence, particularly a lack of sufficient developmental data and
a lack of sufficient dream material in which personified complexes could be
identified, as well as the absence of any clinical contact with the individuals
on my part, my inferences are grounded in my long study of the psychology
of the innate emotions and the complexes that are structuralized by their
activations. This caveat will provide a valid context for my conjectures, and
those of the readers, for: "Experience without speculation leads nowhere"
(Jung 1960: 423, 193).

Chapter 3

Death and rebirth of the life instinct

In this chapter, we will begin by discussing the "case" of someone who is actually a fictional character, Silas Marner, who suffered a severe dissociation of his personality at the age of 24 that persisted for the next fifteen years, upon which the split in his consciousness miraculously healed. Next, we consider a developmental crisis in the life of an actual historical figure, John Stuart Mill, whose severe inner trial began when he was 20 and took three years to resolve. Then, we analyze the clinical case of Mrs A., who at age 33 was treated for a recurrent postpartum psychosis that persisted for five months after the birth of her third child and led to a creative reintegration of her personality. Finally, we review William Styron's account of his own agonizing melancholia, which began in his sixtieth year and lasted eight months before its resolution.

Silas Marner: "and a little child shall lead them"

We meet Silas Marner, the protagonist of George Eliot's 19th century novel of the same name, when he is 24 years old and living in the English village of Lantern Yard. By that age, the young man's life was already "filled with the movement, the mental activity, and the close fellowship, which, in that day as in this, marked the life of an artisan [a linen-weaver who had been] early incorporated in a narrow religious sect" (Eliot 1861: 5). Early in the novel, he suffers a stunning betrayal by a friend, William, who convinces the members of the sect that Silas is guilty of the theft of church money, a crime that in fact William himself has committed. As a consequence, his fiancée rejects the ostracized linen-weaver and marries William instead. After a month of "stunned and benumbing unbelief" at this double abandonment, Silas moves to the rural community of Raveloe "with that despair in his soul – that shaken trust in God and man, which is little short of madness for a loving nature" (ibid.: 10).

Coincident with the move to Raveloe, and as a result of the unceasing affective storm that he has taken with him, Marner's personality becomes markedly contracted. To manage the unbearable affect, he proceeds to lead a life of *social isolation*: "He sought no man or woman, save for the purposes of his calling, or in order to supply himself with the necessaries . . ." (ibid.: 4). The ongoing process of genuinely integrating a subjectivity is also arrested, and Silas's inner life, almost as a consequence of his will to ward it off, is markedly diminished. All of his memories of his life in Lantern Yard are obliterated: "Minds that have been unhinged from their old faith and love have perhaps sought this Lethean influence of exile in which the past becomes dreamy because its symbols have all vanished, and even the present is too dreamy because it is linked with no memories" (ibid.: 12). This profound narrowing of Silas's personality lasts for the first fifteen years that he lives in Raveloe, and during this period he works sixteen hours a day at his craft of linen-weaving "like the spider, from pure impulse, without reflection" (ibid.: 14). His humanity, in other words, has all but vanished, and his life has been reduced to that of a spinning insect. His zest for living, the gift of the life instinct, has vanished.

From a depth psychological perspective, it is reasonable to assume that Silas has experienced a severe *dissociation of his personality*. Jung quoted Janet on this point: "[The] dissociative power which belongs to emotion is never more clearly displayed than in its effect on the memory. This dissociation can act on memories as they are produced, and constitute continuous amnesia; it can also act suddenly on a group of memories already formed" (Jung 1970a: 319, 171).

Marner's practical abilities as a craftsman, however, remain unaltered. As he continues to produce and sell excellent linens, his earning capacity increases. Since he is spending less and less on himself, his heap of golden coins keeps growing. Gradually the accumulation and hoarding of gold becomes his absorbing passion in life, indeed his only delight. Eliot records the revelry that comes for the miser at night, when he is able to contemplate his coins: "He spread them out in heaps and bathed his hands in them; then he counted them and set them up in regular piles, and felt their rounded outline between his thumb and fingers, and thought fondly of the guineas that were only half-earned by the work in his loom, as if they had been unborn children . . ." (Eliot 1861: 19). This is the history of Silas Marner until the fifteenth year after he came to Raveloe.

Then, his golden hoard is stolen by the wastrel younger son of a local squire. When Silas discovered the theft, "he put his trembling hands to his head, and gave a wild ringing scream, the cry of desolation" (ibid.: 41). In the hope that the thief might be caught, Silas breaks through his social isolation and tells his story to those of his neighbors who are assembled at The Rainbow, the local pub. These "regulars" believe him and are sympathetic. Eliot, as psychologically-minded narrator, suggests that it is at this moment that a possible renewal of Silas's life begins:

This strangely novel situation of opening his trouble to his Raveloe neighbours, of sitting in the warmth of a hearth not his own, and feeling the presence of faces and voices which were his nearest promise of help, had doubtless its influence on Marner, in spite of his passionate preoccupation with his loss. Our consciousness rarely registers the beginning of a growth within us any more than without us: there have been many circulations of the sap before we detect the smallest sign of the bud.

(ibid.: 55)

This is as much to suggest that the juice of the innate emotions belonging to the archetypal affect system precedes the consciousness that claims ownership of them. The theft of his hoard of gold that might have been the "last straw" for Marner, and even driven him to suicide, turns out to be the event that leads him to break out of his social isolation.

Even so, after Silas returns home, the agonizing void that had opened up for him in response to his loss persists and becomes *unbearable*:

He filled up the blank with grief. As he sat weaving, he every now and then moaned low, like one in pain: it was the sign that his thoughts had come round again to the sudden chasm – to the empty evening-time. And all the evening, as he sat in his loneliness by his dull fire, he leaned his elbows on his knees, and clasped his head with his hands, and moaned very low – not as one who seeks to be heard.

(ibid.: 76)

(We noted in Table I.1 that the symbol that constellated the innate affect Anguish–Agony was composed of the life stimulus, Loss and the Primordial image "the Void.".) But the kindlier feelings that had been kindled in his neighbors also persist and are expressed in various ways. New Year's Eve is approaching, and they told him that staying up to see the New Year arrive would bring good luck: it might even bring his money back.

On New Year's Eve, the opium-addicted wife of the elder son of the same local squire had set out from a nearby community, with her 2-year-old daughter, bent on finally enacting the fiery vengeance that had been ignited in her months ago when her husband told her "he would sooner die than acknowledge her as his wife" (ibid.: 108). But it is a cold, snowy night and, when she takes a dose of opium and lies down to rest, she freezes to death. The light from the open door of Marner's hut is visible to her child and, unbeknownst to Silas, the tiny girl crawls inside to warm herself at the hearth. The door was ajar because, as Silas opened it to look out at the snowy night, he had had one of the brief lapses of consciousness to which he was susceptible. When he emerges from his cataleptic fit and returns to his normal wakeful attention and turns toward the hearth, it seems to him as if his gold is there on the floor in front of it. His heart beats violently and he stretches out his hand, "but instead of the hard coin with the familiar resisting outline, his fingers encountered soft warm curls" (ibid.: 112):

> In utter amazement, Silas fell on his knees and bent his head low to examine the marvel: it was a sleeping child – a round, fair thing, with soft yellow rings all over its head. Could this be his little sister come back to him in a dream – his little sister whom he had carried about in his arms for a year before she died, when he was a small boy without shoes or stockings? . . . It was very much like his little sister. Silas sank into his chair powerless, under the double presence of an inexplicable surprise and a hurrying influx of memories.
>
> (ibid.: 112)

Marner's experience of Surprise, one of the innate affects, is immediately followed by a flood of early memories, a clear sign that the dissociation that has persisted for fifteen years is beginning to be healed. He wonders how the child has come in without his knowledge, but along with that question "there was a vision of the old home and the old streets leading to Lantern Yard – and within that vision another, of the thoughts, which had been present with him in those far-off scenes" (ibid.: 112):

> The thoughts were strange to him now, like old friendships impossible to revive; and yet he had a dreamy feeling that this child was somehow a message come to him from that far-off life: it stirred fibres that had never been moved in Raveloe – old quiverings of tenderness – old impressions of awe at the presentiment of some Power presiding over his life; for his imagination had not yet extricated itself from the sense of mystery in the child's sudden presence, and had formed no conjectures of ordinary natural means by which the event could have been brought about.
>
> (ibid.: 112)

Now that the dissociation is breaking up, the process of re-integrating his subjectivity is gaining speed.

He feeds and warms the child, and then he discovers her dead mother. He goes to the squire's house to report what has happened. And when the village women suggest he leave the child with them, he replied "It's come to me – I've a right to keep it" (ibid.: 116). This was another experience of Surprise: "The proposition to take the child from him had come to Silas quite unexpectedly, and his speech, uttered under a strong sudden impulse, was almost like a revelation to himself; a minute before, he had no distinct intention about the child" (ibid.: 116).

My conjecture is that the "sudden, strong impulse" is a manifestation of the constellation in Marner of a symbolic "parent–infant" bond (see Chapter 1 of my previous book *The Symbolic Impetus*). He gives the child the name of

Eppie, which is derived from Hephzibah, a name borne previously by his mother and by the sister he had carried in his arms before she died. Silas fosters Eppie's growth and follows it with interest and mounting joy: "[And] Eppie called him away from his weaving, and made him think all its pauses a holiday, reawakening his senses with her fresh life, even to the old winter-flies that came crawling forth in the early spring sunshine and warming him into joy because *she* had joy" (ibid.: 128). The emotions of the life instinct – Interest and Joy – are flowing like a spring freshet.

As Eppie's life unfolds, Silas's soul unfolds too, trembling gradually into full consciousness. Eliot once again comments on the cause of this unfolding:

> In old days there were angels who came and took men by the hand and led them away from the city of destruction. We see no white-winged angels now. But yet men are led away from threatening destruction; a hand is out in theirs, which leads them forth gently towards a calm and bright land, so that they look no more backward; and the hand may be a little child's.
>
> (ibid.: 133)

Despite the Christian overlay ("a little child shall lead them") Eliot is clearly enunciating a psychological truth by noting that what we experience now, in our self-conscious age, is not the angels, but the glorious, affect-laden primordial child, a symbolic expression of the "child's" ability to restore our emotional vitality. When this life-transforming event occurred, Marner must have been on the verge of committing suicide. That he held on without moving toward this option might be accounted for by the fact that he met only three of the four necessary conditions that I have identified for such an outcome. He was socially isolated, there was a dissociation in his personality, and he was experiencing unbearable agony. The condition that was not met was an eclipse of consciousness on the basis of affect possession.

John Stuart Mill: a symbolic death unlocks a cultural attitude

In a section of his autobiography that he entitled "A crisis in my mental history: one step onward," John Stuart Mill describes a transformation of his personality that began when he was 20 years old and did not reach even a provisional equilibrium until he was 23. My interpretation of this as Mill's identity crisis in Erikson's sense (Erikson 1959) will suggest that it marked the completion of his adolescent development.

By the time Mill was 15 years old, he had already developed what Joseph Henderson might describe as a social attitude. This was not unusual for young men of his class in the England of the early 19th century; I would describe his social attitude as an age-appropriate symbolic cultural attitude (see *The Symbolic Impetus*, Chapter 7). Here is how Mill himself saw it:

From the winter of 1821, when I first read Bentham, and especially from the commencement of the Westminster Review, I had what might truly be called an object in life; to be a reformer of the world. My conception of my own happiness was entirely identified with this object. The personal sympathies I wished for were those of fellow labourers in this enterprise.

(Mill 1924: 92)

As is not uncommon for young men, this earliest consolidation of a symbolic cultural identity was organized by the hero archetype. When he was 16, his first realization of this ambition occurred when two of his polemical letters were published in the *Traveller*, a London evening newspaper. For the next four years, Mill actively continued on the course he had charted for himself. But when he was 20 "he awakened from this as from a dream."

What he discovered when he "awoke" was that the usual functioning of his life had ceased: "I was in a dull state of nerves, such as everybody is occasionally liable to; unsusceptible to *enjoyment* or pleasurable *excitement*; one of those moods when what is pleasure at other times becomes insipid or indifferent . . ." (ibid.: 94, emphasis added).

Mill is describing a critical decrease in his experiences of the twin affects of the life instinct, Joy and Interest. This change was followed by an equally critical increase in the frequency, intensity, and duration of his expression of the crisis affect Sadness. (An inversion of the ratio of positive to negative affects had occurred.) As he later put it, he was suffering from the "dry dejection of melancholy." He posed himself a fateful question: "Suppose that all your objects in life were realized; that all the changes in institutions and opinions which you are looking forward to, could be completely effected at this very instant: would this be a great joy and happiness to you?" (ibid.: 94) The answer that came was extremely disillusioning:

. . . an irrepressible self-consciousness distinctly answered, "No!" At this my heart sank within me: the whole foundation on which my life was constructed fell down. All my happiness was to have been found in the continual pursuit of this end. The end had ceased to charm, and how could there ever again be any interest in this means? I seemed to have nothing left to live for.

(ibid.: 94)

As this passage may convey, a cultural attitude is sustained by the happy operation of the innate affects of Interest and Joy, which being innate positive emotions do give someone something to live for. As a result of the collapse of his social cultural attitude and his continuing self-alienation, Mill was cut off from this part of the healthy affective base of his personality. He was also isolated from any relationship that might sustain him during this crisis in his mental history:

I sought no comfort by speaking to others of what I felt. If I had loved any one sufficiently to make confiding my griefs a necessity, I should not have been in the condition I was. I felt, too, that mine was not an interesting, or in any way respectable distress. There was nothing in it to attract sympathy. Advice, if I had known where to seek it, would have been most precious ... But there was no one on whom I could build the faintest hope of such assistance.

(ibid.: 95)

This is a dangerous place to be, psychologically. From the standpoint of our explanatory method, the following necessary conditions for lethal behaviors can be identified: social isolation, self-alienation, and a critical increase in negative affects. In Mill's account of his crisis, however, there is never any indication that he entered that unproblematic state of consciousness, affect possession, which is the final necessary condition for lethal behaviors. When negative emotions were reaching an unbearable level, he asked himself how long he could go on: "I generally answered to myself, that I did not think I could possibly bear it beyond a year" (ibid.: 99). This is the closest Mill came to possession by a suicidal complex.

His creativity was also blocked: "During this time I was not incapable of my usual occupations. I went on with them mechanically, by the mere force of habit" (ibid.: 98). Such a creative crisis, however, can afford the opportunity for the emergence of a radically new insight from more raw and less organized areas of the mind. Mill realized that his education had been based on "the old familiar instruments, praise and blame, reward and punishment" and the habit of analysis "which has a tendency to wear away the feelings" (ibid.: 96). It occurred to him, in the following way, that there might be another basis for the motivation to resume developing himself:

I was reading, accidentally, Marmontel's "Memoires," and came to the passage which relates his father's death, the distressed position of the family, and the sudden inspiration by which he, then a mere boy, felt and made them feel that he would be everything to them – would supply the place of all that they had lost. A vivid conception of the scene and its feelings came over me, and I was moved to tears. From this moment my burthen grew lighter. The oppression of the thought that all feeling was dead within me, was gone. I was no longer hopeless: I was not a stick or a stone. I had still, it seemed, some of the material out of which all worth of character, and all capacity for happiness, are made. Relieved from my ever present sense of irremediable wretchedness, I gradually found that the ordinary incidents of life could again give me some pleasure; that I could again find *enjoyment*, not intense, but sufficient for cheerfulness, in sunshine and sky, in books, in conversation, in public affairs; and that there was, once more, *excitement*, though of a moderate kind, in exerting myself for my opinions, and for the public good. Thus the cloud gradually drew off, and I again enjoyed life: and though I had several relapses, some of which lasted many months, I never again was as miserable as I had been.

(ibid.: 99, emphasis added)

My interpretation of how this remarkable turnaround occurred on the basis of a significant reading is as follows. Marmontel's way of resolving the death of his father showed Mill how to get past his own father complex and yet integrate its essential values, appropriating them for his own future self-development. A psychologist may make this sound easy, but in fact without some form of symbolic experience, of the kind Mill accessed while reading Marmontel, most people get caught in the concrete, either of identification with a parent or object loss when that identification ceases to work for them. Only a symbolic cultural experience enables the energy bound up in the original identification to move into the self. For Mill this had been particularly hard because, not unlike Mozart's early development, the entire initial education of his cultural consciousness had been bound up with his father. His father had begun teaching Mill Greek when he was three years old: ". . . my father in all his teachings, demanded of me not only the utmost that I could do, but much that I could by no possibility have done" (ibid.: 4). Unless, however, Mill could come to feel that such cultural competence and creativity could belong to him and be accessed freely by his own agency, Mill's capacity to contribute from himself was at risk, and by age 20 was threatened with standstill.

Only the metaphorical death of his father made it possible for Mill to proceed. That was the meaning of his depression, but for him to get any immediate benefit from it, he had to find a way to use his Agony and to re-establish contact with his innate Interest and Joy. His reading of Marmontel's solution to the actual death of his own father showed Mill the way to both to mourn and to receive the legacy of his father's own affective energies. Beebe (personal communication) calls this the transfer of the anima from father to son, and indeed in a maturing man it is through the anima that the healthy affective base of the self is accessed. The anima that Mill integrated, however, was not just a replica of his father's. The anima is typically expressed through a cultural attitude, and the cultural attitude emanating from Mill's father had been clearly social. L. H. Stewart has shown that Shame/Contempt is the affect that is drawn upon in the development of a social attitude, and indeed Mill's father had often shamed his son into developing a greater concern for the plight of others. As Mill came into his own, however, Shame/Contempt could no longer motivate him. Instead, he had to get in touch with the Agony of being unable to sustain his relation with his father to find his own cultural attitude. Agony, we know from L. H. Stewart's work, is the affect that shapes the aesthetic attitude.

Following Jung, L. H. Stewart understands the anima as one of the archetypes that function to create a relationship between an individual ego and the unconscious. He assigns to the archetype of the shadow the task of relating to the personal unconscious and the archetype of the self the task of relating to the collective unconscious. He says the anima expresses the way ego-consciousness relates to the cultural unconscious. Beebe (personal communication) has also suggested that Henderson's theory of cultural attitudes can thus be understood as a theory of types of anima.

But at this early stage of his development of a symbolic cultural standpoint, the energies that were liberated from the father complex were now used by Mill to take a major step in the completion of his adolescent development. He records the remarkable transformation in his attitude toward life: ". . . I, for the first time, gave its proper place, among the prime necessities of human well-being, to the internal culture of the individual" (ibid.: 100). He now came to think that it was necessary to maintain a "due balance among the faculties": "The cultivation of feelings became one of the cardinal points in my ethical and philosophical creed . . . I now began to find meaning in the things which I had read or heard about the importance of poetry and art, as instruments of human culture" (ibid.: 101). His great pleasure in music, which had begun in childhood but was suspended during his "gloomy period," revived and began to grow. His reading of Wordsworth for the first time was an important event, for this poet addressed Mill's love of rural beauty. From this juncture, interest and enjoyment in literature and poetry expanded. I believe it is now reasonable to argue that Mill's completion of his adolescence development included not only the symbolic death of his father but also the construction of an aesthetic cultural attitude (see *The Symbolic Impetus*, Chapter 7, for a demonstration of the relationship between innate affects and the development of cultural attitudes, in which I support L. H. Stewart in his view that that the aesthetic cultural attitude is motivated by the innate affect Sadness–Anguish–Agony).

We must remind ourselves, however, that without his capacity to use cultural experience, such as reading, to provide symbolic channels for the transition he needed to make, the same affects could have motivated a suicide. Three of the necessary conditions (social isolation, dissociation from the healthy affective base, and unbearable affect) were present, but not the fourth: he was still able to objectify his affects, and thus never became totally possessed by them. For this, we have to thank the effects of his early education, which had trained him to read, reflect, and write, all activities which favor the objectivation of affect.

All of these developments occurred in a state of relative isolation. Two more years were to pass before Mill, at 25, was able to achieve Erikson's stage of Intimacy, which was marked by his falling in love with a woman who was married to another man and would only eventually become his own wife. We can only speculate that his internal readiness to hold his own in such a complicated, Oedipally-tinged relationship was greatly enhanced by the use he was able to make of his period of isolation, in which he did so much to resolve his father complex from within.

Mrs A.: a psychosis with a constructive outcome

In a chapter of his book *Self and Others* entitled "The coldness of death," R. D. Laing (1969) describes the course of a five-month postpartum illness that was resolved in a constructive manner. Reading his phenomenological account closely, I conceive his patient's disturbance to be an example of what Ellenberger and others have termed a "creative illness" (Bower 1989; Ellenberger 1968; Goldwert 1992), that is, a set of symptoms reflecting, at a personal, psychological level, the self's attempt to reorganize for further growth (Perry 1986).

The patient, Mrs A., was 34 when she gave birth to her third child. Three weeks after delivery she was still unable to get up from her bed. After the births of her two previous children, she had felt somewhat the same, "a complete disinclination to do anything, and no interest in the familiar people and things of her life" (Laing 1969: 68). Jung suggests that this type of "alienation from reality, the loss of interest in objective events is not hard to explain when one considers that [the individual is] under the spell of an insuperable complex" (Jung 1960: 195, 97–8).

In Mrs A.'s case, there was definite evidence that a content of the collective unconscious had been constellated. For two nights in a row, she experienced "a violent storm inside her" with sails crackling and tearing in the wind:

> An infallible sign of collective images seems to be the appearance of the "cosmic" element, i.e., the images in the dream or fantasy are connected with cosmic qualities, such as temporal and spatial infinity, enormous speed and extension of movement, "astrological" associations, telluric, lunar, and solar analogies, changes in the body proportions, etc.
>
> (Jung 1972: 250, 160)

Another well-known collective image is that of the primordial "wind," which the Stoic philosophers called the *pneuma*, the spiritual substance of the universe.

On the second night, she also experienced "a peculiar sense of her thoughts running down and coming to a standstill" (Laing 1969: 69). This depotentiation of her ego-consciousness continued all through the night. When she awoke, her world had changed: "A 'realization' swept over her that nothing had anything to do with her – she was no longer in 'that' world. The room and the baby in the cot suddenly appeared small and far away 'as though seen through the wrong end of a telescope'. She felt completely unconcerned. She was 'absolutely and completely emotionless' (ibid.: 69).

The unconscious had ruthlessly extracted libido from ego-consciousness and the patient had entered the "coldness of death." Jung explains this dynamic as follows:

> The unconscious has simply gained an unassailable ascendancy; it wields an attractive force that can invalidate all conscious contents – in other words, it can withdraw libido from the conscious world and thereby produce a "depression," an *abaissement du niveau mental* . . . But as a result of this we must, according to the laws of energy, expect an accumulation of value – i.e., libido – in the unconscious.
>
> (Jung 1972: 344, 215)

Under the spell of an *abaissement*, psychic activity seems greatly reduced, but it has actually been turned over from the ego to the unconscious, which actually is more clearly perceived than in other states: "Under such a condition unconscious contents become manifest, i.e., can be perceived by the normal sense organs . . . a markedly passive state (trance), which shows that an *abaissement* – the elimination of consciously controlled psychic activity – is needed to give spontaneous phenomena a chance" (Jung 1975: 543). If the patient continues to have access to the unconscious, in the form of dreams, for instance, which can be much more frequent when someone is going through a depression, we can expect the compensatory guiding function of the Self to be progressively more evident. And if we view the patient's illness as a waking dream, then talking to the patient is like talking to a dream-ego that has persisted into waking life and will be able to register the emerging contents:

> Among the first unconscious images to emerge in Mrs A. were strangely altered apprehensions of her body. Although her tongue looked normal in the mirror, it felt like it was paralyzed and twisted. The extremities of her limbs were cold: there was a weight in her arms and legs. It was an enormous effort to make the slightest movement. Her chest was empty . . . To her, her skin had a dying pallor. Her hands were naturally blue, almost black. Her heart might stop at any moment. Her bones, felt twisted and in a powder. Her flesh was decaying.
>
> (Laing 1969: 69–70)

Yet there was a subtle, vengeful grandiosity to her morbidity: "The doctors were tragically deluded by the absence of physical signs of her death. The absence of such signs was the mark of her absolutely unique condition" (ibid.: 70). It was the doctors who were tragically mistaken: "When she had died, the poison lying in her body would give the impression that she had committed suicide, but when the full facts came to light she might be just that unique case which could well revolutionize the whole of medical science. Then the doctors who had been in attendance on her would suffer extreme disgrace" (ibid.: 70).

This inflation of her own importance, which can be thought of as a deformation of the ego, was expressed in her belief, which lasted throughout the five months of her disturbance, that she was being poisoned:

> ... if the individual identifies himself with the contents awaiting integration, a positive or negative inflation results. Positive inflation comes very near to a more or less conscious megalomania; negative inflation is felt as an annihilation of the ego. The two conditions may alternate. At all events the integration of contents that were always unconscious and projected involves a serious lesion of the ego. Alchemy expresses this through the symbols of death, mutilation, or poisoning, or through the curious idea of dropsy ...
>
> (Jung 1966: 472, 263–4)

Although her capacity for integration of unconscious contents was initially impaired, Mrs A. was able to maintain sociable contact with the psychiatric doctors who cared for her in the hospital. Within the context of what she conceived as a physical illness, she was "prepared to talk about her dying state indefinitely, and her movements were not slowed up" (Laing 1969: 70). One's sense, reading Laing's report of her manner at this time, is that her intent was to convince her doctors of the reality of her dying, and that she was prepared to remain firm and clear and calm for as long as it took for them to understand the gravity of her condition.

Laing gives her account of the beginning of her return from the world of death to that of life as follows: "One day, about the middle of March, I became conscious of dreadful coldness in my legs but at the same time noticed that my feet were warm" (ibid.: 70). It was this physical experience that led her to begin to reconsider the nature of her illness. The part of her that had to make the reassessment was of course her ego, which makes its determinations of what reality is on the basis of its experience. Jung explained to an audience of medical psychologists that they actually came to their experience of what they had learned to call ego by "a general awareness of your body, of your existence, and secondly by your memory data; you have a certain idea of having been, a long series of memories" (Jung 1977: 18, 11). The "warmth" in Mrs A.'s feet signaled her resurgent ego's reawakening awareness of her body. Her beginning reconsideration of her illness indicated that the Jungian ego function Thinking was now functioning at the conscious level. The first thought that gave her renewed hope was that "that any illness sufficiently serious to make one 'start' to die would first of all prostrate the person regardless of the strength of that person's will-power" (Laing 1969: 70). Other doubts about her understanding of her disturbance followed, and she realized that she had been in a state of unreality and that she was about to come out of it, which she gradually proceeded to do.

She also found explanations for the "tapestry of symbols" in which her whole body had been enveloped. Laing presents these in tabular form (see Table 3.1).

Laing was able thus to understand each one of her distorted somatic images as an identification with a distressed part of one of her family members. We might therefore see all of her somatic delusions as manifestations of an intensely felt and constellated family complex. Jung has commented on the nature of an individual's possession by their family complex, which he describes as a fall "right back into childhood":

> Wholeness is represented by the family, and its components are still projected upon the members of the family and personified by them. But this state is dangerous for the adult because regressive: it denotes a splitting of personality which primitive man experiences as the perilous "loss of soul." In the break-up the personal components that have been integrated with such pains are once more sucked into the outside world.
>
> (Jung 1968a: 152, 115)

For Mrs A., who emerged from this "fall," or regression, feeling far more in touch with all the parts of herself than before, the regression seemed to be necessary in order for her to complete genuine integration and transformation of the family complex that had emerged from the series of traumas she had sustained within the family. The very same images that at the height of her illness she experienced as somatic delusions, she became able, in the course of her treatment, to experience as parts of her family complex.

Her emotional life began to bloom again. As she lost interest in her symptoms, she became able to recognize and enjoy affects again. Her *excitement* in seeing her husband and children grew. She no longer felt a barrier between her friends and herself. She was surprised that she could feel *pleasure*. In the

Table 3.1 Tapestry of symbols (Laing 1969: 76)

Her tongue felt as twisted, but seen as normal	was	her father's tongue when he had a series of strokes that ended his life
Her chest felt as empty, and her skin seen as yellow	were	her brother's chest and skin on his deathbed
Her hand seen as blue-black	was	her baby's head in a breath-holding attack
Her heart	was	her baby during her last pregnancy when there had been anxiety about something going wrong
Her bones	were	the bones of her mother, who had been crippled with rheumatoid arthritis since the patient's early childhood

morning, she felt *happy* at the prospect of another day. She began to respond to music and regained her sense of humor. She was able to put her trust in God and her psychiatrist. All these were signs that the life instinct has been revived and was energizing both ego functions and cultural attitudes. Longer-term follow up indicated that her striking recovery endured: "After coming out of this metaphorical state, in which she had lived in a state of near death, in her own tapestry of symbols, she felt much more keenly alive than she could remember. Five years later, she still felt well and had had another child without complications" (Laing 1969: 74).

This suggests that her disturbance had been resolved in a creative way, which allowed both for integrative transformation and a new level of personality development. Having experienced "the coldness of death," that is, the constellation of the pathogenic family complex to the exclusion of everything else in her psychic life, she was able to feel grateful for "the warmth of rebirth," that is, the direct access to the healthy affective basis of her personality, which had been blocked to her until her family complex began to be integrated.

Mrs A. had an unusually fortunate outcome to her postpartum psychosis, in that she managed to integrate the experience of death into a genuine rebirth of her affective life that was fortunate for her and her baby, and even avoided a repetition of the syndrome after the birth of her next child. Not all mothers who suffer from this painful condition are able to rebound so decisively. We know that mothers suffering from a postpartum psychosis have on occasion killed their babies, themselves, or both. Mrs A. did not express homicidal impulses and mentioned suicide only once, when she suggested that after she had died, the poison lying in her body would give the impression that she had committed suicide. We have to ask, how is it that she was not motivated to actually kill herself?

An important factor is the absence of social isolation, which we have postulated as one of the necessary conditions for a lethal outcome to an affective crisis. Throughout her five-month period of disturbance, Mrs A. maintained a dialogue with her doctors, although the content of her communications to them were relatively psychotic. Even though she had lost contact with her family and friends, the relationships she was able to sustain with her doctors were sufficient to prevent her from turning destructively toward herself to communicate what she was going through.

Without this sustaining contact, Mrs A. would have been at risk. It is clear that the malignant affective components of her reactivated family complex were sufficient to cut her off from the healthy affective base of her personality. She had lost all interest in the world and no longer experienced her usual enjoyments. At least one, therefore, of the necessary conditions for suicidal behavior, dissociation of the personality from the life instinct, was present throughout most of her disturbance.

As to another of the necessary conditions for the turn to self-injury, unbearable affect, there is no question that Mrs A.'s distress extended beyond the range of normal suffering. But it is not clear from the material we have available whether her experience of crisis affects ever reached a truly unbearable level of frequency, intensity, and duration. She was remarkably calm and matter of fact about being depressed, as if the experience of "dying" was somehow ego-syntonic for her.

Aside from her enduring sociability with caretakers, during her illness, Mrs A. experienced a depotentiation of her ego, which more or less collapsed under the weight of the constellated family complex. The pathological complex that took possession of her consciousness did not include any motivation for impulsive, self-destructive, or violent behaviors, as we sometimes see in people from families where there is a trend toward destructive acting out as a way to escape from suffering. Mrs A.'s particular vulnerability to affect possession, one of the conditions we have postulated as necessary to a lethal outcome, expressed itself in ways that were not only much more benign, but, as we have shown, actually gave her the needed emotional prelude to a constructive reorganization of her personality. Hers, in other words, was the sort of symbolic death experience that is followed by emotional rebirth, and she seemed to know that all along.

We can conclude, then, that one reason that Mrs A. did not make a suicide attempt during her illness is that only two of the four necessary conditions for the turn to a lethal solution of the severe affective crisis was actually present during the five months of her illness. These were dissociation and affect possession, and even these two dysphoric states were remarkably well "held" by her and her doctors, as something they both recognized she just had to go through.

William Styron: the healing potential of self-sacrifice

In his memoir *Darkness Visible*, the well-known American novelist William Styron writes that in June 1985, when he was 60 years old, he entered a period of mental disturbance that deepened in October, had a "near violent denouement" in December, and was resolved by February 1986. He refers to the disturbance of that summer, autumn, and winter as a depression, although he admits that the term melancholia might be more evocative of the "howling tempest" that had raged in his brain.

From our perspective, Styron's account of his ordeal makes it clear that he was never socially isolated. When he lay in a Paris bedroom in October 1985 immobilized by intense misery, his wife, Rose, "sat nearby reading . . ." (Styron 1990: 18). When they returned to their Connecticut home and Styron continued to suffer, he wrote: "As always Rose was present and listened with unflagging patience to my complaints" (ibid.: 45–6). Subsequently he described Rose as "the endlessly patient soul who had become nanny, mommy, comforter, priestess, and, most important, confidante – a counselor of rocklike centrality to my existence . . ." (ibid.: 57). When he attended a dinner party at his home in December 1985 and was nearly mute, he was accepted, "politely ignored" (ibid.: 63), by four good friends who were there.

Styron has described his relationship with a close friend who was hospitalized in the summer of 1985 with severe manic depression, but had recovered by the fall of the same year with the help of medication and psychotherapy. Beginning in this fall, he and Styron were in touch by phone almost every day, support that Styron said, with immense gratitude "was untiring and priceless. It was he who kept admonishing me that suicide was 'unacceptable' (he had been intensely suicidal), and it was also he who made the prospect of going to the hospital less fearsomely intimidating" (ibid.: 77). And from October 1985, Styron had weekly contact with his psychiatrist.

There are certain aspects of Styron's record of his affliction that suggest to me the possibility that he suffered a dissociation from the healthy affective basis of his personality. The life instinct was in abeyance. He was unable to work. His mood was one of "dank joylessness" (ibid.: 5). He felt "less zestful and buoyant" (ibid.: 52). Without amplification of drives by Interest and Joy, his eating was only for subsistence and insomnia was persistent and distressing. His sense of self "had all but disappeared" (ibid.: 56). There was an absence of dreams. His curiosity was not completely extinguished, although it was not at his disposal. He was "accompanied by a second self – a wraithlike observer who, not sharing the dementia of his double, is able to watch with dispassionate curiosity as his companion struggles against the oncoming disaster . . ." (ibid.: 64).

What appear to be alterations in the functional capacity of his ego also suggest a split between consciousness and the unconscious, the source of psychic energy. Styron refers to "confusion, failure of mental focus, lapse of memory" (ibid.: 14). His "lucidity . . . was slipping away . . . with terrifying speed" (ibid.: 4). At times he was a zombie and unable to speak: "Soon evident are the slowed-down responses, near paralysis, psychic energy throttled back close to zero" (ibid.: 47). In my opinion, Styron is describing what Jung and Jungians, using a term borrowed from Pierre Janet, refer to as an *abaissement du niveau mental*, a lowering of conscious functioning:

> *Abaissement du niveau mental* can be the result of physical and mental fatigue, bodily illness, violent emotions, and shock, of which the last has a particularly deleterious effect on one's self-assurance. The *abaissement* always has a restrictive influence on the personality as a whole. It reduces one's self-confidence and the spirit of enterprise, and, as a result of increasing egocentricity, narrows the mental horizon. In the end it may lead to the development of an essentially negative personality, which means that a falsification of the original personality has supervened.
>
> (Jung 1969a: 214, 120)

We can conjecture that another cause for the decline in Styron's conscious functioning is that psychic energy had been high-jacked by monopolistic, affect-toned complexes, which were flooding his consciousness with unbearable emotions.

As part of his research directed toward refining our definition of mental pain, Israel Orbach has reviewed different models of emotional pain, including literary, narrative, phenomenological, theoretical, and empirical models: "The common aspects in all models include intense negative emotions, loss of self, surfeit of the negative" (Orbach 2003: 191). His literary model is based on a content analysis of Styron's *Darkness Visible*, in which Orbach identified ten key categories of mental anguish, which provided the basis for this definition of psychic pain: "Mental pain is *the experience of inner torture, perturbation, and surfeit of negative emotion brought about by an inner estranged and hostile force which destroys the unity of the self and the mind*" (ibid.: 193). Unbearable affect under any other name is just as insufferable.

Looked at from the perspective of unsupportable emotion, Styron's book is an eighty-four page compendium of unbearable affects, so that one must read his entire account to fully appreciate the "storm of murk" (Styron 1990: 47) that engulfed him. Let us, however, consider Styron's descriptions that are expressions based upon weather-related metaphors.

It was while he was in Paris in October 1985, preparing to receive a literary award, that he had a sudden realization that he would not see this city again: "This certitude astonished me and filled me with a new fright, for while thoughts of death had long been common during my siege, *blowing through my mind like icy gusts of wind*, they were the formless shapes of doom that I suppose are dreamed of by people in the grip of any severe affliction" (ibid.: 28, emphasis added).

Styron writes that clinical depression resembles "a veritable howling tempest in the brain" (ibid.: 38). At another point in his account, he contrasts depression with violence: "It is a storm indeed, but a storm of murk" (ibid. 47). He describes his afternoons, which were the worst times of day, when he'd feel "the horror, like some poisonous fogbank, roll in upon my mind . . ." (ibid.: 58). He would lie in this tortured state for as long as six hours, "waiting for that moment of evening when, mysteriously, the crucifixion would ease up just enough to allow me to force down some food and then, like an automaton, seek an hour or two of sleep again" (ibid.: 58). Isn't it possible that during the six hours of intense distress Styron was still capable of integrating some portion of the "poisonous fogbank" and that this accounts for his two hours of sleep? We can agree with Orbach that Styron's mental pain had reached an unbearable level.

In my judgment, if Styron was ever possessed by affect, his capture was only for brief moments. It was just before his trip to Paris in October 1985 that Styron had this thought: "I was still keeping the idea of suicide at bay. But plainly the possibility was around the corner, and I would soon meet it face to face" (ibid.: 50). After he had returned home and was in a meeting with his psychiatrist, Styron reluctantly responded to his question by indicating he was suicidal; they increased their sessions to twice a week. In December 1985, there was a "near-violent denouement," which sent Styron into the hospital. This was also the time when the resolution of the "howling tempest" began.

Styron's trial began in his sixtieth year. He says that he had used alcohol over a forty-year period, often in conjunction with music "as the magical conduit to fantasy and euphoria, and to the enhancement of the imagination" (ibid.: 40). In June 1985, however, he developed a revulsion toward alcohol and overnight became, without the intercession of will or choice, an abstainer. I assume Styron means *conscious* will or choice. He dates the beginning of his depression to this development.

Only in the course of writing *Darkness Visible* did Styron realize that suicide had been a persistent theme in his books and that depression "had been tapping at his door for decades" (ibid.: 79). In "William Styron and the literature of early maternal loss," Melissa Wanamaker wrote that she was "convinced that early maternal loss itself can create a strong predilection in the surviving child not only to become depressed, but also, if sufficiently talented, to become an artist" (Wanamaker 1999: 403). This is in accord with L. H. Stewart's view (see Table 2.2) that the innate affect Sadness–Anguish–Agony is the motivating force for the construction of an aesthetic cultural attitude. Styron was 13 years old when his mother died.

The resolution of Styron's ordeal, I believe, took the form of a self-cure. For years, he had kept a private notebook, which he "fully intended to make use of professionally and then destroy before the distant day when the specter of the nursing home came too near" (ibid.: 59). As his illness progressed, Styron realized that if he "once decided to get rid of the notebook that moment would necessarily coincide with my decision to put an end to myself" (ibid.: 59). One evening during early December 1985 this moment came.

After dinner, he experienced a "curious inner convulsion" that he could only describe as "despair beyond despair" (ibid.: 59). He did not think such anguish was possible. He excused himself, went upstairs, and retrieved his notebook from its special place:

> Then I went to the kitchen and with gleaming clarity – the clarity of one who knows he is engaged in a solemn rite – I noted all the trademarked legends on the well-advertised articles which I began assembling for the volume's disposal: the new roll of Viva paper towels I opened to wrap up the book, the Scotch-brand tape I encircled it with, the empty Post Raisin Bran box I put the parcel into before taking it outside and stuffing it deep down within the garbage can, which would be emptied the next morning. Fire would have destroyed it faster, but in garbage there was an annihilation of self appropriate, as always, to melancholia's

fecund self-humiliation. I felt my heart pounding wildly, like that of a man facing a firing squad, and knew I had made an irreversible decision.

(ibid.: 63–4)

Styron felt he was engaged in a solemn ritual, I believe, because he was! In the next few days, he began preparations for his suicide – rewriting his will and attempting to compose a letter of farewell. Although he had entered a state of possession by a suicidal complex and was no longer ambivalent about ending his life, he was unable to write a suicide note and complete his self-destruction.

It was three days after his "solemn rite" that Styron's renewal began:

Late one bitterly cold night, when I knew that I could not possibly get myself through the following day, I sat in the living room of the house bundled up against the chill . . . My wife had gone to bed, and I had forced myself to watch the tape of a movie in which a young actress, who had been in a play of mine, was cast in a small part. At one point in the film, which was set in late-nineteenth-century Boston, the characters moved down the hallway of a music conservatory, beyond the walls of which, from unseen musicians, came a contralto voice, a sudden soaring passage from the Brahms *Alto Rhapsody*. This sound, which like all music – indeed, like all pleasure – I had been numbly unresponsive to for months, pierced my heart like a dagger, and in a flood of swift recollection I thought of all the joys the house had known: the children who had rushed through its rooms, the festivals, the love and work, the honestly earned slumber, the voices and the nimble commotion, the perennial tribe of cats and dogs and birds, "laughter and ability and Sighing, / And Frocks and Curls."

(ibid.: 66–7)

He renounced his suicidal intentions, woke Rose, and the next day sought admission to a hospital.

Indications of the thawing of the icy state of dissociation are evident in the piercing of his heart, rather than by a knife, perhaps by an arrow shot from the bow of Eros. There immediately followed the recovery of memories suffused with Joy and (in more Freudian terms) work and love. Finally, Styron was flooded by memories all the people who had made his life worthwhile, along with their laughter.

A few days after admission, the fantasies of self-destruction were nearly gone. By early February 1986, his world had brightened: "I felt myself no longer a husk but a body with some of the body's sweet juices stirring again. I had my first dream in many months, confused but to this day imperishable, with a flute in it somewhere, and a wild goose, and a dancing girl" (ibid.: 75). The dissociation between his ego-consciousness and his body had been overcome and his first dream indicates that he has re-established contact with the healthy affective basis of his personality.

My conjecture that Styron's overcoming of his depression was a self-cure is based on the supposition that his ridding himself of his notebook was a self-sacrifice, a symbolic death. As such, it can be thought of as the beginning of an advance in Styron's individuation. With this possibility in mind, we can even speculate that both his involuntary abstinence and his ritual sacrifice were both instigated by the self:

> I have suggested calling the total personality which, though present, can-not be fully known, the *self*. The ego is, by definition, subordinate to the self and is related to it like a part to the whole. Inside the field of con-sciousness it has, as we say, free will. By this I do not mean anything philosophical, only the well-known fact of "free choice," or rather the subjective feeling of freedom. But, just as our free will clashes with neces-sity in the outside world, so also it finds its limits outside the field of consciousness in the subjective inner world, where it comes into conflict with the facts of the self. And just as circumstances or outside events "happen" to us and limit our freedom, so the self acts upon the ego like an *objective occurrence* which free will can do very little to alter. It is, indeed, well known that the ego not only can do nothing against the self, but it is sometimes actually assimilated by unconscious components of the personality that are in the process of development and is greatly altered by them.
>
> (Jung 1969b: 9, 5–6)

From this perspective, we can also hypothesize that Styron's task was to integrate and transform a longstanding, unconscious Agony-complex, which was evoked at the time of his mother's death, but which he had heretofore managed to channel into his writings.

Jung states that the "act of making a sacrifice consists in the first place in giving something which belongs to me. Everything which belongs to me bears the stamp of 'mineness,' that is, it has a subtle identity with my ego" (Jung 1970d: 389, 255). The symbolic nature of the sacrifice "comes about firstly because every human being has unconscious contents, and secondly because every object has an unknown side" (ibid.: 389, 255). The act of self-sacrifice, the renunciation by the ego of its claim, can take two forms. In one, "I renounce my claim in consideration of a general moral principle . . ." (ibid.: 393, 360). In the other, "I renounce my claim because I feel impelled to do so for painful inner reasons which are not altogether clear to me" (ibid.: 394, 360). In the latter case, although there is no moral satisfaction and even some resistance is felt, the self is integrated, "withdrawn from projection and has become perceptible as a determining psychic factor" (ibid.: 394, 360). Jung contrasts these two patterns of self-sacrifice:

These two ways of renouncing one's egotistical claim reveal not only a difference of attitude, but also a difference of situation. In the first case the situation need not affect me personally and directly; in the second, the gift must necessarily be a very personal one which seriously affects the giver and forces him to overcome himself ... The one may be felt very earnestly and experienced with all piety, but the other is the real thing.

(ibid.: 395, 261)

If it is a true sacrifice, the object must be understood to be destroyed: "The parallel to this total destruction of the sacrificial gift by burning, or by throwing it into water or into a pit" (ibid.: 390, n.12, 256). Styron decided against burning and for a pit, a garbage can. Styron's sacrifice of his notebook appears to have been the "real thing" and by the end of February 1986, he had recovered from the "howling tempest" in his psyche.

Chapter 4

Vivienne Loomis: suicide

The epigraph to Part One of this remarkable book-length case history, *Vivienne: The Life and Suicide of an Adolescent Girl*, reads as follows: "At 6:30 on the evening of December 21, 1973, Vivienne Loomis, an attractive ninth-grader, especially gifted in writing, hanged herself in her mother's empty silversmithing studio. She was fourteen years and four months old" (Mack and Hickler 1981).

The book is, in effect, a psychological autopsy, and gives all of us much to ponder. My analysis of Vivienne's life will show that at the time of her suicide she was experiencing all four of the conditions that I have postulated as necessary to account for such a lethal, self-destructive act. I will proceed by discussing Vivienne's preadolescent and early adolescent development and then detail the evidence for the emergence of each necessary condition.

Birth to early adolescence

Vivienne was born on 14 August 1959 into a family which consisted of her father, a Unitarian minister, her mother, a working silversmith, an oldest brother and an older sister.

There are two versions of her earliest manifestations of affective expression. Her mother described her as a quiet baby who was willing to be relegated to the playpen: "You could give her a bunch of toys, a bottle of milk or some orange juice and she seemed perfectly happy" (ibid.: 7). Her brother and sister, on the other hand, recalled a very different picture of Vivienne left to herself: "She would sit on the floor screaming for hours" (ibid.: 7). The unskeptical analyst of affective development would translate mother's account as the recognition that her daughter was possessed of a well-functioning innate emotional life radiating Joy and Interest, play and exploration, in a constructive and self-soothing way. The siblings' account, however, would translate as Vivienne's descent into a maelstrom in which she was potentially beset by all of the innate crisis affects: Loss–Anguish, Restriction–Anger, Rejection–Shame/Contempt, and the Unknown–Fear.

I will argue that in addition to this apparent split in her affective development between affects of the life instinct and crisis affects, there was a traumatic affective complex that began in Vivienne's preschool years and became a major barrier between her ego and the healthy emotional basis of her personality. Although there are the two quite different versions of Vivienne's emotional experience in her infancy, there is agreement that Vivienne had an experience of overwhelming affective intensity when she was 4 and a half years old. Her maternal grandfather died suddenly. On the drive to the hospital, mother got upset and Vivienne began to cry. When they arrived at the hospital and the grandfather's death was confirmed, Vivienne could not be comforted. A month later, upon hearing her mother mention to a visiting friend that she missed her father, the child had the following reaction: "Vivienne cried and cried and cried ... It was just an outpouring. I remember sitting in the rocking chair and rocking her. I thought she was going to be physically sick from the amount of crying she did" (ibid.: 8).

Seven months later, Vivienne's paternal grandfather died, and once again she seemed to absorb the family pain into herself. It is reasonable to infer that these difficult emotional events were structuralized in Vivienne's psyche as an expanding Loss + Void–Anguish complex.

Although middle childhood is a period when children, through social exploration and learning and spontaneous play and games, naturally develop peer relationships characterized by mutuality and equality, this was not to be Vivienne's experience. Commencing in the first grade and lasting throughout elementary school, Vivienne was regularly the butt of other children's jokes. The fact that she did very well academically did nothing to help her social life with her peers. In addition, she developed a devastating, sarcastic wit, which alienated the other children even more. We can conjecture that the five years of almost daily rejection and counter-rejection hardened her social isolation and very likely contributed to the formation of a rejection-complex that carried the affect-tone of Shame (the butt of jokes)/Contempt (her sarcastic wit). She became alienated from other children.

When Vivienne began sixth grade, she and her classmates had to go to a new public school, where they would have to mix with children from other schools. Her old classmates told the new ones, "Don't play with Vivienne Loomis. She stinks" (ibid.: 13). Vivienne responded to their contempt for her by becoming even more sarcastic and biting, which we can surmise indicates that her own Shame/Contempt complex was snowballing. It appears that around this time her social development was at an impasse: I believe she protected herself from further Shame–Humiliation in two ways, by avoiding social contacts and by automatically turning self-contempt, that is Shame, into other-Contempt. Her parents recognized that Vivienne was experiencing a spiraling social decline and transferred her to a private school.

Early adolescence

The intervention seemed to pay off. During the sixth grade at her new school, Vivienne blossomed. She developed her very first emotionally significant friendship with a female classmate and wrote a composition celebrating this event. She took up the flute, started singing in the church choir, began to write poetry, and even entered school dramatics. The primary impetus for this opening up was her relationship with Mr John May, who was the main teacher for the students in her grade. One might guess that Vivienne was in love with Mr May, but this was not abnormal: her sister said that the whole sixth grade loved Mr May, who invited openness and could make you feel better just by listening. He apparently saw Vivienne as someone of special value, who didn't think she was worth much, and he undertook to help her by paying particular attention to her. The authors of the monograph tell us that Mr May complemented her on her work, told her she was pretty, and encouraged her to think well of herself.

One poem that Vivienne considered too intimate to show to Mr May, "Take My Hand," she did share with her family. She begins and ends the poem by asking an unnamed person to guide her through her life. More specifically, she asks to be accompanied through observation to knowledge and discovery. She also hopes that they will discover friends and a lifetime of love. The robust activity of the life instinct, first Interest and then Joy, is evident in her writing.

Vivienne wrote about this poem that it was an account of her ideal life. One might be concerned, on the other hand, that such an ideal might interfere in her bonding with her peers. Her brother and sister certainly thought that Vivienne didn't have any perspective on her idealism and tended to act disappointed (that is, rejecting) when others didn't measure up. The unconscious Shame/Contempt complex appears to have been constellated by the discrepancy between the ideal (Mr May) and the reality (her peers) in which her social development had to proceed.

At this juncture, it is important to understand how Mr May contributed to the remarkable period of growth Vivienne experienced in her eleventh year. Vivienne's relation with Mr May is, I believe, twofold: it is (a) a conscious personal relationship and (b) an unconscious symbolic relatedness. It is the latter that will concern us now.

In Chapter 7, "Rehearsals of identity in early adolescence," of my work, *The Symbolic Impetus*, I identified the *cultural attitude* as the new mode of the symbolic function which emerges at the beginning of this stage of development. In support of this view, I gave examples of individuals developing differentiated religious, aesthetic, philosophic, and social cultural attitudes as they entered adolescence. We have observed Vivienne's construction of an aesthetic cultural attitude during her blossoming in the sixth grade. Like other cultural attitudes first described by Joseph Henderson, such an attitude is a specific function of relation between the ego and the expressive centers of the cultural unconscious and the healthy affective basis of the personality. Henderson, a Jungian analyst, studied the development of all the cultural attitudes as well as identifying an initiation motif in the collective unconscious that helped move the individual into the cultural attitude appropriate to him or herself. This symbolic impetus for psychosocial development in early adolescence could be activated either by collective or by individual initiation rites. Erich Neumann has suggested that when the constellation of a particular unconscious impetus to identity formation occurs, the archetype of the solar hero is drawn upon to organize the personality along differentiated individual lines, creating the basis for a strong ego-identity.

Vivienne's symbolic relatedness with Mr May began when he provided the outer, cultural stimulus, the "teacher," which, I believe, ignited the stage appropriate initiation archetype in the healthy basis of Vivienne's personality. We can conjecture that, at this moment, the imago of a solar hero was activated and projected onto Mr May, so that an unconscious, dynamic symbolic relatedness was formed that provided the impetus for Vivienne's sixth-grade flowering:

> The finest of all symbols of the libido is the human figure, conceived as a demon or hero. Here the symbolism leaves the objective, material realm of astral and meteorological images and takes on human form, changing into a figure who passes from joy to sorrow, from sorrow to joy, and, like the sun, now stands high at the zenith and now is plunged into darkest night, only to rise again in new splendour.
>
> (Jung 1967: 251, 171)

The numinosity of the hero symbol correlates with the intensity of the affects with which the hero is venerated and can be the basis of "love at first sight." This affect is expressed in the first stanza of the poem, "Association with Reality" which Vivienne sent to Mr May for his critique. In this poem, she is liberated from the confining mold of emptiness and enters a world of "everlasting emotion" (Mack and Hickler 1981: 24).

One of the gifts of the hero (which can be received whether one identifies with the hero, as a boy might do, or projects onto him, as Vivienne did) is the capacity to direct the numinous archetypal emotions stirred up by him into developmental channels: "The teleological significance of the hero as a symbolic figure [is that he] attracts libido to himself in the form of wonder and admiration, in order to lead it over the symbolic bridge of myth to higher uses . . ." (Jung 1967: 477, 314). In Vivienne's case, the "higher uses" were the developmental achievements during her eleventh year that we have just described.

At this point, midway through the sixth grade, Vivienne, now age 12, began a personal journal, in which she not only entered her poems but also wrote her thoughts about herself, about life and love, and about ideals and ideal persons. She was starting to think in a more autonomous way and her journal entries record her continuing adolescent development. In her composition, "School," written the following year during the first month of the seventh grade, she indicated that she now had the capacity to shed being a "fake person" and to become "completely Me" (Mack and Hickler 1981: 32). The psychologist will note that she is beginning her struggle to establish her ego-identity. In a letter to Mr May near the end of the sixth grade, she describes her participation in a square dance: "Well, it was exciting for me, because I've never, never been asked by a boy before in my life! They swung me around and we laughed and got all hot and happy . . . Never before in my life have I laughed and joked with someone I never saw before! I've changed" (ibid.: 32).

Vivienne's libido, in other words, has been transferred from Mr May to boys her own age! At the end of the sixth grade, Vivienne rightly judged that Mr May had had a profoundly positive influence on her personality, and she thanked him for it.

Under optimal circumstances, the symbol of the hero would have helped Vivienne to continue to transfer her libido from her family to Mr May and then onto other people in her world. This is because, as her psychological development proceeded, the emotional energies inherent in the projected symbol would provide the impetus for the construction of new adaptive structures and functions of the ego-complex (C.T. Stewart 2001). Such an appropriate channeling of affective energies into realistic projects leads eventually to the natural withdrawal and interiorization of the projected archetypal-symbol that initially led the way. When the process of interioriza-tion of the fantasies that emerge has been completed, the actual personality of the carrier of the imago is more clearly revealed and the personality of the individual who made the projection will have undergone a stage of development.

Social isolation: "you are utterly and absolutely alone"

Vivienne's crush, apparently a projection of a heroic animus onto Mr May, was not to be resolved, however, by a natural process of evolution. In the late fall of 1971, shortly after her beginning seventh grade, Mr May announced that he would be leaving Vivienne's school the following year. Vivienne wrote down her reaction to this unexpected news a few days later, on 9 November 1971:

> He's going to leave me behind as he goes on his merry way. But if he leaves me what way will I have to go? Why won't he stay? When will I die? It seems like I ought to die now while the going's good. While life has still

got some joy. That joy will be gone in a year. Maybe I will be too – oh, ah, silver tears appearing now. I'm crying, ain't I?

(Mack and Hickler 1981: 34)

The progressive decline in Vivienne's well-being that led, twenty-five months later, to her suicide, appears to have begun on this date. Neither during the thirteen months before Mr May's departure nor during the year after it, is Vivienne able to stop her descent into an emotional maelstrom. It will be almost as if the flowering of her early adolescent development during the sixth grade had never occurred. I believe an analysis of the reasons for the tragic impact of Mr May's announcement will help us understand the unremitting psychological decline in Vivienne that ensued.

When Vivienne heard of Mr May's announcement, I believe a new affective relation to her beloved self-object was initiated, for her above reaction to this unwelcome news suggests that an efficient symbol was formed and the innate affect Sadness–Anguish–Agony was activated. The conscious component of this constellating symbol was "Mr May," but now as the life stimulus, Loss, while the unconscious element was the primal image, the Void (see Table I.1, Row 2). We can speculate that this current activation of this crisis affect also awakened the Agony-complex which we have postulated had existed in Vivienne's unconscious perhaps as far back as infancy and certainly from her fifth year, when her grandfathers died and it took on the character of a traumatic complex. The assimilation of the impending loss of Mr May to this complex was why it seemed to her that Mr May had already departed. With this complex structuring her experience, Mr May vanishes into the void. I will present evidence from Vivienne's writings that a progressive increase in the magnitude and intensity of this complex occurred during the remaining months of her life. This, in my judgment, is the primary reason she was unable to recover from the announcement on 9 November 1971.

I believe that with his announcement of his return to California, "Mr May" also was assimilated to the life stimulus, Rejection. This became the conscious component of an efficient symbol for the activation of Shame/Contempt, the unconscious component being the primal image, Alienation (see Table I.1, Column 4). We have argued that during elementary school, Vivienne's rejection by her classmates resulted in the development of a Shame/Contempt-complex of considerable intensity. It seems reasonable to assume that this complex was activated on 9 November 1971. The increase in magnitude of this complex over the next twenty-five months was a secondary reason why Vivienne was unable to reverse her downward course. With the activation of the Anguish and Shame/Contempt complexes, libido was drained from the image of the solar hero as a progressive force in her life. The creative bond between Vivienne and Mr May was now attenuated; in fact, he had come to mean something different to her altogether. There was no question of internalizing what he had once meant to her. Her adolescent development screeched to a halt. During her period of growth, the ratio of positive to negative affects had strongly favored the former, but after the arrest of her development this ratio was reversed.

Vivienne did try to establish a relationship with two other male teachers, either of whom might have replaced Mr May as a source of impetus, but she discovered that both of them were also leaving her school. Nor was she able to develop relationships with other adults or adolescents that might have helped her to withdraw the symbolic projection that was tying her to Mr May and to objectify and integrate the crisis affects that were engulfing her.

By 9 November 1971, Vivienne had experienced a violent rupture of her relationship with Mr May. But, why didn't she withdraw the projection if by now it had turned into such a severe handicap? Certain of Jung's comments about the transference have relevance here:

> Transference, strictly, as I have already said, is a projection which happens between two individuals and which, as a rule, is of an emotional and compulsory nature. Emotions in themselves are always in some degree overwhelming for the subject, because they are involuntary conditions which override the intentions of the ego. Moreover, they cling to the subject, and he cannot detach them from himself. Yet this involuntary condition of the subject is at the same time projected into the object, and through that a bond is established which cannot be broken, and exercises a compulsory influence upon the subject.
>
> (Jung 1977: 316, 138)

The symbolic relation to Mr May has not been resolved, it has been severed: "A violent rupture of the transference may bring on a complete relapse, or worse; so the problem must be handled with great tact and foresight" (Jung 1972: 255, 165). The primary danger for Vivienne at this point of disruption was an acute return of her social isolation:

> The transference therefore consists in a number of projections which act as a substitute for a real psychological relationship. They create an apparent relationship and this is very important, since it comes at a time when the patient's habitual failure to adapt has been artificially intensified by his analytical removal into the past. Hence a sudden severance of the transference is always attended by extremely unpleasant and even dangerous consequences, because it maroons the patient in an impossibly unrelated situation.
>
> (Jung 1966: 284, 136)

Both in her journal and in her letters to Mr May before his departure, Vivienne describes what I believe is her descent into "an impossibly unrelated situation."

In four entries in her journal – on 9 May 1972, about eight months before Mr May's leaving, a few months later during the summer of 1972, in an entry in her diary at the start of the eighth grade in September 1972, and a month after this – Vivienne described her descent into loneliness and social isolation that eventually became "most of the time." She expressed her need for a friend and wrote that she was unable to find one; there was no one with whom to "pour out your heart" (Mack and Hickler 1981: 51). A month after the last entry, Mr May returned to California.

Vivienne's first journal entry for 1973 is undated but coincides with Mr May's departure. It is a short essay titled, "perdre: to lose," in which she indicates, for the first time, that she may "lose her life because [Mr May] is not here" (ibid.: 54–5). She writes that her tangible, true relationship with Mr May is gone forever and she is left with an imaginary one that is too empty to sustain the inner connection to the lost love-object. She has still been unable to withdraw the projection from him and we can infer that the Agony complex continues to snowball.

Vivienne's experience of being in "an impossibly unrelated situation," an increasingly critical state of social isolation, was powerfully expressed in her next poem:

> You reach for a smile
> But there is no one there
> To reflect it.
> You are utterly and absolutely
> Alone.
> Will there never be a hand
> To grasp at yours within the mirror?
>   (ibid.: 55)

The empty hands in this poem are in stark contrast to those in the poem of hope that she wrote in the sixth grade, "Take My Hand."

On 5 June 1973, six months before her death, Vivienne wrote Mr May to tell him that she has been very tearful, continues to feel lonely, and has found no one to turn to. She thinks she has gone to "pieces" and hopes he can send her "something encouraging, positive, anything! for me to live on for a while" (ibid.: 67–8). With the Agony complex continuing to increase in magnitude, Vivienne appears to be searching desperately for connection with Mr May's life instinct. We can postulate that her emotional life was seeking to preserve itself by connecting with Mr May's life instinct. She continues to be reluctant to talk with her family about how she is actually feeling: "I'd talk to my parents, but it would depress them too much . . ." (ibid.: 82).

On 9 July 1973, five months before her suicide, she attempts to strangle herself with her hands and the next day describes this event in a letter to Mr May. In another letter to him two days later, she again writes that she wishes she had some friends, but doesn't. She is unable to mobilize the life instinct she needs to succeed in accomplishing this goal.

The first stanza of the next poem, has a somewhat accusatory tone, but Vivienne is still unable to commit the symbolic murder which would enable her to withdraw her maladaptive projection:

> *Is there no mirror?*
> *Nothing to echo back?*
> *I cannot find you!*
> *I have given all I have!*
> *Gotten nothing back.*
> (ibid.: 97)

Vivienne does not say she is addressing this poem to Mr May, who is disappearing more and more into the void, but it is reasonable to conjecture she is doing so. She seems to contrast the bounty that their relation gave her in the past with her current desolation. In September 1973 as she starts the ninth grade in a new school, she makes a friend named Anne. Their relationship begins when Vivienne reads aloud a composition in English class on suicide and Anne responds with a special interest, revealing that her older sister had committed suicide the month before. Vivienne is soon the only one Anne can talk with about her sister's death. Vivienne confides to Anne her own thoughts about suicide and describes her attempts at self-strangulation, but swears Anne to secrecy. On 2 December 1973, nineteen days before her death, Vivienne writes in a letter to Mr May that her relationship with Anne is limited to school hours as they live quite far apart. In addition, Vivienne mentions that her family would be moving to another community on 28 December 1973, because her father is changing churches. (As it happens, she never makes this move because her suicide occurs on 21 December 1973.) In the 2 December letter she once again tells Mr May she wishes he had returned because he is still her very best friend.

A poem, written during the last three weeks of her life, continues the theme of social isolation:

> Do you love me anymore?
> Are you there?
> You know I need you.
> Whose name can I call out?
> Would anyone come running?
> Because you know I need some one to love me.
> (ibid.: 113)

This poem gives voice, I believe, to Vivienne's desperation over her pervasive social isolation. On 11 December 1973, she tries to hang herself from a tree with her sister's scarf, but is unsuccessful. On 21 December 1973, in her mother's silversmithing studio, she succeeds in hanging herself, using a piece of rope she had obtained from her mother to use in "packing."

Dissociation of the personality: "something lost and never found: a song of joy"

If we accept her siblings' view of her infancy, that she would sit on the floor and scream for hours, and couple this with the extraordinary outpouring of Anguish at the death of her grandfathers during her preschool period, then it is reasonable to assume that by the time she began elementary school, Vivienne had developed an Anguish-toned complex. In the last section, we argued that during her socially compromised five years of elementary school Vivienne had developed a Shame ("Vivienne stinks")/Contempt ("sarcastic wit") complex. That these complexes were not of sufficient intensity or magnitude to cause a complete dissociation of her psyche and block her individual growth is shown by the beginning of a rich and vibrant early adolescent development during her eleventh year in the sixth grade. This blossoming could only have occurred if she was in touch with the healthy affective basis of her personality. This ground was the ultimate source of the Interest and Joy that not only illuminated her relatedness to Mr May, but also provided the impetus for her individual psychological growth during the period she felt he was interested in what she could become.

The dynamic, emotional ground of this growth surge was the symbolic bond that had been established with her sixth-grade teacher, Mr May. When an affect-laden symbol is projected, it serves as a bridge to establish an involuntary emotional tie between subject and object, a bond that extends from the healthy affective base of the projecting individual's personality to the embodied psyche of the other. As we have just explained, Vivienne's projection onto Mr May was not to be resolved by a natural process of evolution.

Jung questions limiting application of the term transference to the process of psychotherapy:

> It is open to doubt whether the transference is always constructed arti-
> ficially, since it is a phenomenon that can take place quite apart from
> any treatment, and is moreover a frequent natural occurrence. Indeed,
> in any human relationship that is at all intimate, certain transference
> phenomena will almost always operate as helpful or disturbing factors.
>
> (Jung 1966: 357, n. 14, 171)

And, indeed, Vivienne's symbolic relation with Mr May, which had been a helpful factor, appears to have become a blocking one. Furthermore, I believe, as the Anguish complex residing in Vivienne's unconscious snowballs and becomes monopolistic in magnitude, it will cause a dissociation between ego-consciousness and the healthy affective basis of her personality. Her capacity for self-vitalization through subjective integration will be critically diminished.

As we noted in Chapter 2, Jung has referred to disturbances caused by affects as *phenomena of dissociation* and has indicated how such psychic splits are brought about: "As we have already explained at some length, affects have a dissociating (distracting) effect on consciousness, probably because they put a one-sided and excessive emphasis on a particular idea, so that too little attention is left over for investment in other conscious activities" (Jung 1970a: 339, 181). During her year of blossoming in the sixth grade, the "image" of Mr May in Vivienne's psyche originated, in my opinion, primarily in a libido-symbol heralding her adolescent development. After she had learned of Mr May's departure, the "image" of Mr May in Vivienne's mind derived primarily from the pathological Agony complex. It is reasonable to argue that Mr May had become "a particular idea."

I will now show that beginning on 9 November 1971, when Vivienne learned of Mr May's upcoming departure, that the snowballing, now monopolistic, Anguish–Agony complex not only led to her social isolation but also caused a severe dissociation of her psyche. We can, I believe, follow the progression of this dissociative process by tracing the eclipse of the sun and moon symbols in her poems, interpreted as expressions of Interest and Joy respectively. Even after Mr May moved to California in January 1973, he continued to be the primary figure in her life. She kept up an active correspondence with him, although he replied infrequently.

During the last thirteen months of her life, from November 1972 to December 1973, Vivienne wrote a series of poems, seven of which contained images of the "sun" and the "moon." These are of course basic images of constellated affective light that have illuminated a variety of human situations in different individuals and cultures. But if one draws on the way the images of the sun and moon are developed by Milton and Blake (see the epilogue to this book), one can see that in the western poetic tradition at least, "sun" often expresses the affect of Interest/Logos and the principle of masculine consciousness, whereas in that same tradition the "moon" expresses the affect of Joy/Eros and the principle of a more diffused feminine consciousness. The series of poems which portray a gradual eclipse of both luminaries depict, I believe, a progressive dissociation, that is cutting off, of the emotional basis of Vivienne's personality. As this dissociation proceeds, Vivienne's ability to see her emotions and experience them in ego-consciousness dims. (Vivienne's diary writing remained to the end somewhat effective, but her expressions were inadequate to keep up with the sheer quantity of crisis emotions pressing for integration.)

On the night of 17 November 1972, a year to the month after the announcement of Mr May's departure (though two months before his actual leaving), Vivienne wrote two poems. In the first of these, a whipping wind, which gathers its strength by taking her life breath away, shatters, smashes, and fells trees as it rushes past. Destructive forces have been unleashed into her ego out of the collective unconscious and they threaten the integrity of her developing ego functions (the branches of the trees) and her very self (her tree of life). In the second poem written the same night there is a stanza that reads as follows:

> And where would you say the
> Moon lies
> With winter on its way?
> Both walls are cold,
> Unblinking off-white.
> (Mack and Hickler 1981: 51)

The significance of the moon for Vivienne can hardly be underestimated. Jung has described the feminine consciousness in lunar terms:

> This is indeed so in the case of woman: her consciousness has a lunar rather than a solar character. Its light is the "mild" light of the moon, which merges things together rather than separates them. It does not show up objects in all their pitiless discreteness and separateness, like the harsh, glaring light of day, but blends in a deceptive shimmer the near and the far, magically transforming little things into big things, high into low, softening all colours into a bluish haze, and blending the nocturnal landscape into an unsuspected unity.
>
> (Jung 1970e: 223, 179)

In Vivienne's case, this description certainly fits: the loss of the moon was for her nothing less than the loss of her female orientation, so that the ego that is left lacks affective color. As the "moon" begins to be difficult for her to locate, Vivienne's consciousness enters a ghostly room where it is surrounded by icy, inhuman ("unblinking"), coldness, an utterly alienated state that has been referred to as "the closed world" of the suicidal person (Alvarez 1971: Part 3). Eros is nowhere to be found.

A poem Vivienne composed a few months later, in early 1973, which has images of both "moon" and "sun," contains this stanza:

> The oddly methodical
> Frenzy builds;
> The terror of the moon is about you.
> (Mack and Hickler 1981: 55)

We can argue now that Hecate (or Luna), the "spook-goddess," has begun to haunt Vivienne: "As the 'spirit-mother' she sends madness, the moonsickness. This idea is perfectly sensible, because most forms of lunacy consist of affections which amount to an invasion by the unconscious and an inundation of the conscious mind" (Jung 1967: 577, 370). Vivienne, however, continues:

> But you will see
> As you hold up your mirror
> That it is only the empty sun
> Which you have found.
> (Mack and Hickler 1981: 55)

By now, Mr May has gone from Vivienne's daily life, and simultaneously, the archetype of the "sun-hero," with its life-giving Interest, appears to have departed from her inner life, leaving a terrible vacancy. Her "sun" itself is an empty void. This suggests a greater dissociation between consciousness and the unconscious.

On 14 May 1973, seven months before her suicide, Vivienne wrote another poem, titled "Where is Night?" which closes,

> You took the sun, but why
> Can't you leave me the moon?
> (ibid.: 64)

My view of this poem is that it expresses, in symbolic form, Vivienne's dilemma. She is now nearing absolute dissociation from both of the primary affects of the life instinct, Interest, "the sun," and Joy, "the moon." In the rest of the poem she sounds spent, like someone who has sensed that her time is running out.

Two months later, on 9 July 1973, Vivienne, for the first time, "practiced" choking herself with her hands. The next day, she wrote a letter to Mr May in which she describes her attempt at self-strangulation and includes four poems. The first, "Empty Sunshine Day," has these first four lines:

> Silence in your ears
> The riots in your tears –
> Just an empty
> Sunshine Day.
> (ibid.: 73–4)

We can surmise that what is absent for Vivienne during these "empty Sunshine Days" is the "sun-hero" as a dynamic libido-symbol. That life-giving symbol, having been projected onto Mr May, who accepted the projection and unwittingly made off with it, has been severed from her psychic landscape.

In "Departure," the second poem she sent to Mr May, "the sun goes down
... to a tune You made up for love" and "the moon weeps in your eyes"
(ibid.: 75). She is now, I believe, addressing herself in the second person here:
it is her own eyes that express the Agony she wishes Mr May could see and
knows he cannot.

On 12 July 1973, she wrote "Empty Sparrow," which contains the following
lines:

> Something lost
> And never found;
> A song of joy
> Yet somehow
> Mimed and mute.
> (ibid.: 77–8)

This imagery rather clearly suggests her soul's loss of contact with the
capacity for emotional expression. The poetry, in fact, works to convey
what she is experiencing because it is so dispassionate in limning her
dilemma. In the terms we have been developing from affect theory, the dissociation of the healthy affective base of her personality is so profound that it
is hard to believe that the innate affect of the life instinct, the "song of Joy,"
still resides anywhere to be found. Only a morbid Interest in its disappearance
remains.

On 8 October 1973, two months before her death, Vivienne wrote, as a class
assignment, an essay on a dream, "On Recognition." Within the dream she
selected to recount, a street cleaner gives her a dream that is also a poem. The
first stanza reads:

> A star unlit
> A child unborn
> The tear inside
> The cry. These things
> Shall make you free.
> (ibid.: 104–5)

We can conjecture that this is a final ambiguous burst of hope for emotional
recovery in the midst of despair. The "star unlit" and "child unborn" symbolize the result of the severance of the bond that had been alchemically forged
in her psyche by her animus and Mr May's anima. The failure of a continu-
ance of this fateful conjunction that had taken place during the year of her
blossoming and born a numinous "child" was now a living death, like the
alchemical *mortifcatio* that follows a first *coniunctio* in the famous series of
illustrations from the Rosarium that Jung used to illuminate the dynamics of
the archetypal transference. In terms of present-day self-psychology, we

would call this the self-object transference. And in affect theory, the conjunction of cosmic principles indicates the healthy dialectic of Interest and Joy, out of which the symbolic impetus for development itself is born. The Renaissance alchemist was intuitively cognizant of the vitality this fundamental process could release when he wrote of the Mercury that is the fuel for the work of spiritual alchemy: "As the little star near the sun, he (Mercurius) is the child of sun and moon" (Jung 1968b: 273, 225–6).

On 21 November 1973, five weeks before her suicide, Vivienne composed the seventh and last poem in this series, "And Where is the Moon?" Now there has been an eclipse of both the sun and the moon, which, as the last stanza indicates, leaves her alone in the void:

> God help me!
> . . . There is nothing.
> Nothing.
> And you have taken the sun
> And
> Where
>   Is the moon!
> (Mack and Hickler 1981: 109)

The total eclipse of both the "sun" and the "moon" indicates that Vivienne's dissociation from the healthy base of her personality has reached its nadir, there is "nothing," only the void. The young woman's desperation is palpable.

Within a subsequent poem, written sometime during the last three weeks of her life, Vivienne describes what I believe has been the consequence for her selfhood of her dissociation, the arrest of her development and the *fragmentation* of her personality:

> The day has splintered
> One thousand pieces
> Beyond recognition.
> And nothing more shall be.
>   (ibid.: 113)

This proclamation turned out to be true. Within a month, Vivienne had committed suicide.

Unbearable affect: "it's strange living with no relief for so long"

I have speculated that there was the development in Vivienne's psyche, by the time she was 11 years old and in the sixth grade, of a Shame/ Contempt complex and an Agony complex, both of considerable intensity.

They were not of sufficient magnitude, however, to block the onset of her normal adolescent development and its poignant unfolding during sixth grade.

I have also argued that when, in November 1971, Mr May announced that he would be leaving her school, a pre-existing Agony complex was immediately constellated. Five months later, on 12 April 1972, Vivienne wrote in her journal that she had "never been more depressed in [her] life [and that she was] developing an inferiority complex" (ibid.: 41). The Shame/Contempt complex, "inferiority complex," was also activated. As a life stimulus for its constellation, we believe that Vivienne experienced Mr May's announcement as both a Loss and a Rejection. We will now follow the gradual build-up of unbearable negative affect, which along with the reduction in the positive affects of the life instinct, as expressed in her writings, made her emotions unbearable.

On 5 May 1972, which she describes as the worst day of the year, she is depressed and thinks that no one really likes her. Vivienne will find to her dismay that many worst days lie ahead of her, for from this time until her death on 21 December 1973 there will be an unremitting increase in unbearable crisis affects. On 12 December 1972, about the time of Mr May's departure, Vivienne wrote a poem indicating that her life had lost its future and she had "nothing" to look forward to. One's life can hardly be bleaker and more insufferable than this. In a journal entry four months later, on 11 April 1973, even suicide seems absurd to her because how can you kill a worthless nothing: "It takes tolerance not to give in to death" (ibid.: 63). She is all but saying that she cannot tolerate much more.

On 5 June 1973, just after her school year had ended, Vivienne wrote a letter to Mr May telling him of her increasing despair: "And now I must say something and it's not easy. You see there have been a lot of tears lately . . . It's funny, but I've really gone to pieces" (ibid.: 67–8). This is an apt description of the fragmentation of the self in the face of self-object failure. The combination of Vivienne's social isolation, the absence of the positive affects of the life instinct, and her increasingly intense Agony are threatening the integrity of her personality. It was four days later that Vivienne "practiced" strangling herself for the first time.

On 2 December 1973, nineteen days before her actual suicide, she sent another letter to Mr May in which she wrote that she had been crying throughout the writing of it: "The funny thing is that crying isn't even a form of letting go anymore. It's just sort of a routine thing like taking orange juice and toast for breakfast every morning. I mean, the pressure is there afterwards, all the time; it doesn't really matter what I do. *It's strange living with no relief for so long*" (ibid.: 111–12, emphasis added).

The magnitude of the Agony complex now seems to be monopolistic, its intensity has become beyond endurance, and it has become continuously active. This entry was made about the same time that she wrote in a poem that the day had "splintered," suggesting either that the complex had a role in fragmenting her self, or that in the face of a fragmenting self, the pathogenic complexes have no barrier to coming forward. But once constellated, they certainly increase the destruction of the self.

On 11 December 1973, a short two weeks before her suicide, she wrote a letter to Mr May which he received the day after her death. In it, Vivienne writes of her fear of her extreme suicidal moods which appear suddenly over a fifteen-minute time span. Just such a mood was the prelude to her most recent, but unsuccessful, suicide attempt. I am arguing that her "extreme" and "terrific" depressions are generated "from the middle of nowhere" by the monopolistic Agony complex.

On 22 December 1973, the day after Vivienne's suicide, her mother found this last poem on the kitchen table. It has no title:

> When you are
> Too weary
> To go on
> And life strikes
> Such a finalizing chord,
> you have a choice.
> > (ibid.: 120)

At one level she means the choice to kill herself, which she made. But in a sense she had no choice. In my judgment, unbearable Agony had now completely overwhelmed Vivienne's ego-consciousness, and her adaptive energies were eclipsed. She was possessed by the complex, which no longer wanted her ego to survive.

Possession by affect: "death is going to be a beautiful thing"

In the first three sections of this chapter, we have postulated the constellation, on 9 November 1971, of an Anguish complex that had snowballed by the time of Vivienne's death to become a pathological, monopolistic Agony complex of such magnitude and intensity that it caused an arrest of her social development, a dissociation of her personality that blocked her subjective integration and growth, and a state of unbearable affect. In this section, we will look at some of her writings that suggest her experience of being taken over by this complex. They begin on 9 July 1973 and ended with her death on 21 December 1973.

The first stanza of a poem composed on 3 April 1973 expresses how tempting death has become to her. At this time she is not yet, in my judgment, possessed by the Agony complex.

It takes tolerance
Not to give in to death,
To resist the temptation
How easy just to die.
To keep on living an empty life
Takes patience from an empty person.
(ibid.: 63)

The self may be empty, but it still has the capacity to endure some things. In the evening of 9 July 1973, Vivienne spent a half hour in the back bathroom of her parents' house "practicing" strangling herself with her own hands. She wrote in capitals across the bathroom wall, "DEATH IS GOING TO BE A BEAUTIFUL THING" (ibid.: 72). This event marked, I believe, Vivienne's first transition from a problematic to an unproblematic state of consciousness. She had gone beyond the objectivation of the Agony complex to an initial rush of possession by it that left her, as possession often does, much less conflicted. This was most ominous. The next day she wrote to Mr May, describing her "practicing" to him, and said: "I know that I will need the knowledge some day soon" (ibid.: 71). But the relief she felt also had its positive side: it appears that it had released a compensatory response from the unconscious, for she now spoke of her decision to live another year. (This estimate of the term of the loan of energy from the unconscious turned out to be overly optimistic on her ego's part: the unconscious would call in the loan, and Vivienne's life would be over, in just five months.)

Vivienne's first paper in her high school freshman English class in the fall of 1973 was about suicide. As we have seen, this captured the attention of a classmate, Anne, whose older sister had actually committed suicide in August 1973. The two girls became friends and Vivienne shared with Anne, after swearing her to secrecy, that she was very serious about suicide and saw a spiritual side to it. In their conversations, the two would go into Vivienne's private world of contemplated death, which Vivienne had kept sequestered from everything else. Vivienne told Anne that she had practiced suicide at least on *five occasions*. I would describe these as brief possessions by the complex. She told Anne she was "calm" each time, which I would interpret as entering the unproblematic state of consciousness that is the hallmark of possession of the ego by a complex (the normal ego must suffer the tensions of opposites, and feel conflict: anxiety and depression are thus, as John Beebe has written, symptoms of the integrity of the ego – Beebe 1992: Chapter 2).

From the standpoint of the dynamics of affect, she was calm because, each time she enacted the suicidal ritual, she entered a state of certainty. Possessed by the conviction that death was her solution, her ego was free of conflict. She would become frightened whenever she found herself home alone, because there was nothing besides the self-strangulation to distract her from her depression. Around others, however, during this time, both at home and at school, Vivienne's persona, an extraverted façade personality, was in full force, leading most of her friends and family to view her as a reasonably normal, healthy teenager. Between each bout of possession, she was able, in her journal entries and in her letters to Mr May, to continue to objectify her emotions.

On 7 December 1973, two weeks before her actual death, Vivienne made a real attempt at suicide, this time going out into the park, wrapping her neck with her sister's scarf, and trying to loop the end of it over a tree branch. The makeshift noose did not immediately work, and she became anxious that others would see her and so left the park unharmed. Four days later, on 11 December 1973, Vivienne wrote a letter to Mr May that he did not receive until after her death. In it she described this suicide attempt in precise detail. She added a comment about the terrific depressions that arose from the middle of nowhere and frightened her. These were less depressions of the ego experiencing conflict than possessions of it. As Jung might have said, she no longer had her emotions: they had her.

While this private drama was approaching its denouement, the family was getting ready to move to another city, where her father had a new job. The date of the actual move was 28 December 1973. Less than two weeks before that, on Sunday, 16 December, Vivienne asked her mother for some rope to use in packing. In fact, she was planning to use it to hang herself, but her mother did not see beyond Vivienne's false explanation, and gave the rope to her. Vivienne will now, I believe, be possessed continuously by the Agony complex throughout the last five days of her life. On Tuesday, 18 December, Vivienne's Christmas vacation from high school began. Vivienne's mother noticed that between Tuesday and Friday Vivienne spent a lot of time re-reading her writing and her journals. Only later did it become evident to her mother that by noon on Friday, 21 December 1973, Vivienne had decided "it was all over":

> I came home on my lunch hour that day, but Vivienne was still in bed. When I got home at suppertime she was sitting in the kitchen – just sitting there. I picked up her hair and gave her a big kiss on the back of the neck. She didn't respond at all. There was a funny smell about her. Now I realize it was the smell of fear. She had decided to do this thing and she had figured out the timing, but she was afraid.
>
> (Mack and Hickler 1981: 4)

That evening Vivienne hanged herself in her mother's silversmithing studio with the rope that she had obtained from her mother. Her parents were at a neighborhood party. Her sister, who had been upstairs playing the piano, sensed that something was wrong and came downstairs to find her sister dead. The day after Vivienne's death, her mother found Vivienne's final suicide poem on the kitchen table. This time I will quote it in full:

When you are
Too weary
To go on
And life strikes
Such a finalizing chord,
you have a choice.

You can either
Take your bow
And leave.
Or carry the tune
appreciating the crescendo
As exactly that.

                    (ibid.: 120)

It now seems clear that at the time of her death, Vivienne was experiencing all four of the necessary affective conditions for the perception of self-destruction as the only possible solution: social isolation, dissociation of the personality from the healthy affective base of personhood, unbearable affect, and affect possession. Her poem hints at her "condition" – the feeling that to go on living, she would have to accept that the present feeling of despair was as much passion as she could ever hope to feel about anything. There would be no further crescendo. When such a terrible, final chord has been struck by the affective instrument, the choice of taking the bow of one's feeling and simply leaving one's emotional life behind begins to seem the obvious one. But this is also the ideology of a complex that has utterly replaced a reasoning ego.

Chapter 5

Kipland Kinkel: killing of parents and others

During the afternoon of 20 May 1998, Kipland Kinkel, a 15-year-old high school freshman, shot and killed his father at their home. When his mother returned home from work in the early evening, he shot and killed her too. He spent the night at home and the next morning, 21 May 1998, went to his school and shot and killed two students and wounded twenty-five others.

This is the note he left in his living room after he had killed his parents and before his rampage the next day at his high school:

> I have just killed my parents! I don't know what Is happening. I love my mom and dad so much. I just got two felonies on my record. My parents can't take that! It would destroy them. The embarrassment would be too much for them. They couldn't live with themselves. I'm so sorry. I am a horrible son. I wish I had been aborted. I destroy everything I touch. I can't eat. I can't sleep. I didn't deserve them. They were wonderful people. It's not their fault or the fault of any person, organization, or television show. My head just doesn't work right. God damn these VOICES Inside my head. I want to die. I want to be gone. But I have to kill people. I don't know why. I am so sorry! Why did God do this to me? I have never been happy. I wish I was happy. I wish I made my mother proud. I am nothing! I tried so hard to find happiness. But you know me I hate everything. I have no other choice. What have I become? I am so sorry.
>
> (Kirk and Boyer 2000d: 1)

He considers his parents blameless for what he has already done and, by implication, for what he is about to do.

In this chapter, I will show that on 20 and 21 May 1998, Kipland was affectively caught in all four of the conditions that I have postulated are necessary for lethal behaviors such as his to emerge. In each of the next four sections, I will consider one of these four conditions and discuss how they apply to and help to explicate this tragic situation. The empirical evidence for this demonstration is drawn primarily from a 167-page transcript written by M. Kirk and P. J. Boyer for *The Killer at Thurston High*, a program aired 1/18/2000 by Frontline (PBS). (The program is divided into seven sections which are identified individually in the text and in the bibliography.)

Social isolation: "I am always alone"

Kipland began keeping a journal when he entered his freshman year in high school in 1997, about eight months before the killings. The quote at the head of this section was written in the fall of that year. I will now attempt to explain how it was that Kipland arrived at this severe degree of aloneness.

When, after the killings, Kipland's sister Kristin was interviewed, she was asked to comment on the parents' method of discipline. She replied that all they needed to do was to let their children know that they were *disappointed* in them. She marveled at the power of this form of discipline. When the interviewer suggested that it was very important, then, for them not to disappoint their parents, Kristen said: "It more than mattered – it was the most important thing" (Kirk and Boyer 2000e: 7). She added that for herself she imagined that at some point disappointing them might have become *unbearable*. Kristin acted as a mediator between her parents and her brother, when she thought they were making a federal case out of one of his minor infractions.

The pattern pointed out by Kipland's sister was also noted by a friend of his mother, who thought that Kipland would have minded if he was a disappointment, as she viewed his parents as a very successful couple with high expectations of others.

Let us recall that the life stimuli for the constellation of the archetypal crisis affects (Fear, Sadness, Anger, and Shame/Contempt) were *the Unknown* (Fear), *Loss* (Sadness), *Restriction* (Anger), and *Rejection* (Shame/Contempt). The spectrum of intensity for Rejection can be conceived as Disappointment–Rejection–Exile. We can conjecture that Kipland's parents' method of discipline can be assimilated to this continuum, which means that the Kinkel family atmosphere was one of potential "disappointment." His sister has indicated that this potential was actualized with considerable frequency and intensity, so that we can conjecture that Kipland was no stranger to constellations of the archetypal affect Shame/Contempt.

Certainly, from the start of his schooling, Kipland was unable to live up to his parents' hopes and expectations for his academic success. Both parents were respected high school teachers and scholastic success was important to them. Beginning in the first grade, Kipland seemed lost at school and had great difficulty with reading, writing, and spelling. Although he was held back a year, the second grade was equally difficult. In the third grade, however, Kipland was placed in special education and from this time on he improved his academic performance.

The parents, particularly the father, were now to become disappointed in Kipland's achievements in another field of endeavor – sports. Athletic prowess was a valued currency in the Kinkel family. The father was a tennis ace, coached the high school tennis team, and was said to be fiercely competitive. When he put a racquet in his son's hand, Kipland just didn't develop any interest in the sport. Nor in middle school was soccer, nor in high school was football, the "tonic" that his father had hoped for. We can infer that disappointments regarding athletic achievement were added to earlier disappointments.

Kipland's relationships with his parents became marred by his tantrums and the threats of further aggression that he would express. He got uncontrollably angry and smashed things when told "No." His sensitivity to rejection was becoming more and more acute. Because of such episodes, Kipland received therapy from 30 January to 30 July 1997, along with a course of Prozac from June to September 1997.

In his first interview, Kipland, who was now 14 years old, became tearful when he characterized his relationships with his parents: "Kip thought his mother viewed him as 'a good kid with some bad habits' while his father saw him as 'a bad kid with bad habits.' He felt his father expected the worst from him" (Kirk and Boyer 2000f: 4). It was now a year and a half before Kipland's final rampage. What was quoted by his therapist suggests that he was experiencing his relationship with his father as one of progressive negativity and alienation.

Kipland's increasing social isolation during this time was noted by several observers. His sister thought that during adolescence he was lonely most of the time. At school, teachers and classmates described him as alternating between being withdrawn socially and playing the class clown. One classmate said being alone was something Kipland himself experienced as weakness: "He was always worried about being alone all the time, isolated and stuff like that" (Kirk and Boyer 2000a: 29–30). If the Shame/Contempt complex was burgeoning, as we are arguing, then Kipland, intensely sensitive to rejection, may have begun to avoid social contacts as a method of self-protection.

During his freshman year, Kipland fell in love with a girl in his class: they attended the school's winter formal, which was held four months before his rampage. He recorded the vicissitudes of this relationship and the mounting pain and despair that its ups and downs engendered in him. He wrote that every time he approached her his hopes were dashed. At such moments he experienced severe heartache accompanied by a rage and animosity so intense that he wondered if he could ever love anyone.

The emotional sequence was reaching out (this was conditioned by the life instinct at low intensity), followed by the familiar response to rejection and its pain, and then (the most painful of all) constellation, at high intensity, of the affect complex of Shame/Contempt. I believe it is the Contempt pole of that constellation that Kipland was experiencing when he refers to his "hate" and "animosity." These feelings were so intense and of such magnitude because they were archetypal, and the inhuman ruthlessness of the archetypal emotion was what made him doubt his capacity for ever loving anyone. There was, poignantly, still hope and it was this, Kipland suggested, that kept him from committing suicide: "Even though I am repulsive [self-Contempt] and few people know who I am [alienation], I still feel that things might, maybe, just a little bit, get better" (Kirk and Boyer 2000d: 2). There were still stirrings of the life instinct.

He sensed his need for help and thought that the positive affects still generated in him by the relationship he was clinging to might be a source of modulation and invigoration. But his agony increased: "Today of all days, I ask her to help me. I was shot down. I feel like my heart has been ripped open and ripped apart" (ibid.: 3). We can conjecture that the intensity of the Rejection–Shame/Contempt experience was expressed through the image of a knife cutting open his heart.

Kipland's sensitivity to rejection, apparent in these entries, was, in my opinion, based on a Shame/Contempt complex that was snowballing into a conscious state of Humiliation and Loathing. This unconscious monopolistic structure had taken over his ego and was now controlling his moment to moment experience. It was no longer reactive to particular life stimuli: it had taken on a life of its own, and was continuously and autonomously constellated. Fear of triggering this complex now became a reason for him to maintain his social isolation.

In Kipland's writings, there is no indication that he was able to learn from the difficulties he encountered with his loved classmate and, thereby, to improve his ability to relate to her. This is unfortunate, because Shame/Contempt is the innate affect that drives the development of the feeling function of the ego (see Table 2.2), and painful interactions might have led to an improved capacity for interpersonal relating (see also *The Symbolic Impetus*: 109–11):

> Disappointment, always a shock to the feelings, is not only the mother of bitterness but the strongest incentive to a differentiation of feeling. The failure of a pet plan, the disappointing behaviour of someone one loves, can supply the impulse either for a more or less brutal outburst of affect or for a modification and adjustment of feeling, and hence for a higher development.
>
> (Jung 1970e: 334, 248)

Such an outcome was not open to Kipland. It appears, rather, that he arrived at an arrest of his emotional development. Jung quotes Neisser's explanation for such a standstill:

The affects which are normally meant to regulate our relations with the surrounding world and to implement our adaptation to it – which act, indeed, as a means of protecting the organism and are the motive forces of self-preservation – these affects become alienated from their natural purpose. The strong . . . feeling-tone of the . . . trains of thought brings it about that, *no matter what the emotional excitation may be, these and these only are reproduced, over and over again.* This fixation of affects destroys the capacity to feel joy and compassion, and leads to the emotional isolation of the patients, which runs parallel with their intellectual alienation.

(Jung 1960: 73, 36, emphasis added)

Kipland's social development was arrested as a consequence of these affective obsessions. It also seems reasonable to conclude that, although Kipland had friends among his classmates (perhaps acquaintances would be more accurate), his most frequent relational experience was one of social alienation: "His social and coping skills were poor, and he was known among his peers for his 'weird sense of humor' and hot temper . . . He complained of being picked on" (Verlinden, Hersen, and Thomas 2000: 38).

There is no indication that he was ever able to share with any adult or peer the homicidal and suicidal impulses he recorded in his journal, nor did he believe that people knew who he was.

On the day he killed his parents, Kipland had been suspended from school for having in his locker a stolen gun he had purchased: "According to police, Kip bought the stolen gun because his father had taken away his .22 rifle . . ." (King and Murr 1998). Just before he was shot and killed by Kipland, Kipland's father had called, in Kipland's presence, "the director of a residential program for troubled teens in Bend, Oregon" (ibid.). Did Kipland experience these actions by his father as further rejections? A long time friend of the father's made this comment about these events: "Knowing Bill, I'm sure he laid down the law at that point . . . 'No driving, no guns, no privileges.' And the kid just felt, 'My world is over' " (Hammer 1998: 32).

In the next section, we will examine how the pathological complex that we postulate interfered with Kipland's interpersonal relations concurrently influenced his intrapsychic life.

Dissociation: "I am repulsive" "you all make me sick"

By the time he started high school, Kipland had developed, I believe, a pathological Shame–Humiliation/Contempt–Loathing complex of sufficient intensity and magnitude that it interfered with interpersonal adaptation. The domination of his psychological life by this complex made it difficult for him to expose himself to the Interest and Joy of others for fear of Rejection, resulting in a paralysis of his social development. This same monopolistic complex also caused a dissociation of his psyche intrapsychically, creating an arrest of his individual psychological growth.

Jung recognized early in his psychiatric career the relation between emotions and intrapsychic dissociation: "As we have already explained at some length, affects have a dissociating (distracting) effect on consciousness, probably because they put a one-sided and excessive emphasis on a particular idea, so that too little attention is left over for investment in other conscious activities"(Jung 1970a: 339, 181). Jung explains the mechanism for the "excessive emphasis" on certain themes caused by the complex:

> The ego-complex is, so to say, no longer the whole of the personality; side by side with it there exists another being, living its own life and hindering and disturbing the development of the ego-complex, for the symptomatic actions often take up a good deal of time and energy at its expense . . . Anything that does not suit the complex simply glances off, all other interests sink to nothing, there is a standstill and temporary atrophy of the personality. Only what suits the complex arouses affects and is assimilated by the psyche. All thoughts and actions tend in the direction of the complex; whatever cannot be constrained in this direction is repudiated, or is performed perfunctorily, without emotion and without care . . . The flow of objective thought is constantly interrupted by invasions from the complex . . .
>
> (Jung 1960: 102, 47–8)

In the note that Kipland left on the coffee table in his home after he had shot and killed his parents, he insisted that he had done so to protect them from unendurable embarrassment. From this excessive emphasis on Shame to the exclusion of the normal human consideration toward preserving the physical lives of others under any circumstances, we can see that the "particular idea" of Shame generated by the pathological complex had led to a logical, if self-defeating, strategy: to keep Other-Contempt conscious at all costs while repressing Self-Contempt, that is the Shame that might have prevented Kipland from enacting such a reprehensible crime. There is always a high cost to the life instinct inside the person who takes up such an attitude:

> The individual who must minimize negative affect at any cost may pay the price of surrendering not only the maximizing of positive affect but even the price of abandoning completely all excitement and enjoyment. There is no zest in his life, because its pursuit might entail punitive negative affect. He dare not seek positive affect lest he become afraid, and lest this turn to terror and panic. He dare not seek excitement

nor enjoyment lest it entail risk, which threatens utter humiliation or overwhelming anguish or blind rage.

(Tomkins 1963: 262–3)

We turn now to Kipland's journal to observe how these conflicts and defensive maneuvers played themselves out.

The emotion he writes most often about is "hate," which is alternately directed at himself and at everyone else. I believe that his word "hate" is to be understood as an expression derived from the Shame/Contempt complex. The slash that separates these two parts of the complex is important: in Kipland's case, Shame would refer to the times when Contempt is directed toward himself, Contempt to when the affect is directed toward others. "I am repulsive," "You all make me sick," Kipland wrote side-by-side in his journal, clearly conveying the close proximity of these alternating expressions of the Shame/Contempt complex in his psychological life.

But Shame/Contempt can also take the defensive form of Pride/Contempt. In another entry, he describes himself as strong and others as weak. That this is what Freud would have called a reaction formation comes through because, in the main, he realizes he is pitiful and thinks that people would laugh at him if they read his journal. Here is how he defends himself against the possibility of such Humiliation: "But they won't laugh after they're scraping parts of their parents, sisters, brothers, and friends from the wall of my hate" (Kirk and Boyer 2000d: 3). The Loathing directed toward others must now become lethal to be effective in suppressing his Self-Loathing. He thinks that one reason he hates so much is because "everything I touch turns to shit" (ibid.: 4). This is Shame–Humiliation talking.

On nine other occasions in his short diary, he expresses homicidal impulses, mostly directed at schoolmates. Suicidal impulses are recorded on three occasions. There are no indications that exciting or enjoyable moments occurred with any frequency, even though they are most likely still present in the healthy affective basis of his personality.

A rough draft of a school essay on the theme of "love at first sight," which he titled "Love Sucks," was found in Kipland's room after his arrest. He wrote that although he didn't believe in love at first sight, he did believe in hate at first sight. This seems to express Kipland's alienation from his own innate Eros, which would have contributed to his difficulty in relating positively to others as well as himself. Kipland concluded his essay by referring back to its theme and then making a reference to guns as a solace for his aloneness:

I really wouldn't know how to answer this question because my cold black heart has never and never will experience true love . . . I plan to live in a big black hole. My firearms and [illegible] will be the only things to fight my Isolation. I would also like to point out Love is a horrible thing. It makes things kill and hate.

(ibid.: 4–5)

He was living a loveless, hate-filled life, and it hardly seemed worth the effort to try to connect with others, or even to the idea of love itself. But there were, in my view, other manifestations of the pathological monopolistic complex that were plaguing him.

Kipland told Dr Bolstad, one of the psychiatrists who interviewed him after the shootings that, ever since he was 12 years old, in the sixth grade, he had heard voices. One of he voices said "You need to kill everyone in the world," while another said "You are a stupid piece of shit" (Kirk and Boyer 2000g: 2). We can interpret the first "voice" as Other-Contempt and the second as Self-Contempt (Shame). Tomkins has described the dissociative civil war that occurs in such circumstances:

> When an individual with such a personality structure is forced to dir-
> ectly confront the internal oppressor, and to become aware of the full
> measure of contempt in which be holds his other self, the dialogue of
> the two selves has the characteristic unrelenting ferocity of civil war.
> Two caricatures of the self now compete openly for permanent posses-
> sion of the self. One is a derogating, unrelenting critic, and the other is
> an arrogant affirmer of the glory of the self. Both selves have been
> hardened by the protective armor of mutual distrust to such an extent
> that there can be no experience of unity within such a personality.
> Only if neutralization of both self-contempt and arrogance can be
> achieved through sustained painful confrontation of self before self
> can civil war surrender to self-government. Failing this, the arrogant
> self will be forever vulnerable to vicarious insult and humiliation from
> without.

(Tomkins 1963: 280–1)

He didn't tell anyone about the voices because he was afraid that that they meant he was mentally ill. He particularly didn't want girls to think that he was mentally ill, because had become interested in them. He said that there were times that he came close to telling his mother about the voices, and that he wanted to, but that he was afraid to.

Kipland described one time when an interaction with his parents seemed to evoke the second voice. He was in the sixth grade and had received, as a "referral" to his parents, a formal reprimand from his school for some misbe-havior. When his parents saw the referral they became angry and began yelling at him. When he went to his room, the voice followed up, yelling over and over, "Stupid shit, you can't do anything right" (Kirk and Boyer 2000g: 4).

It is helpful to recognize that both of these voices belong to the same complex. Jung's analysis of a severely disturbed patient, which included the use of the word association test, concluded that "the psychic activity of the patient is completely taken up by the complex: she is under the sway of the complex, she speaks, acts, and dreams nothing but what the complex suggests to her" (Jung 1960: 208, 109). In the above vignette, Kipland's thoughts are, I believe, "under the sway" of the Shame/Contempt complex, and he is already at risk for acting out his Contempt, not just feeling paralyzed inside by Shame.

Finally, there is no evidence of the diversification of Kipland's interests and symbolic and cultural advance that we might expect as indications of the beginnings of his adolescent development. His individual psychological progress had been arrested by the dissociation of his personality. And in spite of his attempts at emotional self-regulation and self-soothing, he could not escape a crescendo of painful affects.

Unbearable affect: "why did God want me to be in complete misery?"

As the intensity and magnitude of the pathological affects increases and the availability, both interpersonally and intra-psychically, of the Interest and Joy needed to integrate and modulate these emotions decreases, the level of distress we refer to as *unbearable affect* results.

In his journal, Kipland records emotional states that I believe fall outside the range of normal suffering. He wrote that he felt like his "heart was breaking" and had been "ripped open and ripped apart" (Kirk and Boyer 2000d: 2). I think to differentiate this account of authentically anguished suffering from adolescent hyperbole, we need to keep in mind that Kipland's self-report is part of the overall pattern of expressing, almost exclusively, negative affective states throughout his diary. The heart that is "ripped open and ripped apart" is an image of the critical intensity of emotional distress that accompanied Kipland's feeling of rejection by the girl he had fallen in love with. The quote at the beginning of this section expresses his unbearable emotion in a manner that has an eerie similarity to the sufferings of Job.

In the last section, we suggested that Kipland was beset by a Shame–Humiliation complex of considerable magnitude, which at its greatest intensity was manifest in "voices," alternately expressing Other-Contempt and Self-Contempt, the latter experienced as Humiliation. Under such circumstances we can expect him to adopt what Tomkins refers to as "anti-humiliation strategies":

> The personality which contains an internalized oppressor is governed in large part by the wish to minimize the experience of humiliation, by the wish not to bear the rasping, tongue-lashing voice of the internalized

shamer and condemner; but, it may also be governed by identification with that not so small voice. The same process whereby the parent who humiliates one takes up permanent residence in the self of the derogated one powers the derogatory thrusts not only against the self but against others as well.

(Tomkins 1963: 265)

Whenever he could, Kipland would have been motivated to turn Self-Contempt into Other-Contempt, the latter taking the form of various aggressive fantasies.

We conjectured in the last section that Kipland's fascination with guns and his desperate need to obtain more and more of them had become an anti-humiliation defence. Tomkins comments on the transformation of a defence against Shame–Humiliation into an ominous pattern:

> We will now consider a less benign consequence of the power strategy to minimize humiliation inhibition. Whenever this strategy operates exclusively, without benefit of leavening by the image of maximizing positive affects and when the only positive affects experienced are consequences of reducing his humiliation, expressing it or humiliating others, the individual is then caught up in the most deadly of human aims.

(ibid.: 296)

The "most deadly of human aims" is the elimination of the "oppressor," either in the form of homicide, suicide, or both: "Finally, when humiliation reaches a maximum, whether in fact or in the imagination of the oppressed one, and no relief is in sight and anger is recruited by the continuing high level of negative stimulation from the feelings of humiliation, it may appear to the individual that there is no alternative but to destroy the oppressor" (ibid.: 298).

We can interpret the note that Kipland wrote after he had killed his parents as indicating that, by then, his experience of Shame–Humiliation had reached "a maximum." When he explains the killing of his parents to spare them unbearable embarrassment, he is projecting onto them his own insufferable feelings of Shame–Humiliation. The likely sequence was as follows: (a) Kipland experienced an unbearable level of Humiliation; (b) because it was unendurable, he unconsciously projected it upon his parents; and (c) then killed them to wipe this "embarrassment" from the face of the earth. One would have to add to this model the caveat that it is a bit too contrived and logical-sounding until the emotion that grounds the logic is underlined. We have, all of us, a tendency to think that others experience the same emotions that we do. Someone in the grip of an affective complex assumes that everyone else in the world is governed by the thinking and logic that pertains to the complex. Thus Kipland would have assumed that his parents could only be as ashamed as he.

In an interview with a detective the day after the rampage, Kipland repeated this explanation on two occasions.

> AW ... Now you shot your mom to save her the embarrassment and that sort of stuff, right?
> KK Yes.

> AW When did you decide in your mind that you had to kill your mom, before you shot your dad?
> KK Afterwards.
> AW Afterwards.
> KK My dad kept saying how my mom ... how embarrassed she was going to be and how horrible I was and I couldn't let my mom feel like that. I couldn't do anything else.
>
> (Kirk and Boyer 2000c: 10–11, 16–17)

That Kipland had projected the unbearable Humiliation that he was experiencing onto his parents was, I believe, the reason that he failed in his efforts to shoot himself after he had killed them. Had the original level of Shame he felt still been directed only at himself, it seems to me very likely that he would have committed suicide at once. I will now attempt to explain how Kipland, during the last phase of his psychological decline, became possessed by the pathological complex we have been describing.

Possession by affect: "I didn't know what else to do"

We have already presented our view of the relation between Kipland's struggle to minimize his experience of Shame–Humiliation and his obsession with guns. This turn to weapons as an anti-humiliation strategy is, however, not sufficient to account for Kipland's rampage. At the time of Kipland's killings, the Humiliation/Loathing complex that I have conjectured had caused his social isolation, the dissociation of his personality, and an unbearable intensity of negative affect, had taken possession of him and directed his homicides. Let us describe more of the prehistory of the killings, in order to understand how a complex moves from a dominant to a possessing place in a psyche vulnerable to its effects.

When Kipland was 13 years old and in the seventh grade, 1995–6, he and some of his friends ordered books with instructions for making bombs. The next year, he bought his first gun from a friend and hid it from his parents. Although in January 1997, Kipland's mother had expressed her concern about her son's fascination with guns, on 27 June 1997, at Kipland's request, his parents bought him a pistol, with the not so easily enforced stipulation that it was to be used only under his father's supervision. A month or so later, Kipland bought from a friend another pistol, which he kept hidden from his parents. Three months later, on 30 September 1997, when Kipland was 15 and starting high school, his father bought him a semiautomatic rifle that again was to be used only under adult supervision. By now, Kipland had become a competent marksman. When he went with a friend and the friend's father on a shooting weekend, and shot a relentless barrage of bullets at tin cans and targets, the father commented: "Kip was good. He'd shot that gun enough to where he knew how to shoot" (Hammer 1998: 32). In his literature class this same year, Kipland told his classmates that "he dreamed of being a killer and had admired the Unabomber" (Rogers 1998: 64). In his high school speech class that year, the 15-year-old Kipland gave a talk on "How to make a bomb."

This prehistory is important, because it was the events following his secret purchase of another gun, this time a stolen one, which Kipland acquired during the following spring, on 19 May 1998, that proved to be the precipitant for his two-day killing rampage. From a Kohutian self-psychological perspective, the guns he collected can be viewed as self-objects for Kipland, that is, as important extensions of his affects and fantasies. Behind all of the above, I believe, is the pervasive experience for Kipland of intensely felt rejection.

We have observed the linkage he made between these feelings and consoling weapons. Weapons are not only fascinating objects in their own right but can also serve as symbols of *invulnerability*. It is likely that at this stage of his adolescent development, Kipland was identifying with some legendary hero whose enchanted objects – armor, sword, spear, belt, etc. – could provide him with physical invincibility and invulnerability. Jung was particularly insightful about the turn to heroic fantasy, which is not uncommon in the face of actual vulnerability:

> But if a man is a hero, he is a hero because, in the final reckoning, he did not let the monster devour him, but subdued it, not once, but many times. Victory over the collective psyche alone yields the true value – the capture of the hoard, the invincible weapon, magic talisman, or whatever it be that the myth deems most desirable.
>
> (Jung 1972: 261, 170)

Kipland, however, was not able to achieve the symbolic victory he wanted. In his psychic economy, it was not mastery, or even self-possession, but emotional invulnerability to rejection that he was seeking. In adolescence, that is a goal doomed to fail without superhuman support. The veritable arsenal of weapons – explosives, guns, ammunition – that the police found in his home after the killings attested less to the adequacy of these magical instruments enabling both heroic defense and heroic retaliation than to the intensity of the feelings of alienation and powerlessness the boy had come to experience chronically in his relationships with others.

There is, however, another aspect of Kipland's relationship to guns which give them such fascination for him. It was only in relation to them that he was able to freely express the emotions composing the life instinct, Interest and Joy. The prehistory I have recounted indicates that bombs, as well as guns, were a focus of intense Interest for him. He was able to find Joy in his weapons, because he felt he could relate to them without fear of Rejection, that is, being "stabbed . . . in the back." They were the only objects that could be trusted and were safe to love. It is in this context that we can understand the anguish that accompanies the fear he confesses to his journal that his parents are about to take them from him.

When Kipland's sister was home from college for a visit in March 1998, just two months before the killings, she was surprised at how much better he seemed. She noted that he was more positive and would make jokes, displayed increased self-confidence, and entered into all the family conversations. She added that he did not mention guns or bombs. Perhaps his sister, Kristin, who had intervened with their parents on his behalf on so many occasions, was the one human person toward whom he felt freest to express his positive emotions without fear. Or perhaps she was merely observing the security the guns had brought him, which was now the best-kept secret of his life.

The following entry in his journal indicates how actually close he was, at the time of her positive impression of him, to losing control over his vengeful impulses:

> I know everyone thinks this way sometimes, but I am so full of rage that I feel I could snap at any moment. I think about it everyday. Blowing the school up or just taking the easy way out, and walk into a pep assembly with guns. In either case, people that are breathing will stop breathing. That is how I will repay all you mother fuckers for all you put me through.
>
> (Kirk and Boyer 2000d: 2)

Even in this entry, however, Kipland reveals an ongoing cognitive capacity to observe his rage and even to compare it to what he believes is the norm. The intellectual insight did little to modulate the strength of his affect.

In an interview with a psychiatrist after his rampage, Kipland recounts an exchange with his father just before he killed him which appears to mark the transition from consciousness of homicidal affect to possession by it. The spark that ignited this invasion of lethal motivation in Kipland was, we can argue, his father's escalating disappointment in him. This occurred on the day that the school had called the police, after the father of another boy had called to say a gun of his had been stolen by someone in his son's circle of school acquaintances. After the gun was found in Kipland's locker, and Kipland's father had been notified by the police of his son's arrest, Kipland's father picked Kipland up at school and they drove home together. On the way, they stopped for lunch and his father apparently said: "You're only 15 and you've already got two felonies . . . You disgust me" (Kirk and Boyer 2000g: 16). Then the father went to the car to eat his lunch by himself. Kipland said that on the drive home from the diner the voices were all over him: "B was saying, Look at what you've done, you stupid piece of shit, you're worthless. The A voice said, You'll have to kill him, shoot him. C was repeating this over and over. They got louder and louder. I went into the house. I was crying" (ibid.: 16). Kipland told the interviewer that there was a change in the content of the comments by the "voices" at the moment of entering the house: "The voices told me, 'You have no choice.' I had never heard that before, 'You have no choice' " (ibid.: 17). This conveys well how someone experiences the moment of possession. Kipland's monopolistic complex had assimilated his ego-complex and was commandeering its executive functions, insisting that the ego had no choice of its own in what would happen next. After Kipland's father called, in his son's presence, a residential center in Oregon and discussed the possibility of sending him there, reality seemed to agree with the thinking of the voice. Kipland, following this logic, went and got a rifle and shot his father. Again a voice repeated the fateful statement before he shot his mother: "You have no other choice" (ibid.: 17). The voices seem to articulate both the fact and the *raison d'être* of possession. The unstated part of the logic that reveals the identification with the possessing complex is, ". . . if you are to avoid the experience of humiliation you have agreed you cannot allow yourself to bear."

In the note Kipland wrote after he had killed both his parents but before his rampage at his school he said, ". . . I have to kill people, I don't know why . . . I have no other choice" (Kirk and Boyer 2000d: 1). This statement was repeated throughout the night by one of the voices: "You have no other choice. Kill everybody. Go to school and kill everybody" (Kirk and Boyer 2000g: 17). And the next day, possessed by what I believe by now was a monopolistic Humiliation/Loathing complex, he went to his high school and shot and killed two students and wounded twenty-five others. In a long interview the day after the killings with a detective who was trying to get at what had motivated Kipland to take so many lives, Kipland repeated the statement, "I had no other choice," eleven times. He was recalling, and probably reexperiencing, his state of possession.

I think it is clear that at the time of his lethal acts, Kipland was experiencing *all four* of the necessary conditions for homicidal behaviors – social isolation (rejection and loneliness), dissociation (including hearing his thoughts as voices), unbearable affect (the misery associated with the Humiliation/Loathing complex), and possession by affect (the feeling that he had no other choice). In the next chapter we will look at another case involving two teenagers in which these four elements are also strikingly present.

Chapter 6

Eric Harris and Dylan Klebold: multiple homicides followed by suicides

Eric Harris and Dylan Klebold were seniors at Columbine High School in Littleton, Colorado, when, on 20 April 1999, they entered their school and shot and killed twelve students and one teacher, wounded twenty-three others, and then shot and killed themselves. In our attempt to understand the forces that compelled these shootings, we will draw upon articles in newspapers, magazines, and police reports, some of which include interviews with those who knew the killers. Moreover, both Dylan and Eric kept diaries, and portions of these have been made public. They also created documents to memorialize their intentions that they wanted the world to see. In 1997 and 1998, Eric maintained a website where he posted statements on a variety of topics; transcriptions of this material are available. In March and April 1999, the two adolescents made a series of videotapes in which they discussed what led up to what was to come, and parts of these, too, have been made public. The last of these videotapes was filmed on the very morning of their rampage. From this material, it is not too difficult to reconstruct the emotional background of the tragedy, in which the four necessary conditions we have postulated to account for this type of violence are all present. So using the different conditions to organize the material, let us proceed through what has been established.

Social isolation: two overly shy teenagers keep a dark secret

Eric was born on 9 April 1981, and Dylan was born on 11 September 1981. Both boys were raised in intact families and were the younger of two sons. Both boys grew up shy.

In his book *Introduction to Structural Psychology*, Roger Muchielli (Professor of Psychology, Faculty of Letters and Humanities, Nice) summarized "the famous analysis of the *shy man*" made by Dugas in his 1898 classic, *Timidity, A Psychological and Moral Study*:

If in reading this document we put aside the author's personal opinions

... and restrict ourselves to his observations related to "shyness," we have to remark that everything is organized "logically" for the shy man, beginning with a certain way of experiencing relations with others. This relation with others, as well as corresponding situations, is experienced as a danger of unfavorable judgment handed down by others, whoever they may be, this judgment therefore being dreaded as an existential risk (injury, collapse, diminution of self, bound up with the fear of rejection or of scorn).

(Muchielli 1970: 121–2)

This existential risk accounts for the subject's attitude of "anxious vigilance" in interpersonal situations, which, in turn, is based upon the subjective certainty of the "perception of rejection or contempt on the part of others" (ibid.: 123). Muchielli attributes these characteristics of the shy man to a " 'dynamic' of the personality – that is, an affective-motor constant – all of which escapes the waking consciousness, concerned with *variable contents*" (ibid.: 124). In the context of contemporary affect theory, I would designate the unconscious "affective-motor constant" as a feeling-toned complex, in this instance composed of the innate affect Shame/Contempt. We can find evidence of such a complex in both boys.

In elementary school, middle school, and high school, Dylan was observed by others, including his parents, to be inordinately shy. In middle school and high school, Eric was similarly observed by classmates to be overly shy. My view of their "shyness" is that it was, in both of them, a self-protective avoidance of relationships. For each of them extreme reserve was a strategy designed to avert painful constellations of a Shame/Contempt complex. The social isolation that ensued, however, deprived them of "Emotional Dialogues with Others framed by Interest and Joy," which might have helped them in integrating Shame/Contempt in a more developmentally adaptive way.

A classmate of Dylan and Eric at Columbine High School who met Dylan when they were in the first grade recalled that "Dylan was a shy kid" (Brown and Merritt 2002: 23). He noted that Dylan was able, however, to develop a circle of friends until he was transferred to an accelerated program, where competition was the ruling principle among the students. The classmate, who was also in this program, which was known as CHIPS, said: "Finding friends in the CHIPS program was virtually impossible" (ibid.: 31). The parents of this classmate also recalled Dylan at the time he was in elementary school with their son. The father said: "He was really shy . . . and it would take him fifteen or twenty minutes to warm up to us every time he came over, even though we knew him and were close to him" (ibid.: 30). The mother observed that he was a sensitive child "who worried a lot about what other people thought – perhaps too much for his own good" (ibid.: 30). This sounds very much as if already Dylan was exhibiting "anxious vigilance," which is highly suggestive that a Shame/Contempt complex had been structured by the time he was in elementary school.

Eric's shyness was also evident to others. When Eric was 12 years old, he played Little League baseball in Plattsburgh, New York. One of his former Little League teammates, a senior at Plattsburgh High School at the time of the killings, remembered Eric as "a player whose shyness crippled his ability . . . He was the shyest out of everybody when it came to just talking" (Simpson and Blevins 1999). When at bat, Eric was reluctant to swing and tried instead for walks. Another Little League teammate remembers Eric as a reclusive, quiet 12-year-old, who "struggled to make friends" (ibid.).

Achievement was very important to both boys. A Columbine sophomore, who had played baseball with Dylan in elementary and middle school, remembered Dylan as a hard-throwing pitcher: "He was the kind of kid that, when he played, he had to win. Whenever he got pulled from a game, he'd come off and actually cry" (ibid.). He found it kind of weird when Dylan quit playing altogether in middle school: "It was just boom, Dylan's not playing any more" (ibid.). Tomkins's linkage between Shame and Defeat may apply here:

> What of the feeling of shame following defeat? Suppose one has struggled long and hard to achieve something and one suffers failure upon failure until finally the moment is reached when the head gives way and falls forward, and, phenomenologically, the self is confronted with humiliating defeat . . . Defeat is most ignominious when one still wishes to win.
>
> (Tomkins 1963: 138)

As Dylan "had to win," we can conjecture that he quit baseball because he had reached that "moment" when the Humiliation he experienced upon losing a game had become more than he could tolerate. Eric's inability to swing his bat and his strategy of trying to get pitchers to "walk" him, so he wouldn't strike out, may also have been Shame-avoiding behaviors.

When Dylan and Eric were approaching the day of their killings, both of them recalled experiences that we can easily interpret as humiliating, and it is not hard to locate the archetypal expression of Shame/Contempt in their utterances. On one of the videotapes made in the months before their rampage, Eric expressed bitterness toward his military family, which was often required to change location, saying he always had to start over "at the bottom of the ladder" and that people in each new school would constantly make fun of him: "my face, my hair, my shirts" (Seibert 1999). On another tape, Dylan recalled that he had "hated the stuck up kids" in a day care center he attended when a child, who he thought had scorned him, uttering vengefully, "I'm going to kill you all . . . You've been giving us s -- t for years" (ibid.). Dylan also pointed angrily at his popular athletic brother, Byron, and Byron's friends who "ripped" on him. He said: "If you could see all the anger I've stored over the past four f --- ing years" (ibid). Dylan said that except for his parents, all of his extended family had treated him like the *runt* of the litter.

When Eric was a freshman in the High School, he was still tongue-tied and meek. He did, however, take a girl in his class to that year's homecoming dance. When she was interviewed three days after the shootings, on 23 April 1999, she remembered that on their date he had been nervous and quiet. She also recalled how, after she broke up with him a few days after the dance, he faked his suicide. "He had his friends take me over to his house. When I went there, he was laying with his head on a rock, and there was fake blood around him, and he was acting like he was dead" (Briggs and Blevins 1999). At that time Eric would have been 14 years old, and we can argue that by then the Shame of rejection was becoming an unbearable experience.

During his freshman year, Eric formed a best-friend relationship with the same classmate who had known Dylan from the time they were in the first grade together. When their relationship fractured two years later, Eric posted a message on his website urging others to kill his estranged friend and wrote in his diary of his own wish to kill him. This rejection struck as deeply as the one by his freshman girlfriend, but now his lethal emotion (I would surmise it is Contempt) is expressed outwardly.

During his senior year, Eric was still sensitive to the possibility of rejection. In a letter that he sent to a girl at the pizza parlor where they both worked, Eric began this way: "Hi. I have a few things I want to say but I never seem to be able to say them in person" (*Columbine Report* 2006: 715). In the body of the letter he says he hopes they could get together some time. He ends by asking for a response, but hedges this request, almost courting rejection: "If you don't [want to go out] . . . just don't say anything. I'll understand, I'm used to it" (ibid.). Eric occasionally dated girls he met outside of school, but was unable to obtain a date for the senior prom. A co-worker at the pizza outlet where they both worked said, "He fretted about not having a girl friend and was 'just a lonely kid' " (Briggs and Blevins 1999).

On 31 March 1997, now 15 years old and completing his sophomore year in high school, Dylan began to keep a journal. In it he wrote that this period of his life was a "weird time, weird life, weird existence." He indicated that he felt he didn't fit in socially, was alienated and depressed, hated his existence, and had thoughts of suicide: "I swear – like I'm an outcast, & everyone is conspiring against me . . ." (*Columbine Report* 2000). By the time he was 16 and in his junior year (1997–8), Dylan was writing in his academic day planner, "The lonely man strikes with absolute rage" (ibid.).

In a paragraph titled "My 1st love???," Dylan begins "OH My God . . . I am almost sure I am in love . . ." (*Columbine Report* 2006: 480). He continues by enumerating what he likes about a girl's physical appearance and her personality, including as one of her charms "her NOT being popular" (ibid.). He continues: "If soul mates exist, then I think I have found mine" (ibid.).

There is no indication that he was able to initiate a relationship with her. In a subsequent entry, which may or may not be related to this one, Dylan draws a heart and writes above it, "I now know the final battle – the pain of humanity is our love . . ." (ibid.: 509). He attended the senior prom, which was held three days before the shootings. On the videotape made the morning of his rampage with Eric, Dylan addressed his date and said: "I didn't really want to go to the prom. But since I'm going to die, I thought I might do something cool" (Lowe 1999b).

Dylan's mother and father were interviewed by the police in November 2000, the year following the shootings. The parents said that "Dylan was extraordinarily shy in high school" (Obmascik, Simpson, and Oulton 2000) and never had a girlfriend. They referred to his friends more as a circle of acquaintances than close friends, and said that some members of this group were also quite shy.

Monopolistic complexes

To turn the facts and observations that I have presented so far into indicators of the constellation of unconscious, archetypal affect complexes is of course a deduction. Neither Eric nor Dylan was ever a patient of mine. But I feel, reading their material in the light of my clinical experience working with early adolescents, that by the time Eric and Dylan had completed their sophomore years in High School, a good two years before their enacted revenge, both had developed recognizable Shame/Contempt complexes, which were at the very least of considerable magnitude. I would go so far as to say that these complexes had begun to monopolize the boys' psychic economy. They were certainly already generating suicidal and homicidal thoughts in both adolescents. During their junior and senior years, an affect theorist can observe snowballing of these unconscious structures. I believe that this malignant progression was due, in part, to the scornful verbal and physical bullying the boys had to endure on a daily basis from some of their classmates.

If this analysis is correct, another contribution to the snowballing would have to have been made by the dynamics of the complexes themselves. Tomkins provides us with insight into this factor, in a passage that reveals that any affect generates a theory that makes it inevitable that the same affect will be replicated. Tomkins calls this an *affect theory*, noting that all persons entertain theories that explain their affects to them. As he puts it, "An affect theory is a simplified and powerful summary of a larger set of affect experiences. Such a theory may be about affect in general, or about a particular affect" (Tomkins 1963: 230). Tomkins illustrates with what he calls "shame theory," meaning the theory that develops in a person who has repetitive shame experiences as to where his shame is coming from. Tomkins's eerie conclusion is that such a theory is actually a way of perpetuating the emotional experience, turning it into a way of life:

> Shame theory is one such source of great power and generality in activating shame, in alerting the individual to the possibility or imminence of shame and in providing standardized strategies for minimizing shame. Although shame theory provides avoidance techniques, it is also one of the major sources of the experience of shame, since it provides a shame interpretation of a large number of situations ... The existence of a shame theory guarantees that the shame-relevant aspects of any situation will become figural in competition with other affect-relevant aspects of the same situations.
>
> (ibid.: 230–1)

Tomkins's theory, like Ribot's "anxious vigilance," is in accord with Jung's notion of "complex-sensitivity," which also contributes to the magnification of any emotionally charged issue. When complex sensitivity reigns, "A single word, a gesture, if it touches the sore spot, reveals the complex lurking in the depths of the psyche" (Jung 1960: 106, 51). In this way, a vicious circle develops – the complex sensitivity leads to more discharges of the complex, which increases the strength of the complex and increases the likelihood of the complex being constellated, which leads to an increase in complex sensitivity on the part of the embattled ego that wants to avoid such discharges. The result is the personality starts to be ruled by the complex.

But when two people share such complex sensitivity, there can also be mutual contagion between them. Mutual contagion, I believe, was certainly a factor that led to an increase in the magnitude of complex discharge in both Eric and Dylan, well before their final blowout. Eric and Dylan became friends in Middle School and close friends in High School, so that by the end of their sophomore years they were observed to be inseparable. Their cars were always parked side by side in the school parking lot. They ate lunch by themselves at a separate table. After school they worked at the same pizza parlor. They took the same bowling, creative writing, and videotape classes. A classmate in the writing class said that if they didn't put their names on the top of their papers, you would not be able to tell them apart: "They wrote about the same stuff – rocket launchers, grenades, shotguns, zombies killing people, ripping people's flesh. Everybody thought it was pretty funny at that time. Nobody really took it seriously" (Briggs and Blevina 1999).

In their videotape class, the friends made videos in which they starred themselves as protectors of weak and bullied students. Yet after the rampage, one student said she thought Eric "was the greatest actor she had ever known, he never deviated from being a 'bright, smiling kid' " (ibid.). This was because, by the time Eric and Dylan had reached their senior years in high school (1998–9), they had both developed pleasing façade personalities. Their classmates had no idea of what was to come. By April 1998, they had become much more secretive, which contributed further to their social isolation.

A dark secret

Eric and Dylan began planning their attack upon their High School in April 1998, one year before they carried it out. They used the twelve months that followed to formulate their assault plan and gather the materials necessary for its execution. Throughout this period, they told no one but each other of their intentions. Ironically, keeping such an all-consuming planning process secret for an entire year contributed to both boys' social isolation, increasing the likelihood that the plan would move toward action. The most revealing clue as to what was to come was a series of videotapes that they made in March and April 1999, which they knew would only be viewed after their homicides and suicides had been carried out. All through this planning year, their individual and joint sense of their superiority over others was increasing, and this made any notion of either one of them reaching out socially seem like a humiliating concession that would be unthinkable. At the time of their killings, neither adolescent was engaging in meaningful dialogues with others framed by Interest and Joy. Both were experiencing a standstill in social development. Although they had each other, they were both stuck in their social isolation. Any Interest and Joy they had was devoted to planning their rampage.

Dissociation of the personality: arrest of development

In lieu of a normal American teenage social adaptation, Dylan and Eric flirted with Nazi mannerisms, calling out *Sieg Heils*! after they made strikes in their bowling class, recalling Hitler's birthday and his deeds with admiration, speaking German phrases, and announcing on their last videotapes that their plan was to advance Hitler's "final solution" a bit further. They were going to kill mankind at large!

The identification with Hitler was telling. From a depth psychological perspective, both Eric and Dylan were struggling against a very powerful, unconscious internal "dictator" – the archetypal affect complex of Shame/Contempt. Jung has spoken of the situation that ensues when any complex gains such an ascendancy:

> Now when there is a marked change in the individual's state of consciousness, the unconscious contents, which are thereby constellated, will also change. And the further the conscious situation moves away from a certain point of equilibrium, the more forceful and accordingly the more dangerous become the unconscious contents that are struggling to restore the balance. This leads ultimately to a dissociation: on the one hand, ego-consciousness makes convulsive efforts to shake off an invisible opponent ... while on the other hand it increasingly falls victim to

the tyrannical will of an internal "Government opposition" which displays all the characteristics of a daemonic subman and superman combined.

(Jung 1966: 394,195)

I believe that during the time their "Hitler" fantasies were generated Eric and Dylan were experiencing dissociation of their psyches, which only worsened by the time of their rampage.

Dissociation between consciousness and the collective unconscious

Jung has indicated how such psychic splits are brought about: "As we have already explained at some length, affects have a dissociating (distracting) effect on consciousness, probably because they put a one-sided and excessive emphasis on a particular idea, so that too little attention is left over for investment in other conscious activities" (Jung 1970a: 339, 181). It is reasonable to argue that during the year preceding 20 April 1999, the day of the killings, the "particular idea" that dominated both Eric and Dylan, monopolizing their psychic energies and bringing about their dissociations, was the need for "retribution." Their dedication to evening the score with those who had, or were perceived as having, scorned or bullied them, was manifested throughout this last year of their lives in their formulation and planning of their revenge.

On his 1997 website, Eric made a list of the things "I HATE," which consisted of "stupid things" done by "stupid people," both of which he found contemptible. A year later, on his March 1998 website, there was a change in tone. He stated his wish to "kill almost all of the residents [of Denver]" and added this tirade:

> Well all you people out there can just kiss my ass and die. From now on, i dont give a fuck what almost any of you mutha fuckas have to say, unless I respect you which is highly unlikely. but for those of you who happen to know me and know that I respect you, may peace be with you and dont be in my line of fire. for the rest of you, you all better fucking hide in your houses because im comin for EVERYONE soon, and i WILL be armed to the fuckin teeth and I WILL shoot to kill and I WILL fucking KILL EVERYTHING! No I am not crazy, crazy is just a word, to me it has no meaning, everyone is different, but most of you fuckheads out there In society, going to your everyday fucking jobs and doing your everyday routine shitty things, i say fuck you and die. if you got a problem with my thoughts, come tell me and ill kill you, because . . . god damnit, DEAD PEOPLE DONT ARGUE! God Damnit! I AM PISSED!!

(Harris 1998)

These diatribes are prime examples of how a "particular idea" can hijack psychic energies to the degree that a dissociation of the personality results. I believe that these thoughts were generated within the pathological complex that had taken over Eric's mind, but it should be emphasized that this complex was not exclusive to Eric. Rather, as its archetypal energy might suggest, it was a defiant complex rooted in adolescent issues that had descended upon both Eric and Dylan, who were equally in the grip of it. A comparison of the 1997 and 1998 postings indicates that there has been a snowballing of this pathogenic complex, resulting in an increase not only in its intensity and its magnitude but also in the frequency of its discharges, all of which led to further dissociation of Eric's psyche from anything resembling insight and self-restraint. The rise in intensity is apparent in the progression from the habit of calling people "stupid" to direct expressions of homicidal impulses toward them. Jung developed a formula to account for the overall capacity of a complex to become constellated and gain ascendancy over the horizon of psychic life: "The constellating power of the nuclear element corresponds to its value intensity, i.e., to its energy" (Jung 1970b: 19, 12). This power of the complex to constellate itself is directly related to the increase in the number of situations toward which the complex began to assert its attitudes. This ever-increasing constellation of the complex is evident in the way Eric expands his initial contempt for just a certain number of stupid people to expressions of his strong wish to kill "EVERYONE." Jung used such evidence to gauge the strength of a complex: "The data required to determine the relative number of constellations may be obtained partly by direct observation and partly by analytical deduction. That is to say, the more frequent the constellations conditioned by one and the same complex, the greater must be its psychological valency" (ibid.: 21, 12).

Eric's diary: 10 April 1998–3 April 1999

In the material released by the Jefferson County Sheriff's office on 6 July 2006, there is a document that consists of twenty serial entries by Eric in his journal, the first written on 10 April 1998 and the last on 3 April 1999 (seventeen days before the rampage). These writings cover the year that is most often given as the time Eric and Dylan spent planning for the rampage. The excerpts that I have selected for our review will show the increase in intensity of the pathological complex over this year, which led to an expansion of the dissociative split in Eric's personality.

One of the most frequent topics in these journal writings is Eric's persistent belief in his intellectual superiority over most other people, which is an indication of his desperate need to fend off intrapsychic experiences of Shame and Humiliation. Again and again in these writings, Eric proclaims his superiority over others. He has "SELF-AWARENESS" while others are "STUPID." He feels like God and only the people he deems worthy should escape extermination. He is higher in terms of "UNIVERSAL INTELLI-GENCE" than almost anyone in the world. He "thinks" and asks "why," while others are robotic conformists. He is proud to be "different," although this may get him labeled " 'unusual' or weird or crazy." He wonders "if anyone will wright a book about me, sure is a ton of symbolism, double meanings, themes, appearance vs. reality shit going on here. Oh well, it better be good if it is writtin" (*Columbine Report* 2006: 98, 17 December 1998). On 12 November 1998, however, another aspect of his inner life breaks through:

> everyone is always making fun of me because of how I look, how fucking weak I am and shit, well I will get you all back: ultimate fucking revenge here. You people could have shown more respect, treated me better, asked for my knowledge or guidance more, treated me more like a senior, and maybe I wouldn't have been so ready to tear your fucking heads off. then again, I have always hated how I looked, I make fun of people who look like me, sometimes without even thinking sometimes just because I want to rip on myself. That's where a lot of my hate grows from, the fact that I have practically no self-esteem, especially concerning girls and looks and such. Therefore people make fun of me constantly . . . therefore I get no respect, and therefore I get fucking PISSED.
>
> (ibid.: 95)

In this passage, Eric vacillates between self-reflection and adamant projection. On 17 November 1998, five months before the rampage, he continues these themes: "If people would give me more compliments all of this might still be avoidable . . . but probably not. Whatever I do people make fun of me, and sometimes directly to my face. I'll get revenge soon enough. Fuckers shouldn't have ripped on me so much huh!" (ibid.: 96).

Then Eric makes a direct link between people's tendency to make fun of him and his repeated statement "KILL MANKIND": "Then again it's human nature to do what you did . . . so I guess I am attacking the human race. I can't take it, It's not right . . . I fucking hate the human equation" (ibid.). We can also observe that the Shame–Humiliation that is invading his consciousness is quickly becoming unbearable. So it is that at this moment he draws back: "This is beginning to make me get in a corner. I'm showing too much of myself, my view and thoughts, people might start to wonder, smart ones will get nosey and something might happen to fuck me over, I might need to put on one helluva mask here to fool you all some more" (ibid.).

By his senior year, his façade personality was indeed "one helluva mask." In another excerpt from his journal, written on 20 December 1998, we can observe how the pathological complex, not Eric's ego-consciousness, can determine the meaning of events. One of his favorite bands is releasing their new album, *Adios* in April 1999, the month of their killings. Eric comments: "how fuckin appropriate, a subliminal final 'Adios' tribute to Reb [Eric] and Vodka [Dylan], thanks KMFDM . . ." (ibid.: 98).

Dylan's writings

Again, the complex that had this strength, or power to constellate itself, was not just in Eric's psyche. In November, 1997, Dylan had written in his journal that he wanted to die, but also expressed a wish to get a gun and go on a killing spree. In April 1998, Dylan put several comments in Eric's Columbine High School 1998 yearbook: "One such entry referred to '*the holy April morning of NBK (Natural Born Killers).*' Another entry says in part '*killing enemies, blowing up stuff,* killing cops!! *My wrath for January's incident will be godlike. Not to mention our revenge in the commons* (the school cafeteria)" (*Columbine Report* 2000). (The incident for which Dylan promises revenge was the police arrest of Dylan and Eric in January 1998 for entering an unlocked car and stealing electronic equipment.) This suggests that the snowballing monopolistic complex has also increased its grip on Dylan's psyche between November 1997 and April 1998. It is interesting, theoretically, to consider whether this snowballing of the same pathological complex in the psyches of both boys is happening through contagion, or through the fact of a common disposition to entertain the same complex. In either case, the same complex was clearly causing a dissociation in each boy's psyche, and massively contributing to both boys' social isolation. This alienation from their classmates was a further factor in their developing *folie à deux*, since the complex was rapidly replacing contacts with other High School students as their main social reality. Eric wrote that he and Dylan were engaged in "a two-man war against everyone else."

Eric and Dylan

In their senior years, Eric and Dylan took the same creative writing and videotaping classes. They made a video, *Hitmen for Hire*, which depicted them as available to be employed by those students who were picked-on and oppressed to drive off or kill the bullies who were tormenting them. This was less than three months before they would themselves unleash death at Columbine High.

Eric wrote a school paper about a battle between Marines and Aliens, which contains a scene with eerie similarities to the 20 April 1999 rampage. In it, he depicted shattered glass, dead bodies scattered around him, and a carpet of blood. "The deathly dark glow of light from above was barely enough to notice the blood and flesh splattered on the large slabs of granite that passed for walls" (Vaughan and Kass 2003). (Dylan wrote a story for this same class, which we will review in detail at the end of this chapter.)

For another writing assignment, students were asked to pretend they were inanimate objects and describe themselves. A classmate later described Eric's essay: "Most people would choose a bicycle or something. He chooses a shotgun shell and writes about his relationship with the barrel. He often wrote about shotguns" (Brooke 1999).

The fantasy materials that Eric and Dylan were producing in these courses were not constructed, in my judgment, by the creative imagination that these class assignments were hoping to constellate, but rather by the pathological complex that was increasingly dominating both boys' psyches:

> The complex forms, so to speak, a miniature self-contained psyche which, as experience shows, develops a peculiar fantasy-life of its own. What we call fantasy is simply spontaneous psychic activity, and it wells up wherever the inhibitive action of the conscious mind abates or, as in sleep, ceases altogether. In sleep, fantasy takes the form of dreams. But in waking life, too, we continue to dream beneath the threshold of consciousness, especially when under the influence of repressed or other unconscious complexes.
>
> (Jung 1966: 125, 56)

On the other hand, both Eric and Dylan were able to maintain their excellent academic performances throughout High School. Dylan was accepted to a college and only shortly before their rampage visited it with his father. In spite of a 3.8 average, all of Eric's applications to college were turned down. It is likely that both boys' pleasing façade personae provided only a thin veneer over their formidable shadow sides.

Mostly, the boys were setting the stage for enacting their revenge. Beginning in April 1998 and up until 20 April 1999, the day of their assault, Dylan and Eric invested vast amounts of energy in planning and preparing for their killings. They built and detonated bombs; they collected an arsenal of guns and ammunition; they drafted precise itineraries for the day of their action; and they made goodbye videotapes. They expected that these videotapes, the last of which was recorded the morning of their attack, would be viewed after their deaths. During this period, virtually all their thoughts, fantasies, and actions were driven by Shame–Humiliation/Contempt–Loathing complex. The complex had hijacked the life instinct and subordinated the executive functioning of their egos. Neither Eric nor Dylan was any longer able to sustain emotional dialogues with the healthy affective bases of their personalities and the progressive forces of Interest and Joy that resided there.

Arrest of individual development

Another sign of dissociation produced by the complex is that we do not find in either Eric or Dylan during the last two years of their lives any evidence of real psychological growth. There was simply no diversification of interests, and there was no construction of cultural attitudes. The complexes that had led to arrests in their social development had also blocked individual differentiation. Again, this is a phenomenon Jung recognized as a consequence of the dissociation of a psyche:

> I seriously consider the possibility of so-called "arrested development," in which a more than normal amount of primitive psychology remains intact and does not become adapted to modern conditions. It is natural that under such conditions a considerable part of the psyche should not catch up with the normal progress of consciousness.
>
> (Jung 1960: 529, 244)

A further clue is that neither Dylan nor Eric gave much indication that they were cognizant of their shadow sides. Under such circumstances, there occurs what Jung refers to, citing Neisser, as *affect fixation*:

> The affects which are normally meant to regulate our relations with the surrounding world and to implement our adaptation to it – which act, indeed, as a means of protecting the organism and are the motive forces of self-preservation – these affects become alienated from their natural purpose. The strong . . . feeling-tone of the . . . trains of thought brings it about that, no matter what the emotional excitation may be, these and these only are reproduced, over and over again. This fixation of affects destroys the capacity to feel joy and compassion, and leads to the emotional isolation of the patients, which runs parallel with their intellectual alienation.
>
> (ibid.: 73, 36)

"Intellectual alienation," however, is too mild a word for what can ensue. When Dylan and Eric were in the grips of their complexes, they exulted in the power the complexes conferred on them. This is a distortion of the life instinct, not, as Jung suggests, healthy, innate Joy, which might foster development. Rather, the boys' dissociations eventually led to developmental standstills of the sort Jung describes when he writes:

> The ego-complex is, so to say, no longer the whole of the personality; side by side with it there exists another being, living its own life and hindering and disturbing the development of the ego-complex, for the symptomatic actions often take up a good deal of time and energy at its expense. So we can imagine how much the psyche is influenced when the complex gains in intensity . . . Anything that does not suit the complex simply glances off, all other interests sink to nothing, *there is a standstill and temporary atrophy of the personality*. Only what

suits the complex arouses affects and is assimilated by the psyche. All thoughts and actions tend in the direction of the complex; whatever cannot be constrained in this direction is repudiated, or is performed perfunctorily, without emotion and without care . . . The flow of objective thought is constantly interrupted by invasions from the complex.

(ibid.: 102, 47–8, emphasis added)

From the standpoint of affect theory, the boys' developmental blocks were due to the dissociation between their pathological consciousness, more and more structured by the complex, and the potentially growth-inducing influence of the twin affects of the life instinct, Interest (encouraging healthy curiosity/exploration) and Joy (stimulating healthy fantasy/play).

Unbearable affect: immunization against humiliation

All of this makes more sense if we realize that Eric and Dylan were engaged in a continuous effort to avert catastrophic invasions of consciousness by the innate affect Shame–Humiliation. These threatened eruptions from the unconscious had their origins in the same suppressed and repressed Shame–Humiliation/Contempt–Loathing complexes that had led to their social isolation and the dissociations of their psyche in the first place. Silvan Tomkins developed his theory of monopolistic humiliation to account for such a paradoxical phenomenon: "We might say humiliation becomes monopolistic when the individual never experiences humiliation because he is forever vigilant and so always successfully avoids the feeling of shame" (Tomkins 1963: 379). I will now examine the anti-Shame–Humiliation strategies that the natural defensive capacities of their psyches developed and how both Dylan and Eric reinforced them intentionally. I should point out that some of their statements already quoted make more sense when looked at from the perspective of warding off intolerable emotion.

During the last year of their lives, the monopolistic complex besetting Eric and Dylan had produced a state of malevolent watchfulness:

As monopolistic humiliation theory deepens and becomes unified and stabilized, the general direction in which such unification necessarily moves is analogous to warfare between nations. A permanent state of vigilance is created in which every precaution is taken lest the self be overwhelmed. The assumption of the complete malevolence of the other no longer needs documentation. The unified strategy tends toward an unrelenting hostility and counter-contempt in which every attempt will be made to save the self by destroying the power of the other.

(ibid: 478)

Driven by persistent states of darkly anxious vigilance, Dylan and Eric went so far as to declare war on everyone. This war talk began in 1997 when Eric commented on his website about his hate (an affect theorist would say Contempt) for all the stupid people and the stupid things they do. The scope of the war was expanded on his 1998 website when he expressed his wish to kill everyone. Dylan said on one of the videotapes made in the months before their killings that it was humans that he hated, clearly implying that the enemy of his complex was the human race (and presumably what was left of his own humanity). Eric later wrote: "I declared war on the human race and war is what it is" (Lowe 1999a). In one of his journal entries Eric expanded on the magnitude of their war: "It will be like the L.A. riots, the oklahoma bombing, WW II, vietnam, duke and doom all mixed together, maybe we will even start a little rebellion or revolution to fuck things up as much as we can" (*Harper's Magazine* 2002).

To sustain the momentum of their "two-man war against everyone else," they sensed the need to keep magnifying their lethal animosity. On one of the last videotapes Eric said: "More rage. More rage . . .Keep building on it" (Gibbs and Roche 1999). Utilization of such an externalizing strategy, however much it evacuates the contents of the complex onto others, does not, however, enhance one's overall life: "Although it is more comfortable to be disgusted by others than by the self, it is nonetheless an experience of negative affect. To be continually outraged and disgusted by the shortcomings of others is not to lead a rewarding life" (Tomkins 1963: 266). Rather, this defense leaves the individual walking a fine line, for the innate affect Contempt–Loathing is a punishing emotion, whether directed toward others or oneself, and can reach intolerable levels. Part of the problem is that the contempt is directed toward what the individual sincerely feels is wrong: "Such individuals are truly outraged and disturbed by the evidence, to which they are especially sensitive, that human beings are worthy only of contempt. The continually outraged piety of such a one need not be much less uncomfortable than finding the self forever worthy of self-contempt" (ibid: 266).

In general, however, Other–Contempt is at least temporarily less destructive to the individual's sense of well being than its bi-polar counterpart, Self–Contempt. Eric and Dylan got a certain amount of energy, and an elevation of self-esteem, from the "outraged piety" in their attitudes toward the inferior humans by whom they felt surrounded.

When Eric and Dylan unwittingly identified with the grandiose fantasies originating in their complexes, they were also engaged in anti-Humiliation strategies typical of the person indulging in delusions of grandeur:

> Without his knowledge, the idea of grandeur enables him to immunize himself against all influences from his surroundings; nothing penetrates his skin, and he can thus keep aloof from obligations that would be binding to other people. He does not feel in any way called upon to prove

to himself or his fellows that this superior judgment is based on corresponding merits.

(Jung 1977: 509, 221–2)

One form that Dylan and Eric's ideas of grandeur took was their anticipation that their exploits would be made into a movie. They imagined that famous directors would fight over the opportunity to make the film. In line with this inflation, Eric, on one of the last videotapes, pointed to the journal that had an entry outlining the Columbine attack and said: "This is the book of God" and added, "Somehow I'll publish this" (Lowe 1999a). Dylan said, "I know we are going to have followers because we're so fu---ing God-like" (Lowe 1999b). When they invoked their special evolutionary status, Eric and Dylan were clearly motivated to keep their unbearable feelings of inferiority at bay. Dylan even said: "We're not actually human – we have human bodies but we've evolved into one step above you f---ing human s----. We actually have f---ing self-awareness" (ibid.).

Based on these observations, I think it is reasonable to assume that during the last year of their lives, the pathological complexes that had continued to snowball had produced a defensive inflation:

> The smoldering ashes of humiliation recruit images and re-interpretations of the antagonist so that he grows more and more offensive. As this happens, the embers of shame and self-contempt are fanned into hot flames which in turn recruit cognitive reappraisals that provide fresh fuel for the magnification of the negative affect. Just as individuals fall in love at a distance, so may they fall in hate with one who has humiliated them.
>
> (Tomkins 1963: 283)

When there is a progressive increase in the intensity of Shame–Humiliation, individuals may become irreversibly vengeful:

> As the oppressor grows more formidable and the role of positive affects diminishes even more, the power strategy takes the form of pure revenge and reversal of roles. The formula now is "You cannot humiliate or condemn me, but I can humiliate and condemn you" ... No animal other than man is capable of so long sustaining a grudge or wounded pride, and a biding of time for the appropriate moment for turning the tables on the oppressor.
>
> (ibid.: 298)

Eric and Dylan wanted to take revenge on the policemen who arrested them after their theft from a car. Dylan said they wanted to take revenge on the commons (the student gathering place), and Eric reportedly said: "I hate you people for leaving me out of so many fun things" (*Columbine Report* 2000).

He railed, for instance, against five girls who did not answer his phone calls: "I hate you people for leaving me out of so many fun things. And don't fucking say 'well that's your fault' because it isn't, you people had my phone #, and I asked and all, but no, no no no don't let the wierd looking Eric KID come along, ooh fucking nooo" (ibid.)

Dylan also directed his vengeful rage at the members of his family who treated him as the runt of the litter as well as at the stuck-up kids in his early day care setting. Eric commented on the frequent moves of his military family and the vengeful feelings evoked when he had to start over each time at the bottom of the ladder and kids made fun of his clothes and appearance. Eric made shooting noises while aiming his shotgun and said: "Isn't it fun to get the respect we're going to deserve" (Gibbs and Roche 1999).

All this suggests the enormous effort the boys were making to fight off the humiliation they felt at being outsiders in their high school. This was an unbearable affect, which in Tomkins's view can have the effect of making it but a short step to lethal enactment to make the pain go away once and for all: "Finally, when humiliation reaches a maximum, whether in fact or in the imagination of the oppressed one, and no relief is in sight and anger is recruited by the continuing high level of negative stimulation from the feelings of humiliation, it may appear to the individual that there is no alternative but to destroy the oppressor" (Tomkins 1963: 298).

It was on 20 April 1999, I believe, that Eric and Dylan finally felt they had no alternative but to attack their fellow students, as well as the teachers who had failed to protect them. There was, however, one last obstacle in the way of their execution of their rampage: fear of reprisal. This last hurdle was removed, I believe, by their recognition of the immanence of their suicides.

In this evolution, we can see how an affect-complex that is unbearable can become a route to possession by that very same complex, so long as the most intolerable part of the affect can be located in other persons. The result of being unable to bear the pain of the affect, however, is a marked diminution of personal responsibility.

Possession by affect: Eric: "I can't help it." Dylan: "It's what we had to do."

At the time of their violent assault on their school, both Dylan and Eric were possessed by the very same pathological complex that had contributed to their social isolation, dissociation, and anti-humiliation behaviors. This follows the general

> . . . rule [that] there is a marked unconsciousness of any complexes, and this naturally guarantees [the subjects who are unconscious] all the more freedom of action. In such cases their powers of assimilation become especially pronounced, since unconsciousness helps the complex

to assimilate even the ego, the result being a momentary and unconscious alteration of the personality known as identification with the
complex. In the Middle Ages it went by another name: it was called
possession . . .

(Jung 1970b: 204, 98)

On the other hand, unless the necessary conditions we have been tracing –
social isolation, dissociation, and unbearable affect – are all present, possession by affect does not occur.

During the summer of 1997, between their sophomore and junior years of
high school, Dylan and Eric began to make and explode pipe bombs. On his
website, in the fall of 1997, Eric wrote that a secret "clan" had formed to
carry out "missions," during which he and Dylan would vandalize the homes
of classmates who had offended them at school:

> We are more of a gang. We plan out and execute missions. Anyone pisses
> us off, we do a little deed to their house. Eggs, teepee, superglue, busy
> boxes, large amounts of fireworks; you name it and we will probly or
> already have done it. We have many enemies in our school, therefore we
> make many missions. It's sort of a night time tradition for us.
>
> (Harris 1997)

Let us not contend the fact that bullying was endemic at Columbine High
School and that Dylan and Eric were among the favored recipients of such
aggression, and that all students would have been best served if such
behaviors had been effectively minimized. But I think that whatever others
did to torment Eric and Dylan, the slights they actually suffered had also to
be amplified through the activity of archetypal complexes before they could
be seen as justifying such harsh retaliatory "missions." Their use of the word
"enemies" is an example of such magnification. The fact that the missions
undertaken in retaliation were carried out in the dead of night indicates the
level of arousal the complexes produced. One can hear the ominous contribution of the complex in the account Eric and Dylan gave to a few of their
classmates after their 1997 Halloween "prank": "That night, the two of them
went up on the roof with a BB gun and took shots at little kids who were
trick-or-treating. They said the kids would look around, all confused at what
had hit them . . . They told us this over lunch, laughing like it was the funniest
joke in the world" (Brown and Merritt 2002: 72). It is reassuring to note
that the classmates were shocked rather than amused, but it does not seem
that this lack of social validation much retarded the growth of the complex that
had learned it could discharge itself and make an impression. Similarly, the
intensity and content of their vituperative screeds and the grandiose expressions of their evolutionary superiority in their journals and on their videotapes were certainly determined by the unconscious and now monopolistic

complex, but at the time of the writings and tapings neither boy was yet possessed by that complex.

In his diary, Eric also describes both the objective aspects of planning for the assault and his own subjective experiences as this process proceeded. In the context of our previous discussions of the necessary conditions that prevailed at the time of the rampage, Eric's descriptions of the planning process and his inner life depict his progression toward possession by affect. One year before the killings were carried out, on 21 April 1998, Eric predicted that he would be dead before his journal was ever read.

And when they spent a year secretly planning their assault on Columbine High School and assembling the arsenal they needed to carry it out, Eric and Dylan were certainly driven by their Shame–Contempt complex, but even then they were not yet possessed by it. Even when they made a *Rampart Range* videotape, two months before their killings, a videotape which showed them carrying out target practice with their various guns, they were certainly discharging their complex, but they were still not possessed by it.

On 23 October 1998, six months before the assault on Columbine High School, Eric predicted, "someone [is] bound to say 'what were they thinking?' when we go NBK or when we were planning it, so this is what I am thinking" (*Columbine Report* 2006: 93). "I have a goal to destroy as much as possible so I must not be sidetracked by my feelings of sympathy, mercy, or any of that, so I will force myself to believe that everyone is just another monster from Doom like FH of FS or demons, so It's either me or them. I have to turn off my feelings" (ibid.). Although this statement is dictated through Eric by the complex, he is not yet possessed by it.

On 17 November 1998, five months before the assault, the tension continues to mount: "It'll be very fucking hard to hold out until April" (ibid.: 96). A tipping point occurred on 22 November 1998, when Eric crows that he and Dylan have obtained the guns they needed for their attack, "Its all over now, this capped it off, the point of no return. I have my carbine, shotgun, ammo and knife all in my trunk tonight . . ." (ibid.: 97).

In a diary entry on 3 April 1999, Eric acknowledges that NBK came quickly and described his state of mind seventeen days before the rampage: "The amount of dramatic irony and foreshadowing is fucking amazing. Everything I see and hear I incorporate into NBK somehow. Either bombs, clocks, guns, napalm, killing people, any and everything finds some tie to it. Feels like a Goddam movie sometimes" (ibid.: 99). This is a precise description of the fact that the complex is now assimilating all of reality.

In the tape they made the morning of their assault, Tuesday, 20 April 1999, however, there is clear evidence that they were finally possessed by the strong, monopolistic Shame–Humiliation/Contempt–Loathing complex. We recognize this when Eric says, in no way trying to rationalize or provide a legal defense for what he is about to do: "I can't help it." Dylan follows, "It's what we had to do" (ibid.). If we take this state of the self-description at face value, rather than attempt to write it off as a defensive rationalization for behavior the boys could still choose to control, we have to ask, "Why couldn't they 'help it'? Why was it something they 'had to do' "? I think it was because, phenomenologically, in the reality of the psyche, they were both possessed by the innate affects at the core of the monopolistic complex: like planetary bodies drawn into the gravitational field of a larger star, they were too close to the archetypal field of the complex to be able to maintain an independent ego position like choice.

In these videotapes in which they recorded their last words, the boys did manage to exonerate their parents from any responsibility for their actions: " 'It f --- ing sucks to do this to them [his parents]', Harris said. 'There's nothing you guys could have done to prevent this.' Klebold told his mom and dad they have been 'great parents. I'm sorry I have so much rage,' he said" (Seibert 1999).

In a section that I find very poignant, the possessed boys concluded their last tape by telling their parents they were sorry and saying goodbye. This was their egos' last word. After the rampage, Dylan's parents revealed in an interview that they had noticed a change in their son during the week before the shootings. Dylan's father told their pastor that he had detected "this slight tension" in his son a few days before the attack. His mother said that something in her son's voice spooked her Tuesday morning. "The goodbye had an edge to it." The edge belonged to the complex.

Eric's dream and Dylan's Story

I have acknowledged a difficulty, because of a lack of sufficient developmental evidence, in demonstrating with any certainty the origins of the unconscious pathological complexes that overwhelmed Eric and Dylan. Within the 946-page *Columbine Report* released on 6 July 2006, there is, however, a dream recorded by Eric and a copy of a story Dylan wrote for his creative writing class, which give us a direct look into the unconscious of each boy. In these expressions, their pathological complexes appear in personified form.

This is consistent with Jung's view that complexes of this strength will inevitably express themselves in some way:

> . . . an unconscious event which eludes the conscious mind will portray itself somehow and somewhere, it may be in dreams, visions, or fantasies . . . Such a content is an autonomous complex divorced from consciousness, leading a life of its own in the psychic non-ego and instantly projecting itself whenever it is constellated in any way . . .
>
> (Jung 1968a: 410, 301)

As these complexes have opened up in consciousness as personified images, we need to understand the process that Jung and Hillman call "personifying." Personifying of our emotions and complexes is a spontaneous activity of the psyche that can occur in the unconscious without any conscious effort on the part of the subject: "Dream psychology shows us as plainly as could be wished how complexes appear in personified form when there is no inhibiting consciousness to suppress them, exactly like the hobgoblins of folklore who go crashing round the house at night" (Jung 1970b: 203, 97–8). We can identify such a personified unconscious complex in a story that Dylan wrote two months before he and Eric went on their rampage (*Columbine Report* 2006: 28–9). Similarly, an unconscious complex of Eric's makes its appearance in personified form within an undated account of one of his dreams (ibid.: 739).

We do not know for sure when Eric's dream occurred, although some of its content and the direction of his associations indicate to me that he wrote it down between April and October 1998. It was in November 1998 that Eric and Dylan obtained the guns they needed for their attack: "Its all over now, this capped it off, the point of no return. I have my carbine, shotgun, ammo and knife all in my trunk tonight . . ." (ibid.: 97). In February 1999, Dylan wrote the story that described rather closely what the two boys would go on to do.

Eric's dream

The first segment of Eric's dream depicts a successful ascent up a hill toward a goal, which is made difficult by the narrowness of the road and the press of other cars:

> The dream started out in my car. Dylan and me were trying to drive up a very steep hill to get to some event at the top. The road up was barely wide enough for two lanes of traffic and there were lots of other people that I recognized mostly from my bowling class trying to get up the hill also. The road was dirty, and the sides of the road sloped upward, so there wasn't much room at all. After lots of honking, yelling, aggressive driving and racing we made it to the top of the hill and parked my car.
>
> (ibid.: 739)

My interpretation of the dream so far is that it depicts a concentration of a high level of will, as would be necessary to bring off any enactment, whether positive or negative, of energy emerging from the unconscious. For Eric, this was experienced as a compensatory impetus from the unconscious which offers Eric the possibility of a step forward in his psychological development. For us, with twenty-twenty hindsight, it represents a peak of regressive development. But we can only determine which meaning is correct by continuing to follow the dream. In the next section of the dream, the task awaiting Eric at the top of the hill, the "event," begins to show itself: "The next event I remember was struggling to get a bowling ball from an old rack sitting near the wall of a large, open room. If you have ever seen a movie called Demon Knight, it was like the main room in the hotel in that movie. After getting a ball, we ran up an open Staircase" (ibid.). A ball used in a sport is a basic motif in many cultural contexts, where it often has sacred overtones, and Jung has interpreted it as a symbol of the Self that is transpersonal to the ego. Eric's acquisition of the ball, enabling the game to begin, may indicate that a connection has been established between his ego-consciousness and the Self. Interpreted thus, the ball contains his coiled developmental potential, as well as the energy for realizing it. Since it is in this dream a bowling ball that rolls down lanes, one can say that the boy has discovered the *path-finding* ball of fairytale, that is, a symbol of the Self's dynamic potential to motivate and direct action.

Eric's possession of the ball, however, is brief, and its disappearance signals a dramatic change in the ensuing action of the dream:

> All the while people that I don't like in school were taunting us and I had a sense that things were starting to get tense. At the top of the stairs we no longer had the bowling ball for some reason, and we looked over the railing and fights and brawls were starting downstairs. We ran over to the corner of the ledge and lots of gunfire broke out. We heard several people being shot and a lot of evil growling and yelling. We telepathically seemed to understand that we should stay where we were and wait for a SWAT team to arrive and help us out. A few times we peaked over the ledge and bullets shredded the railing and walls around us. The downstairs was empty, but had several shadows that seemed to have evil, demented inhabitants.
>
> (ibid.)

This is a remarkable development, for it documents that in the inner world, Eric felt victimized and appalled by the evil that was taking possession of his soul, something the world could not have known. I believe that in this dream Eric is being confronted by the pathological complex incubating in his unconscious.

Jung has written about the perspective that such psychic objectivity can offer: "What, on the lower level, had led to the wildest conflicts and to panicky outbursts of emotion, from the higher level of the personality now looked like a storm in the valley seen from the mountain top" (Jung 1969a: 17, 15). This element of perspective does not mean that the storm is robbed of its reality to inflict harm, but at least in the dream there is still a part of Eric that is not identified with its destructive potential. It is this perspective that a therapist hearing such a dream tries to convey to a client. The client who accepts the message of such a dream certainly does continue to feel the force of violent affect and is shaken and tormented by it, yet at the same time is aware of a higher consciousness looking on which checks the temptation to become identical with the affect. This would be a consciousness that regards the affect as an object and can say, dispassionately, "I *know* that I suffer." That the ball disappears in Eric's dream suggests to me that this perspective, which depends upon a healthy relation to the Self, will also disappear. From now on, Eric will gradually become identified with the violent complex, incapable of standing outside it.

When we speak of containing strong affect from a theoretical perspective that honors emotion, the subject's task is to remain in contact with the complex, without being annihilated by it, and to await further developmental guidance from the unconscious. The ball, had it remained in play in the psychic field, would have been a source of just such guidance. I believe the disappearance of the ball is a consequence of the capacity of the complex to induce a dissociation of the psyche. The subjective sense of injury and desire to seek a proper revenge was strong enough to create a complex ego that had no relationship to the objective Self that could keep things in perspective and enable Eric to outgrow the complex. This loss of objective self-restraint is mirrored in the dream by the destruction of the SWAT team that was attempting to restore order: "After a long time of waiting a team of SWAT guys came into the ledge from a door beside us and hurried us out of the building. Somehow we were on the ground level as we ran to a few cars and vans parked outside. We looked back and the SWAT team was being shot apart by gunfire" (*Columbine Report* 2006: 739).

Without any help from this supraordinate order-restoring force, Eric is left to face the complex on his own, stuck with the probability that he will be overcome by it, despite his individual efforts to escape it. Here is how he tries to handle himself in the dream:

> We knew that we had to rescue ourselves since the actual rescue team was being destroyed. We hopped into a bulky white car and sped off down the hill, just as some sort of rocket flew out of the door of the building and nuked the SWAT team. Somehow I recalled some old sheriff guy in a bronco saying something about how he would escape the mountain roads by cutting across the switchbacks, no matter how steep they were. Next thing I knew we were in this bronco truck and we did a 180 on the dirt road and started to free fall down a few levels of the mountain. We landed on a road and sped off to a quiet little mountain a few minutes down this road.
>
> (ibid.)

That the confrontation between dream-ego and complex has been abandoned and the descent takes on a magical, unrealistic character suggests that Eric's further attempts to dissociate himself from the complex will finally be unsuccessful. If the dream had been presented during a psychotherapeutic process, it might have been possible for the therapist, as Jung has pointed out, to provide the kind of support that might have strengthened Eric's ability to objectify the complex that had begun to possess him. Jung speaks hopefully of the effects of consciousness in this regard:

> We psychologists have learned ... that you deprive a man of his best resource when you help him to get rid of his complexes. You can only help him to become sufficiently aware of them and to start a conscious conflict within himself. In this way the complex becomes a focus of life. Anything that disappears from your psychological inventory is apt to turn up in the guise of a hostile neighbour, who will inevitably arouse your anger and make you aggressive.
>
> (Jung 1970c: 456, 225)

But let us look at how Eric's dream ends:

> After this my memory gets a little foggy, but I remember Dylan and I standing behind a large, senile mountain man who was buying a ton of groceries at a lodge. He left a sack of liquor and a pistol on the counter as he left, and I walked up and said something like too bad he forgot these, and paid for my things and left with all the stuff.
>
> (*Columbine Report* 2006: 739)

Instead of an emergence of a new awareness, Eric's level of consciousness has diminished. It is at that point that he meets the old man who has also suffered a lowering of the level of consciousness. Significantly, the old man has with him the instruments for both intoxication and aggression. We could describe him as a cultural complex (Singer and Kimbles 2004) that simply took over Eric's consciousness, in his already compromised state of mind. Had there been other values in the collective around them, another form of the "old man" might have appeared at this moment, a wisdom figure who might have lent his energy to self-restraint on the part of the boys and thus encouraged a more positive outcome to their flirtation with revenge:

> Often the old man in fairytales asks questions like who? why? whence? and whither? for the purpose of inducing self-reflection and mobilizing the moral forces, and more often still he has the necessary magic talisman, the unexpected and improbable power to succeed, which is one of the peculiarities of the unified personality in good or bad alike.
>
> (Jung 1969a: 404, 220)

Instead, this old man has lost his mind, and gives them what they need to enact their worst fantasies. What seems true is that a lowered level of collective consciousness, symbolized by the old man, offers an additional danger to individual consciousness losing ground because of the various personal conditions we have been detailing.

Dylan's story

The premise for our analysis of Dylan's story, written for his creative writing class and found among his personal papers, is that it is close to a dream (closer than to a conscious daydream). It is, of course, only in retrospect that we can conclude that the complex we are about to identify in Dylan's narrative is causally related to the rampage that occurred on 20 April 1999.

The story Dylan turned in to his creative writing teacher is set after midnight in a town that even at 1:00 a.m. is still bustling with activity. The moon was "barely visible, hiding under a shield of clouds, adding a chill to the atmosphere" (*Columbine Report* 2006: 28). A man's arrival in this town is announced by the sounds he makes as he walks down its streets: "Behind the conversations & noises of the town, not a sound came from him, except the dark monotonous footsteps, combined with the jingling of his belt chains striking not only the two visible guns in their holsters, but the large bowie knife, slung in anticipation of use" (ibid.).

His wide-brimmed hat, spiked gloves, spiked overcoat, and duffel bag were all black. He was over six feet tall, strongly built, and the observer "could feel his anger rising, cutting thru the air like a razor" (ibid.). Dylan's narrator observing him thought that he "looked ready for a small war" and that he was "fueled by some untold purpose. What Christians would call evil" (ibid.).

This sinister man stops in front of a popular bar and waits until nine college-preps come out: "They knew who he was, & why he was there" (ibid.). One of the preps says, "You still wanted a fight huh?" (ibid.), while another says, "Dude we were jus messin around the other day" (ibid.). When one of the youths challenges the man to shoot, the narrator hears a laugh coming from the man:

> It was faint at first, but grew in intensity and power as I heard the man laugh. This laugh would make Satan cringe in Hell. For almost half a minute this laugh, spawned from the most powerful place conceivable, filled the air, and then the entire town, the entire world. The town activity came to a stop, and all attention was now drawn to this man.
>
> (ibid.)

Once he has finished laughing, the man proceeds to kill the nine college boys – shooting seven, knifing one, and killing the remaining boy with a blow to the head. Then the killer detonates several bombs by remote control in an effort to divert the police while he leaves the scene of his carnage.

The man picks up his belongings and walks back the way he came:

I was still, as he came my way again. He stopped, and gave me a look I will never forget. If I could face an emotion of god, it would have looked like the man. I not only saw his face, but also felt emanating from him power, complacence, closure, and godliness. The man smiled, and in that instant, thru no endeavor of my own, I understood his actions.

(ibid.: 29)

The creative writing teacher was concerned enough about the content of this story to talk with Dylan and bring it to the attention of his parents. Dylan maintained it was just a story.

In the story, the college-preps knew why the dark man was there and that it had to do with a previous confrontation between them. They knew that he was seeking to avenge himself for what had occurred in that first meeting, though this is never revealed in the story. We do know, however, that Dylan himself, in the videotapes that Eric and he made in the two months just before their killing spree, proclaimed his motivation for the rampage was to avenge himself for all of the slights he had incurred over the years. This suggests, I believe, that within Dylan's story the merciless man seeking retribution is a personification of a Shame–Humiliation/Contempt–Loathing complex.

One of the most powerful events in Dylan's narrative is the protagonist's world-encompassing laugh. This is reminiscent of a patient of Jung's whose conscious mind grieved at her father's death, but whose unconscious shadow manifested itself in a sudden fit of laughing. Through this symptom, her repressed will to power, her longstanding wish to surpass her father was revealed: "She had finally arrived on top" (Jung 1972: 51, 39). This clinical incident is presented in the context of Jung's discussion of the *will to power*. Jung considers his patient's hysterical laughter as a symptomatic act, resulting in part from the patient's repression of her dark side:

It was an hysterical laughter, a psychogenic symptom, something that sprang from unconscious motives and not from those of the conscious ego. That is a difference not to be made light of, and one that also tells whence and how certain human virtues arise. Their opposites went down to hell – or, in modern parlance, into the unconscious – where the counterparts of our conscious virtues have long been accumulating. Hence for very virtue we wish to know nothing of the unconscious, indeed it is the acme of virtuous sagacity to declare that there is no such thing as the unconscious. But alas! It fares with us all as with Brother Medardus in Hoffmann's tale *The Devil's Elixir*: somewhere we have a sinister and frightful brother, our own flesh-and-blood counterpart, who holds and maliciously hoards everything that we would so willingly hide under the table.

(ibid.)

Indeed, it was from Hoffman that Jung may have derived some of his notion of the shadow. Another source, of course, was Nietzsche, who had noted the will to power in certain individuals, an idea that Adler was to develop in his theory. Jung understands those individuals driven by power motives to have certain characteristics: ". . . those who want to be 'on top' are mostly people who are either the under-dogs in reality or fancy they are not playing the role that is properly due them. Hence they often have difficulty in adapting themselves socially and try to cover up their inferiority with power fictions" (Jung 1966: 24, 19). This is a good way to understand the defenses created by both Dylan and Eric to try to stay afloat in the dark waters of their maladaptive interpersonal and intrapersonal relations. We must understand, however, that the complex that took over the two of them, and was personified by the character in Dylan's story and the figures in Eric's dream, was not simply idiosyncratic to them. It is a cultural complex, ubiquitous in American life, that is frequently constellated in situations where shaming has occurred. One classic personification of this cultural complex is "Dirty Harry," the vengeful homicide detective played by Clint Eastwood in a series of movies that made him famous. The shame he carries is in his very nickname, "Dirty." But he enjoys the position others put him in when they try to put him down. They give him the chance to express his contempt for those who attempt to shame him, through homicidal revenge, which feels like justice. Go ahead, he tells them, "Make my day!"

In his article titled, "The laugh of Satan: a study of a familial murderer," Robert S. McCully (1978) presented the case of an 18-year-old teenager who killed three family members – his mother, his half-brother, and his stepfather. After these acts he reported hearing "the laugh of Satan" ringing in his *ears*. (Dylan heard the "laugh [that] would make Satan cringe in hell" before his killing spree.)

McCully examined this adolescent after the murders using three different editions of Rorschach inkblots, each of which yielded remarkably similar image-associations from the patient. In associating to the inkblots, the patient thought he saw two types of images that the tester, McCully, found especially significant: supernatural "evil" images and "pleasant" images. An example of the former type of association was: "Seems some supernatural being with wings . . . I guess it will put the straight jacket on me. The Devil, something with great powers, evil powers, evil, gloomy, yet seems majestic and wears crown" (McCully 1978: 88). Examples of images that McCully designated as pleasant were "flowers, trees, and various pleasant neutral images" (ibid.).

The "evil" images were the more profound in their intrapsychic effect: "His super-natural-evil images excited him visually. This was not feigned, he appeared to identify with them" (ibid.). We have already observed a similar pattern in Dylan before he committed the murders. We recall him saying of the dark man in his story that "Thru no endeavor on my own, I understood his actions." This suggests to me that he was in a state of deep identification with the dark man in his fantasy. Identification means in practice adopting all the object's ways of behaving, as though the subject was the same as the object and not a separate individuality.

McCully emphasized that "the satanic-supernatural images tended to virilize the subject and provide him with an hypnotic-like sense of immediate kinship or identity" (ibid.). He treated images of flowering trees and various pleasant images with disdain. The author made the following interpretation: "Yet, their symbolic significance would mean one thing to him, the one thing he could not tolerate in himself: *weakness*" (ibid.: 86). He concluded that the flowers represented the psychological remains of a struggle between two inner opposites, weakness and power, which had held the subject in constant tension: "Power won, and the subject became the pawn of an inflated paranoid compensation" (ibid.).

By the time the patient reached the final stages of this conflict, just before the killings resolved his inner tension, relatedness had come to symbolize weakness. McCully speculates that "the laugh of Satan" that the patient had heard inside just after the killings "may have symbolized the death knell of relatedness and the triumph of evil over good" (ibid.). One particular murder in which we can feel the Satanic solution is the patient's killing of his mother. Mother had become "a scapegoat symbolizing a capacity to elicit in him an intolerable sense of weakness" (ibid.). The point of killing her, then, was to kill off that weakness. McCully speculates that in this form of murder, the underlying pathological complex is "*an obsession for power*" (ibid.: 84).

Classmates of Eric and Dylan who were in Columbine High School at the time of their rampage have reported that both laughed as they went about their killings.

Chapter 7

Sinedu Tadesse: homicide followed by suicide

On 28 May 1995, the last day of her junior year at Harvard University, Sinedu Tadesse, a 20-year-old student from Ethiopia, killed her Vietnamese roommate, stabbing the other young woman forty-five times with a knife as she lay sleeping in her bed in the room next to Sinedu's. Sinedu then hanged herself in the bathroom they had shared.

My presentation of the conditions that were operative at the time of Sinedu's lethal behaviors is based on the material made available by Melanie Thernstrom in her account of this tragedy, *Halfway Heaven: Diary of a Harvard Murder* (1997). I will show that at the time of the murder and suicide, Sinedu was experiencing every one of the four conditions that the reader will now recognize as basic to the emergence of such lethal behaviors.

Social isolation: "I am unable to make friends over the years"

Like most of the other subjects of the present study, Sinedu Tadesse kept track of her inner life through journals. In her case, these documents achieved voluminous proportions, and they provide a rich source of data about her affective history. According to Sinedu's accounts of her development, her social isolation began in her family, continued in her community and schools in Ethiopia, and reached its apogee at Harvard.

Family

In more than one place in her diaries, Sinedu attempts to describe her experience of the family atmosphere within which she grew up. She wrote questions to herself, "asking whether anyone had ever made her feel special, loved, comforted; inspired trust or admiration; offered wisdom; or taught her how to be 'sweet' " (ibid.: 187). Each question was answered, "No." In a letter, she elaborated on her experience: "I have been raised in what you might be able to call an abnormal situation. I don't understand what people mean by the warmth of a family, the love of the mother and the security of their home. I grew up feeling lonely and cold amidst two parents and four siblings. I had no one to rely on for warmth" (ibid.: 188).

She thought her parents' marriage was conflicted: "We never had warm family days because all conversation was tainted with the irritating arguments between my parents" (ibid.: 192). She wrote that her parents quarreled, nagged the children, and abused them emotionally: "There was no comfort to seek from them, no warmth. Life was cold & hopeless & annoying" (ibid.: 193). Another comment that Sinedu made is of particular interest from our perspective: "They never involved themselves in our emotional world. They acted as if emotions did not exist" (ibid.: 188).

In this portrayal of her family atmosphere, it is what is lacking that is most salient in her thoughts. From the perspective of the innate affects, it is the twin affects of the life instinct, Interest and Joy, that are absent. She is not describing a family life which is continuously enriched by mutual curiosity and play, as well as cultural experiences. This means that her social and symbolic development is already at risk.

In repeating these appraisals here, it is important to stress that they do not have to be objective to express what Sinedu herself experienced psychologic-ally in relation to her parents. We cannot know what the parents actually did, or tried to do, for Sinedu emotionally, and one has to assume that they were, at the very least, supportive of her educational aspirations and the edu-cational efforts that got her to Harvard or she would not have been likely to become a student at such a good university. But the impression given, reading Sinedu's subjective account, is that the parents were unsuccessful in making Sinedu feel cared for, even if they in fact were doing a number of things for her, that many another child or parent would have interpreted as caring.

She characterizes the relation with her mother as one of unrelenting mutual hostility. Her mother told her not to trust anyone outside the family, no one at all. Before her father's political imprisonment in Ethiopia when she was 7 years old, Sinedu had been proud of her father. When he was released two years later, a broken man, she despised him and felt humiliated by him. During her adolescence, her older brother and sister "began mercilessly mock-ing her appearance – calling her big-bottomed, big-headed, and huge" (ibid.: 193). A friend of her father's used to call her "very black," and her mother used to tease her about being a "no-nose" (ibid.: 193). Sinedu felt that her siblings' teasing was not part of the usual brother and sister and sister and sister bantering, but "had a more malicious damaging spirit" (ibid.: 193).

These recollections by Sinedu of her family life allow us to suggest that a negative construction was happening, which would have been exacerbated by the lack of robust interpersonal dialogues under the aegis of the life instinct. Without ruling out the emergence of one or more complexes, each composed of a crisis affect, we can surmise that the structuralization of a pathological Shame/Contempt complex was most evident. This complex may have already attained an unmanageable excess of intensity.

It was during her father's absence, starting at age 7, when she was entering middle childhood, that she experienced what I believe was a compensatory reaction from the unconscious: "She began to spend hours daydreaming about herself as a happy, wealthy student living in a happy, wealthy family" (ibid.: 193). This sort of fantasy was consistent with the results of my study of the development of the symbolic function (C. T. Stewart 2001), in which I identified the characteristic symbolic mode at the beginning of the stage of development appropriate to age 6 or 7 as the "symbolic community." Unfortunately, Sinedu misinterpreted these fantasies in two ways. She labeled her "daydreaming," which in fact was a breath of fresh air from the unconscious, as "the worst of all habits" (Thernstrom 1997: 193). Worse, she began to take her daydreams literally, so that when she was 10 or 11 "she actually wrote a good-bye note to her family so that she could go live with her fantasy family and then waited for God to transport her" (ibid.: 193).

Her literalization of the symbolic community suggests a deficit in the development of the symbolic function, which is not surprising as the innate affect Joy and its dynamisms, fantasy/play, seem absent from her life. If she had been able to realize these compensatory fantasies and emotions in a progressive series of symbolic realizations, the outcome of this period of her symbolic development might have been more truly reparative in allowing her to become part of a meaningful peer community rather than just a high achiever without a socially supportive context.

School in Ethiopia

Sinedu chose as the epigraph for her high school year book, "Friendship is life's most precious treasure" (ibid.: 38). In the primary grades, her relations with her peers were, in her terms, "hellish":

> Year after year, I became lonelier and lonelier. I see friends deserting me. They would take every chance to show me that they did not have any love or respect for me. They made me sit by myself when we went for long school trips. I stared out the window while they had fun sitting together. I had to swallow my pride to start talking to them to prevent pitying looks from other students.
>
> (ibid.: 102)

Sinedu's experience of rejection by her elementary school classmates would have further augmented the pathological Shame/Contempt complex that we believe was already being structuralized in her family relationships.

As a clue to what in Sinedu may have elicited her social isolation, a high school guidance counselor said, "She didn't seem to want friends" (ibid.: 39). I suspect that this counselor may have been observing Sinedu's social avoidance defenses which served to protect her from the pain and alienation that would result from additional rejections. Another adult from her high school years, one of her teachers, noted the quality of self-containment that may have belied Sinedu's actual need for people: "She was resourceful, meticulous, poised, mature, never goofy or silly – I never remembered her laughing or goofing off or attending to her personal happiness. I think it would have gotten in her way" (ibid.: 37).

Now we can see Sinedu's own lack of playfulness, which we indicated above was seemingly lacking in her family milieu. The same teacher commented on the way she pursued her studies: "She was one of those little academic machines – academically focused to the point of tunnel vision. Her papers were methodical, played it safe, never delved" (ibid.: 37). Playing it safe academically minimized the likelihood of critical feedback from her teachers that might have resulted in painful constellations of the Shame/Contempt complex. Her quest for scholastic perfection was successful, as she was accepted by twenty-four American colleges. She told people that the day she was admitted to Harvard University was the happiest day of her life.

Harvard University

At Harvard, Sinedu ate her meals alone and spent the weekend nights studying by herself in the dormitory library or watching TV, again alone. Her brother, who attended Dartmouth, once asked if she didn't have friends she spent time with. She said, "No," and wrote in her journal that she wished to "illude [sic] to myself as reaping friends like wheat (ha ha)." She hated to reveal "the image of a lonely girl, but I know that is the truth . . . I am unable to make friends" (ibid.: 100). At her wake, a mourner said: "Sinedu didn't have any friends" (ibid.: 13).

A lot of students in Sinedu's position used the African Students Association as a nexus for dating, but Sinedu showed no interest in any of that. Faced with an upcoming school dance, she recorded an exchange with a male cousin, already married, in which he told her how attractive she would be if she had a beautiful dress, and a new hairstyle. Melanie Thernstrom comments: "The complimentary, flirtatious banter . . . left her at a loss: she could feel herself glaring at him with 'annoyance' and a 'dead' expression. She knew she should have said something '*playful*,' she writes: 'But what? What kind of words, tone . . .?' " (ibid.: 97, emphasis added).

Sinedu is aware of what we might refer to, applying Erikson's concept, as a severe play inhibition. Her annoyance is defensive, but her deadness is a clear indication of the absence of that vitality which only the life instinct, Joy and Interest, can give any of us. She lived with this cousin and his family during the summers before and after her freshman year at Harvard, but spent more time playing with his children than with him and his wife. This was just what she needed to begin to break out of her social isolation, but it turned out to be too little, too late.

Nor was she able to connect with her classmates, who evoked a fair degree of social anxiety. Sinedu's class presentations evoked such distress that this avenue for breaking out of her isolation and letting people get to know her was denied her: "As she muddled her way through her material, groping for English words, she became paralyzed by the fear that she could not hold the attention of the class: they were bored, perhaps even laughing at her" (ibid.: 93). Jung has emphasized how important it is to have – and take – the opportunity to express one's views and be heard:

> For, to have an audience is agreeable – it always proves something to you – while if you are alone you lose your self-esteem. It is as if you become smaller and smaller and finally are a mere speck in an awfully extended cosmos, and then you either develop megalomania or become a nothing-ness. Therefore it is advisable to have a certain audience, if merely for the sake of demonstrating that you know who you are, that you become something definite, that you are just as ordinary as other people, and that you are living in your body. You lose all these considerations when you are alone with yourself.
>
> (Jung 1988: 844)

All Sinedu could imagine from her classmates at this juncture in her life was boredom, that is, lack of Interest, or scornful, not shared, laughter. At this point, Sinedu was experiencing herself in social contexts as a "mere speck," a "nothingness." It is hard not to surmise that by this time the Shame/Contempt complex had snowballed into a monopolistic Humiliation/Loathing one:

> We might consider humiliation monopolistic whenever the individual is perpetually humiliated, as we define an anxiety neurosis by the presence of chronic anxiety. We might define it by the exclusive interpretation of stim-uli in terms of their relevance for humiliation, independent of whether this leads to humiliation or to successful avoidance of the affective experience.
>
> (Tomkins 1963: 379)

Two of Sinedu's diaries entitled "My Small Book of Social Rules" and "The Social Problems I Faced," record her own attempts to find a solution to her social isolation by trying to establish for herself the rules of American social life. One topic that preoccupied her was conversation, that is, what people talk about with each other. Sinedu set as her task to come up every morning with three topics of conversation. But she was never able to find topics that she thought would bring her closer to other students. Thernstrom has summarized Sinedu's description of what happened to her internally in social interactions:

There was a terrible feeling of dissociation: what she calls "this heart-failer thing" – how at some point in a conversation the thread gets lost and she "stops caring." She feels "dead and it is hard to warm myself up." She also writes that she often finds she has difficulty listening because she is so consumed by the anxiety of formulating an appropriate response.

(Thernstrom 1997: 99)

The "heart-failer thing" resulted, at least in part, from Sinedu's inability to reveal to others any of her weaknesses or faults. And this had serious consequences for her emotional development. Jung stated in one of his letters: ". . . without relatedness individuation is hardly possible. Relatedness begins with conversations mostly. Therefore communication [with others] is indubitably important" (Jung 1975: 609).

Jung was also of the opinion that relationships are not built on our strengths but on our imperfections:

A human relationship is not based on differentiation and perfection, for these only emphasize the differences or call forth the exact opposite; it is based, rather, on imperfection, on what is weak, helpless and in need of support – the very ground and motive for dependence. The perfect have no need of others, but weakness has, for it seeks support and does not confront its partner with anything that might force him into an inferior position and even humiliate him. That humiliation may happen only too easily when high idealism plays too prominent a role.

(Jung 1970c: 579, 301)

Sinedu was much too concerned with the potential embarrassment revealing her insecurities to others might evoke to ever do so. Here is Thernstrom's summary of what Sinedu wrote when she considered revealing her vulnerabilities:

She must never, ever let on her desperation or others will feel superior, gloat at her patheticness, and expect her to "grovel." At every point she must guard her back and watch that she not become "the butt" of people's jokes or let others "cross that boundary." If she allows herself to show others how she really feels about them, they will "attack and hate and defend [sic] you." . . . "Watch out!" she warns herself.

(Thernstrom 1997: 99–100)

Earlier, she had written, "Do not show off what you really think. Put on a mask" (ibid.: 96). If she had been able to construct a workable social persona, this might have helped her to take her first steps into the college social milieu. In what I think was a fateful decision, she conceived her social task as to perfect the façade personality that she began to craft in her childhood and adolescence. This façade, which was primarily an anti-humiliation strategy – "Watch out!" – worked all too well to keep her human vulnerability out of view. But, it really cut her off from others, and also put them off from her.

When her freshman year roommate decided not to live with her during the following year, Sinedu became aware of still another block to social relations, the diffidence of others. She reacted to the perceived rejection by her on-again off-again potential roommate with fury, writing that the other young woman "had pranked over her prostrated body" (ibid.: 106) and resolving for the first time to someday avenge herself. We can argue that at this moment the pathological Shame/Contempt complex has now been directed outward. Rather than Shame, Sinedu's conscious experience is near lethal Contempt for her erstwhile roommate. She also recognized that her inability to forgive anyone who had hurt her feelings interfered with the development of relationships with others. This was an insight that might have helped her. As William Blake has said: "Friendship cannot exist without Forgiveness of Sins continually."

As we have noted, Sinedu spent the summer between her freshman and sophomore years living with her cousin and his wife and playing with their children. From the standpoint of the symbolic development of her affective system, this is exactly what she needed to do to break out of her isolation. Not coincidentally, during this same summer she wrote a letter addressed to anyone who might be able to respond to it, posting it on the web as well as mailing it to names she had drawn from the phone book. Within the letter itself, she states that she is writing the letter because she is desperate: "My problem is that I am not bonding with people" (ibid.: 101). She describes the persistent psychic distress that has accompanied this lifelong difficulty and indicates that she has worked very hard to overcome her social inhibition, but that her efforts have not been successful. She feels like she is drowning. She admits that she has always thought it would be helpful to have someone who will check in on her:

> ... one ordinary person who will invite me for jogging or taking a walk, for shopping, for watching TV together, for having dinner together a few times, etc. in these petty, but constant activities, the tips about living that I would pick up, the skills that I would develop and the peace of mind that I would get are immeasurable. After all a pat on the back means a whole lot more than a recorder that squeaks when it is done. ...
>
> (ibid.: 103)

One woman the letter reached corresponded briefly with Sinedu, but stopped when Sinedu sent her, as she put it, a "weird cassette tape and these weird journal writings" (ibid.: 104). Another woman who encountered the letter knew someone at Harvard and passed the letter on to that person, who passed it on to a dean, who read it and passed it on to Sinedu's dormitory, where it was placed in her file.

As Sinedu was about to enter her sophomore year at Harvard, a Vietnamese classmate, Trang Ho, agreed to room with her. Sinedu's hopes for this relationship bordered upon the ecstatic. The first four days after hearing of Trang's decision were the "highlight" of Sinedu's life. She wrote in her diary that for the first time she knew what it was like to be happy, and she became quite expansive in her appreciation of the new roommate's potential contribution to her life: ". . . my rooming problem was solved in the best possible way saving my face and also with a girl I thought I would really enjoy to be with, with a girl I would make the Queen of my life. I could just see myself raising my head proudly whenever people ask me who I'm rooming with" (ibid.: 106). She thought that the main problem in her life was going to be solved, although she did fear that if the rooming arrangement did not work out she would again experience that "shitty cringing feeling" (ibid.: 106).

Jung has sounded a warning over the individual's placing the guarantee of self-worth in the hands of another:

> In the last resort the value of a person is never expressed in his relation to others but consists in itself. Therefore we should never let our self-confidence or self-esteem depend on the behaviour of another person however much we may be humanly affected by him. Everything that happens to us, properly understood, leads us back to ourselves; it is as though there were some unconscious guidance whose aim it is to deliver us from all ties and all dependence and make us dependent on ourselves.
>
> (Jung 1973b: 78)

As attempts to derive self-esteem from the actions of other persons are based on projections, this type of relation actually increases the individual's social isolation:

> The effect of projection is to isolate the subject from his environment, since instead of a real relation to it there is now only an illusory one. Projections change the world into the replica of one's unknown face. In the last analysis, therefore, they lead to an autoerotic or autistic condition in which one dreams a world whose reality remains forever unattainable. The resultant *sentiment d'incompletude* and the still worse feeling of sterility are in their turn explained by projection as the malevolence of the environment, and by means of this vicious circle the isolation is intensified. The more projections are thrust in between the subject and the environment, the harder it is for the ego to see through its illusions.
>
> (Jung 1969b: 17, 9–10)

Sinedu was to be led back to herself, but not in the constructive way that Jung describes.

Sinedu was incapable of feeling that she was developing a truly close relation with Trang, which in her mind would mean a more exclusive one. She became jealous of Trang's many friends and of Trang's family, who occupied a great deal of Trang's attention. Pages of Sinedu's diary are devoted to the question of how to deal with this problem. We are safe in assuming that her feelings of Humiliation were doubly painful as they followed such high hopes for this relation. The relationship deteriorated over the next two years and came to its deadly impasse two months after Trang announced to Sinedu that she would be rooming elsewhere for her senior year. Soon, both Sinedu and Trang would be dead.

Dissociation: "there is no power that lies in me that I could use however I want to"

In the last section, we conjectured that Sinedu's interpersonal growth was held back both by her family's seeming lack of support for her social play and exploration and by a pathological complex, which appears to have begun to be structured in the relations with her parents and siblings. We argued that this complex drove her into a pattern of social avoidance, which was intended to protect her from rejection induced Shame and Humiliation. This self-imposed social isolation, however, deprived her of the Interest and Joy of others which might have helped her overcome her social inhibitions.

In this section, I will argue that Sinedu's personal development was blocked because her adaptation to her inner life was stultified by her lack of the capacity for individual exploration and play, which mirrored her social deficit in these growth promoting dynamisms. She was unable to command the life instinct on her own behalf. Jung has commented on the interrelation between social and individual adaptation:

> Regression, on the other hand, as an adaptation to the conditions of the inner world, springs from the vital need to satisfy the demands of individuation. Man is not a machine in the sense that he can consistently maintain the same output of work. He can meet the demands of outer necessity in an ideal way only if he is also adapted to his own inner world, that is, if he is in harmony with himself. Conversely, he can only adapt to his inner world and achieve harmony with himself when he is adapted to the environmental conditions. As experience shows, the one or the other function can be neglected only for a short time.
>
> (Jung 1970b: 75, 39)

Sinedu's limitations in adapting to her inner world stemmed, I will argue, from her lack of symbolic development and from a dissociation of her psyche caused by the monopolistic Shame/Contempt complex, both of which cut her off from the healthy affective basis of her personality.

Cognitive development

During her educational years in Ethiopia, Sinedu excelled. As she was completing high school, she received the second highest SAT scores in the nation. She applied to twenty-four universities in America and was accepted by all of them. She entered premedical studies at Harvard and maintained her level of performance throughout her three years there. This pattern of dedication and achievement is based both on an established interest, that is, "becoming a physician," and the availability of sufficient Interest to realize this goal. There is no indication, on the other hand, that there was that development and diversification of her intellectual interests, which we might have expected during her adolescence or her time at Harvard. Her cognitive horizon was a narrow one.

One of her high school counselors has noted that she was an "academic machine," with little time for teenage fun and games. Someone who knew her as a classmate, both in high school and at Harvard, described her as the most rational and least emotional person he had ever known. Her lack of imaginative playfulness imposed another restriction on the character of her intellectual pursuits: "I may add here that the ideal Logos can only be when it *contains* the Eros; otherwise the Logos is not dynamic at all. A man [or woman] with only Logos may have a very sharp intellect, but it is nothing but dry rationalism" (Jung 1984: 701).

In Sinedu's life, the dialectic between Interest and Joy that is characteristic of the life instinct and guarantees that Logos contain Eros, was severely restricted by the lack of Joy, and its dynamism, fantasy/play, in her psychic life. As L. H. Stewart has suggested, any block to the individual's ability to move freely *from play to exploration and back from exploration to play* should be seen as evidence of psychopathology.

Symbolic development

In the material available to us, Sinedu's symbolic life consisted of three disparate occurrences. The first, which we described in the last section, was a period of intense daydreaming about an ideal family that persisted throughout her middle childhood, but was developmentally sterile. The second, also referred to in the last section, happened during summer between her freshman and sophomore years at Harvard when she lived with her cousin and his wife. She spent more time playing with their children than she did relating to them. This, it seems to me, might have been the beginning of a period of self-healing play, but it ended when Sinedu returned to Harvard after the summer break. The third, which occurred during the final months of her life, consisted of her participation in an evangelical Bible study group. From a developmental perspective, this indicates the emergence of a new potential for symbolic growth, in the form of a religious cultural attitude. This suggests that Sinedu was able to at least embark on her long delayed adolescent development. The surprise that this new activity evoked in those who knew her is further evidence for its individual character. In general, however, her symbolic development was blocked. She spent her time outside of classes studying or watching television by herself. She did not read books or go to movies.

Jung has addressed the abrasiveness of life, individual or societal, that lacks a rich symbolic dimension

> Now, we have no symbolic life, and we are all badly in need of the symbolic life. Only the symbolic life can express the need of the soul – the daily need of the soul, mind you! And because people have no such thing, they can never step out of the mill – this awful, grinding, banal life in which they are "nothing but." They are simply sick of the whole thing, sick of that banal life . . .
>
> (Jung 1977: 627, 274)

Jung uses the term "nothing but" to refer to an attitude that under-estimates anything psychic, which is regarded as "personal, arbitrary, and therefore completely futile" (Jung 1954: 302, 177): "The unconscious, after all, is 'nothing but fantasy.' We 'merely imagined,' so and so, etc. People think themselves magicians who can conjure the psyche hither and thither and fashion it to suit their moods" (ibid.:).

Jung offers a counterposition to this orientation, that at its root is a negation of the creative aspect of psychic activity:

> All the works of man have originated in creative imagination . . . In the normal course of things, fantasy does not easily go astray; it is too deep for that, and too closely bound up with the tap-root of human and animal instinct. It has a surprising way of always coming out right in the end. The creative activity of imagination frees man from his bondage to the "nothing but" and raises him to the status of one who plays. As Schiller says, man is completely human only when he is at play.
>
> (Jung 1966: 98, 45–6)

Although Sinedu left a voluminous collection of journals in which she described her attempts to find a solution to her social problems, there is little evidence in these records that she had an inner world of creative fantasy. She was caught in the everyday world: "Trust in the imaginal and trust in soul go hand in hand, as depth psychologists have recognized. The reverse is also true: when imagination is not evoked, there is a deep-seated lack of confidence to imagine fantasies in regard to one's problems and to be free of the ego's literalizations, its sense of being trapped in 'reality' " (Hillman 1975: 51).

It seems that one of the realities she was trapped in consisted of the affects and fantasy-images of a pathological Affect-toned complex. It is only symbols formed by the creative activity of the unconscious that connect us with the healthy basis of our personality.

Psychic dissociation

As her diaries indicate, Sinedu was able to deploy the same Interest that motivated her pre-medical studies to sustain her journal writing. Neither her academic studies nor her writings, however, seemed to afford her much in the way of heartfelt Excitement or Joy.

I will now argue that the same monopolistic Humiliation/Loathing complex that handicapped Sinedu in her encounters with others also interfered with her dialogue with the healthy affective basis of her personality, that is, engendered a dissociation between ego-consciousness and the Self. It was this complex that dissociated her ego from the affects of the life instinct, so that to others and to herself, her life was boring rather than interesting and joyless rather than joyful. The "power" that Sinedu was aware she lacked was the energy of the twin dynamisms of the life instinct, which were bottled up in her dissociated unconscious.

By the time Sinedu was in high school, the conscious manifestations of a pathological complex seemed apparent to herself and others. She knew she was painfully shy and blushed at the slightest provocation. Her teachers knew her feelings were easily hurt and that she was hypersensitive to rejection. (Rejection, we recall, is the life stimulus that triggers the Shame/Contempt complex to discharge.) By the time Sinedu got to Harvard, even the thought of revealing herself to others evoked fears of Humiliation.

In her diaries, Sinedu directs Contempt at herself for minor social gaffes and refers to herself as a "cuckoo," a "crawling insect," and, in contrast to a lollipop, "cooked Asparagus." She wished to be seen as a "rose in a sunny garden."

In the titles that Sinedu gave to two of her journals, "My Small Book of Social Rules" and "The Social Problems I Faced," we can note the extent to which her individual efforts were aimed, in a quasi-therapeutic self-help mode, at developing her capacity for objective relationships. But the contents of the journals and tapes were highly rationalized, obsessive ruminations about herself, not emotional dialogues with the self-healing and compensatory functions of the unconscious framed by Interest and Joy.

Jung has pointed out the distinction between a truly helpful self-knowledge and what he calls the knowledge of the ego, implying a rational activity that is dissociated from the needs and desires of the total self:

It [self-knowledge] is manifestly *not* a knowledge of the ego, though this is far more convenient and is fondly confused with self-knowledge. For this reason anyone who seriously tries to know himself as an object is accused of selfishness and eccentricity. But such knowledge has nothing to do with the ego's subjective knowledge of itself. *That* is a dog chasing its tail . . .

(Jung 1969b: 251, 163–4)

Trapped in fantasies generated by the pathological complex, Sinedu was chasing her own tail in her diaries: "By means of these fantasies people can easily slip into an unreal and completely unadapted attitude to the world, which sooner or later must lead to catastrophe" (Jung 1961b: 298, 131). Sinedu was never able to integrate the painful emotions that bedeviled her and thereby break through the dissociation in her personality and reach an authentic understanding of the healthy affective basis of her personality, which I believe was still there in spite of all the evidence to the contrary.

Developmental arrest

Sinedu's psychological development was blocked by her inability to generate emotionally meaningful dialogues with others or herself. This meant that a fully functioning life instinct, the motor of development itself, was seldom robustly constellated. Here is a diary entry, previously cited, which exemplifies her difficulty. A male cousin engages her in flirtatious banter, which left her at a loss:: ". . . she could feel herself glaring at him with 'annoyance' and a 'dead' expression. She knew she should have said something 'playful,' she writes: 'But what? What kind of words, tone . . .?'" (Thernstrom 1997: 97).

In this vignette, Sinedu's lack of spontaneity is apparent. In a section of her journal where she is attempting to forge a normal mask for the world, she exhorts herself: "She begs herself to learn the art of false merriment, instructing herself to laugh 'falsely' regardless of her feelings, and smile at appropriate moments" (ibid.: 97). A spontaneous smile or laugh is beyond her grasp. This is reminiscent of Winnicott's middle-aged schizoid patient, who had lacked the capacity for spontaneity his entire life. His dedication to his analysis was strengthened when he surprised himself by *laughing* while at a movie (C. T. Stewart 2001).

Jung has spoken knowingly of such rigidity and deadness and told us how he thinks it might be overcome. His comments were based on a text by a 17th century alchemist with the pseudonym, Eirenaeus Philalethes, which he interpreted as if it were a dream. (The text itself is not relevant for our purposes.) First, he makes a diagnosis: "You are sterile because, without your knowledge, something like an evil spirit has stopped up the source of your fantasy, the fountain of your soul . . . You wish to have results that flatter your pride, you expect something useful, but here can be no question of that as you have realized with a shock" (Jung 1970e: 191, 161).

I am suggesting that in Sinedu's psyche, this "evil spirit," which she never got close to confronting in the alchemical way Jung suggests here, was a monopolistic Humiliation/Loathing complex, that had produced the severe dissociation in her personality and the attendant developmental arrest of which she was painfully aware, but which she could do nothing to alleviate. Next, Jung suggests a treatment for this condition:

> If you will contemplate your lack of fantasy, inspiration and inner aliveness, which you feel as sheer stagnation and a barren wilderness, and impregnate it with interest born of alarm at your inner death, then something can take shape in you, for your inner emptiness conceals just as great a fulness if only you will allow it to penetrate into you. If you prove receptive to this "call of the wild," the longing for fulfilment will quicken the sterile wilderness of your soul as rain quickens the dry earth.
>
> (ibid.: 190, 160–1)

The "fulness" that is concealed is, I believe, the affective basis of the personality which includes a vital and ever-flowing life instinct. Another statement by Jung even suggests a dynamic for her rampage:

> The unconscious demands your interest for its own sake and wants to be accepted for what it is. Once the existence of this opposite is accepted, the ego can and should come to terms with its demands. Unless the content given you by the unconscious is acknowledged, its compensatory effect is not only nullified, but actually changes into its opposite, as it then tries to realize itself literally and concretely.
>
> (ibid.: 192, 162)

In Sinedu's case, we are arguing that her inability to integrate the primitive affects composing the monopolistic complex burst forth in the form of homicidal and suicidal impulses: Loathing toward Trang, then Loathing toward herself.

Conclusion

Sinedu spent most of her life with one-half of the life instinct, Joy–fantasy/play, absent from her consciousness. There was no symbolic space for play and culture to flourish. Every morning, she awakened to face another grim and joyless day.

Unbearable affect: "despite the outward glory, I live in pain"

In her many journals and in the letter she sent to strangers, Sinedu recorded the course of her emotional development, beginning with her "hellish" childhood. By the time she was in school in Ethiopia, her experiences of negative affects had already extended beyond the range of normal suffering: "Day in and day out, I cried my head off; I was so lonely. If I went early or, left late I would be roaming the yard and deserted hallways alone while other students roared with laughter and talked their hearts out standing in groups" (Thernstrom 1997: 102).

During her three years at Harvard, her suffering mounted. Thernstrom summarizes the pattern that emerges in the diaries from this period: "Her days are long and boring. Even her best days are pierced by pain, when she realizes she is 'laughing standing on thin air' " (ibid.: 101). When she moved among others, Sinedu described a distress that was even more marked: "When I am with a group of people, I keep so quiet (I have nothing to say) that I send chills through those who notice me. Then I cry when people forget about me, or dislike being with me. When I am with one person, I shake with nervousness fearing that we will run out of things to say and she or he will be bored" (ibid.: 102–3).

She was preoccupied, in fact, with the feeling that she had reached the limit of her inner resources. In the section documenting Sinedu's social isolation, I indicated that her most extreme act between her freshman and sophomore years was to broadcast her despair to a number of people she didn't know at all, in the form of a letter sent to strangers whose names and addresses she found at random, in the telephone directory and on the web. To all of them, she sent the same letter, which begins with the explanation that she is writing because she is desperate. She is becoming overwhelmed by the magnitude of her despair.

Making friends, of course, was not a solution for someone so severely cut off from the possibility of a healthy social attitude. Shortly after she began to room with the Vietnamese classmate whom she had imagined would solve her social problems, Sinedu found herself beset with envy, jealousy, and hate because of her roommate's relationships with family and friends, from which she was usually excluded in a manner not inappropriate in a roommate situation, but devastating to her:

> Even more painful to Sinedu than being alone . . . were times when [her roommate] would have friends over. They would hang out laughing and talking in the next room, while Sinedu sat alone, pretending to study and garnering grievance. It was the situation, somehow, she had been in all her life – the laughter sounding to her like everything that had been denied her, all the joy and communion of life from which she was mysteriously and permanently excluded.
>
> (ibid.: 109)

She is laid low by despair and hopelessness: "What makes her feel the most hopeless, she writes, is the sense that the situation will never 'reverse': others will continue on, 'tucked in their rich full lives', and she will 'cry alone in the cold' " (ibid.: 114). The frequency, intensity, and duration of negative emotions is now reaching an unbearable level.

In these excerpts from Sinedu's writings, we can discern reference to the innate affects Anguish and Fear, as well as the complex emotions such as despair, hopelessness, envy, jealousy, and desperation. It was, however, Humiliation that she dreaded the most, as this citation indicates:.

> She continually writes about the fear that were she to expose herself – her needs, her loneliness, her envy, and her aggression – others would ridicule, exploit, or destroy her. She should present herself as powerful and confident, and when she speaks about herself she must never reveal her insecurities. When she talks about how she dresses or eats or does things, she should not "grimace" lest she "dishonor" herself. She admonishes herself to avoid an entreating tone of voice and tells herself that it is better to be alone for twenty four hours than to allow others to drag her around wherever they want to go.
>
> (ibid.: 99–100)

The only sure protection against Shame that she can think of is to assume a false mask, which, of course, leads to increasing social isolation: "I live in my own shell, afraid to reveal my personality and to express my opinions. Although it took me a long time to realize, I am very shy. I blush at every little thing . . ." (ibid.: 101).

When her roommate tells her she is moving out, Sinedu records in her journal the emergence of homicidal and suicidal impulses. Her roommate's decision means that Sinedu was left to be randomly paired with a roommate by the Dunster House office. An editorial written by a Harvard student stated that he understood how Sinedu felt, for floating was worse than death. As Leslie Dunton-Downer put it, "To float for your senior year – to suddenly face the possibility of being stuck in a room with random sophomores who can't find Ethiopia on a map – that's a tough thing" (ibid.: 112–13).

On the morning of the day before she enacts her lethal impulses, Sinedu's roommate, Trang, went out in the morning and came back at midday: "As [her roommate] opened the door to Sinedu's room to leave, [she] could see Sinedu hunched on the bed, in a fetal position, her knees up, holding her head in her hands, looking down and crying. When [she] returned at noon, Sinedu was still in the same position" (ibid.: 121). When Sinedu was asked if she was okay, she "silently waved her away" (ibid.: 121). Sinedu's experience of still being alive, although her life was over, was insufferable.

Possession by affect: "the bad way out I see is suicide & the good way out killing, savoring their fear & then suicide"

When Sinedu's freshman roommate, Anna, with whom she had not been close, announced that she had chosen a new roommate for her sophomore year, Thernstrom recorded her response: " 'Damn you, you bitch!' Sinedu wrote in her diary with fury, saying that she would never forgive her, for Anna had 'pranked over [her] prostrated body.' " She resolved to someday make Anna regret her decision (ibid.: 106). If this was not a momentary possession by the Humiliation/Loathing complex, it was very close to it.

In the letter she sent to strangers, penned two years before her rampage but at a similar time of anguish between her freshman and sophomore years, Sinedu had written: "I probe deeply into myself to solve the emotional pains I go through" (ibid.: 103). And, indeed, in this letter and in the voluminous diaries she kept both before and after writing it, Sinedu was still able to describe her emotional experiences in an objective manner. Two months before the turn to lethal acting out, even though her initial emotional reaction to the rejection by her Vietnamese roommate was one of great intensity, she was not at that time entirely possessed by it. In order to preserve her ego upon learning that she had not been chosen, she initially displaced her homicidal rage reaction onto another classmate that she hardly knew: "I hate . . . If I ever grow desperate enough to seek power & fearful respect through killing, she will be the 1st one I would blow off . . . The way she acts, she acts as if I am no more importance than a crawling insect" (ibid.: 114).

The "If" indicates an ongoing consciousness of her affect. Then she contemplates the two solutions she sees left for her:

> The bad way out I see is suicide & the good way out killing, savoring their fear & then suicide. But you know what annoys me the most, I do nothing. You would think I was both hand & leg-cuffed to a couch stuck in the ground. Sometimes even if a bomb falls beside me, I would be scared at first and then not even bother to see what happened.
>
> (ibid.: 114–15)

Sinedu was, unfortunately, liberated from the cuffs, her inhibitions, when, in my judgment, a bomb, the pathological, monopolistic Shame–Humiliation/Contempt–Loathing complex exploded *inside* her.

After her roommate's decision, the transition within Sinedu from what we are calling "awareness of emotion" to what we would describe as "possession by affect" began. This shift was heralded by several behaviors. The first was withdrawal: "Instead of strengthening her other relationships that spring, Sinedu withdrew from everyone" (ibid.: 113). There were also what might be referred to as end of life behaviors: "She wrote to a relative that she had always promised them a *gabe* blanket . . . and that she wanted to give it now. She sent her sisters in Ethiopia a present. Two weeks before the end of the semester she packed up her computer . . . and sent it to one of her cousins" (ibid.: 117). Then, she called a cousin and arranged to have brunch with him.

In retrospect, this cousin was certain that she was saying goodbye. During the brunch he was struck by the transformation in her appearance and behavior: "She was wearing makeup, high patent leather heels, and shorts . . . Surprised, he told Sinedu she looked 'spectacular.' He asked after [her roommate] and Sinedu said she was fine. She told him a guy had invited her to a prom and she had said no . . . There was an air of happiness about her. She seemed lighter" (ibid.: 117).

Sinedu was free of conflict not because her difficult emotions had disappeared but because she was now possessed by them, and had in effect given up struggling with them or fearing what people would think if they knew what she was feeling. She now simply was the emotion, and this gave her a certain lightness and even attractiveness to others, although she was beyond longing for that or even caring. In a sense, she had made an identification with the Self that is at the core of even the darkest emotions. Jung has described this state in his commentary on the *manipura* chakra:

> When you are in *manipura* you have no conflict, because you are the conflict itself, you just flow like water or fire; you can be exploded in ten thousand pieces yet you are one with yourself because there is no center from which to judge, there is nothing in between the pairs of opposites. For you are everything, you are also the pairs of opposites, you are this and that when you are emotional. It is not I who realize, it is the emotion that realizes.
>
> (Jung 1976: 420–1)

If we recall that at one time she had written in her journal that she wanted to be a lollipop but had had to settle for being cooked asparagus, now, at the end of her life, on the verge of a violent resolution to her feelings of isolation, envy, and self and other hatred that had taken possession of her, she had become the lollipop. Others could enjoy her.

In the week before the killings, Sinedu could even take one exam and receive an A grade on it. But then she missed two exams and students saw her in the library "distracted, with a glazed look" (Thernstrom 1997: 118). Whatever consciousness had been associated with the high of having become her own emotions was fading.

During the same week, Sinedu purchased the knife with which she was to kill Trang and the rope with which she was to hang herself. She wrote a letter that was never mailed to one of Trang's future roommates, commenting on Trang's "betrayal" and how it had caused so much "evil" between them that rooming with her these final weeks had been like "burning in hell." Yet she ended the letter by asking the addressee to plead her case with Trang, to get her to change her mind. This indicates a final ambivalence about the steps she was about to take, and suggests that possession by a monopolistic complex is never total. There is always a sliver of ego capable of making a choice to feel and act differently. In Sinedu's case, she herself was holding out the hope, however faint, of a nonviolent resolution to the intolerable situation into which she felt Trang had suddenly placed her.

In the middle of her last week of life she dropped off a photograph of herself at *The Harvard Crimson*, the student daily newspaper, with the typed message: "KEEP this picture. There will soon be a very juicy story involving the person in this picture." On the outside of the envelope she typed "IMPORTANT" (ibid: 119). The *Crimson* editors had no idea what to do with the letter and it was eventually thrown out.

On the Friday before her murder, Trang invited a friend to stay with her for the weekend and help her move. Sinedu's behavior on Saturday night, to the degree that it was observed by others, was atypically extroverted:

> No one knows exactly how Sinedu spent her last night. A Harvard-security guard told the police that at 6:30 P.M. that night Sinedu had come and requested a key to her room, telling him that she had locked herself out. He had seen her throughout the year and she had always appeared lonely to him, but that night she was smiling and in a jovial mood. A little while later she returned again and asked if he would let her into the weight room, which he found unusual, as she had never made the request before and students who used the weight room knew how to get in without a key. Around 8:30 P.M. he saw her standing on the street outside [her dormitory]. He asked what she was doing, and she told him she was waiting for a friend to pick her up. It struck him as unusual, he told the police, that he had seen Sinedu three times in a short period of time that evening. The police were unable to locate anyone else who saw Sinedu that night or discover who, if anyone, she had been waiting for.
>
> (ibid.: 122)

When Sinedu's roommate and her friend returned in the middle of the night (about 2 a.m.), they noticed that Sinedu was lying on her bed with the light on. The next report we have of her is from later that same Sunday morning: "Some time before eight in the morning an alarm went off . . . Sinedu was already in the bathroom. They heard her cross through their room to turn off the alarm and then go back into the bathroom" (ibid.: 123). Then Sinedu's roommate and her friend went back to sleep: "[The visitor] awoke to see Sinedu standing over [her roommate], stabbing her silently with a huge knife and a fixed, glazed expression – intent, like she really knew what she was doing" (ibid.: 123). The visitor left to get help. When the police arrived, they found Sinedu's roommate dead and Sinedu hanging from a rope secured to the shower curtain rod. Although she was still alive when they discovered her there, she died shortly after while being administered to by an ambulance crew.

We have already established that by the time she turned toward violence, Sinedu had long been under three of the conditions that I believe are necessary if an emotional conflict is going to succeed in provoking this level of concrete lethal action: social isolation, dissociation, and unbearable affect. The fourth condition that ensured the lethal outcome was affect possession, an altered, ego-less state of mind that came over her only at the very end of this malignant process, and might yet have been reversed had anyone been able to recognize it for what it was.

Chapter 8

Gloria: panic and homicide
Peter: fury and killing of mother and sisters

One criterion I used for the selection of the cases discussed in Chapters 4–7 was that writings by the individuals, in the form of journals or diaries, etc., were available. These subjective materials contributed to the validity of my analyses of the presence or absence of the conditions postulated as necessary for their lethal behaviors. These personal records also increased the likelihood that my speculations about the unconscious emotional complexes that were at the root of their enactments were reasonable deductions.

No such subjective expressions are available from the two cases discussed in this chapter. My justification for this modification of method is based on these considerations. The reader will have made note of the fact that in Chapter 4 I argued that the pathological complexes that haunted Vivienne and drove her to suicide were composed of the crisis affects Agony and Shame/Contempt. In Chapters 5–7, I conjectured that the unconscious complexes that eventually impelled Kipland, Eric, Dylan, and Sinedu to their lethal behaviors were composed of the crisis affect Shame–Humiliation/ Contempt–Loathing. On the basis of the analyses so far, then, are we to assume that the two other crisis affects never contribute to individuals killing others, themselves, or both? I think not. In this chapter I will argue that the pathological complex in the case of Gloria was composed of the crisis affect Fear–Terror–Panic, while in the case of Peter it was composed of the crisis affect Anger–Rage–Fury. If my presentation is persuasive, then we can conclude that in the presence of the four necessary conditions for lethal behaviors, pathological complexes composed of any one of the crisis affects, accompanied by a decrease in the vitality of the life instinct, may motivate lethal enactments. These cases are drawn from Muriel Gardiner's *The Deadly Innocents: Portraits of Children Who Kill* (1985).

Gloria: a panic complex that leads to homicide

When she was 15 years old, Gloria, in a state of panic fearing for her life, shot and killed her uncle, Albert. She had intended to kill his wife, Ethel, who was threatening to murder her with a butcher knife. We have noted that the

Unknown is the life stimulus for the crisis affect Fear. I think it will become apparent that for Gloria the Unknown took the form of life-threatening behaviors toward her by adults in her milieu.

From birth until she was nearly 4 years old, Gloria lived with her parents. Her mother was away most of the day working as a domestic, so Gloria was deprived of maternal care. Her father, a railroad train porter, was frequently absent, so she also suffered from a lack of paternal care. She was barely 4 years old when her father was killed in a train wreck and she was abruptly sent to live with her maternal grandmother. There, she found the warmth and love she had been missing in her own home.

When she was 6 years old, her mother and stepfather appeared one day at the grandmother's home and took Gloria to live with them. There she soon became the babysitter for her younger brother and a series of half-siblings. Her mother continued to be frequently away and she was critical of Gloria. Her stepfather was emotionally and physically abusive, frequently beating Gloria. Tomkins has stated that constellation of the innate affect Fear–Terror–Panic occurs when a child is exposed to a parent "who relies upon terror as a technique of socialization . . . to guarantee norm compliance" (Tomkins 1991: 514). Terror is the higher octave of Fear, just as Panic is the next octave of intensity after Terror. We can assume the beatings Gloria received were terrifying and resulted in the formation of a Fear–Terror–Panic complex capable of discharging at different levels of intensity in response to life-stimuli at different levels of provocation. In spite of a family atmosphere replete with all levels of provocation, Gloria had been able to maintain an adequate academic performance at school, even though her social adaptation lagged. At 14, after having been terrorized at home by her stepfather for eight years, Gloria finally stood up to him when he threatened yet another beating. She was abruptly sent to live with her grandmother.

Although Gloria was delighted to be with her beloved grandmother, she was more than a little troubled by the presence of her maternal Uncle Albert, his wife, Ethel, and their children, who had moved in during her absence from this home. She was soon put in the familiar role of babysitter and accepted this with grace and continued to maintain an average school record.

Gloria's room was next to her uncle and aunt's and was separated from them by only a paper-thin wall. As they were both alcoholics, she was bombarded daily by their drunken, raging arguments and equally distressing loud raucous laughter. We don't know the precise time from her return to her grandmother's to the day she killed Albert, but it seems that she suffered this contagious exposure to the negative emotions of Ethel and Albert for about a year.

The day on which Gloria killed Albert was a hot Saturday in August. This is how the day began: "Albert, who did not work on that day, had been drinking along with Ethel since early morning. By afternoon they were screaming and quarreling. Albert began brutally beating one of his sons" (ibid.: 30). It is reasonable to assume that with her own experiences of step-father brutality, Albert's beating of his son would have constellated in Gloria the pathological Terror complex and increased its magnitude. On that day, when their child escaped to the grandmother's part of the house, his parents came after him. Then, Ethel and Albert got into a heated argument. At a later time, Gloria described the continuation of this dispute:

> Albert was shouting that Jack wasn't his son. I felt ashamed, and sorry for Jack. I don't like to see kids hurt. Then Albert and Ethel began hitting each other. There was blood all over the place, and my grandmother can't stand blood; she started screaming and told them to get out of the house. Ethel went into the kitchen to get an ice pick and came back to stab Albert.
>
> (ibid.: 30)

At this juncture, Gloria felt driven to act, even placing herself in danger: "I screamed at her to stop, and I jumped and grabbed her. Then they went back next door and kept on fighting. They were real drunk, just crazy, I was scared" (ibid.: 30).

These events would not only have continued to elicit Gloria's Fear–Terror–Panic complex, but as they escalated also would have stepped up the level at which it discharged within her own psyche. As with many storms, there was an ominous period of quiet that ensued. Then, Gloria heard her uncle and aunt raging in their room:

> "There ought to be some way of getting rid of that girl," Albert was saying. "She's just a bloodsucker. Mom's saving her money for her, not for us and our children. We've got to get Gloria out of the house somehow. Why doesn't Mom send her back to Viola? *She*'s her mother . . . "You know she never will," replied Ethel. "The only way we can get her to leave is to make life so miserable for her that she'll want to go."
>
> (ibid.: 30–1)

Ethel and Albert had now joined forces to direct their irrational rage toward Gloria, who became enraged, frightened, and in tears.

Throughout all these events, Gloria was preparing for a special date that evening. When she went to retrieve her freshly laundered dress from the clothesline, she found one of Ethel and Albert's children playing with it in the mud. She yelled at him, but did not strike him. The following exchange with Albert occurred next: " 'What do you mean hitting Junior?' Albert shouted. 'He's not your son. You have no right.' Gloria replied: 'I didn't hit him I just yelled at him.' Albert retorted: 'You're a liar. He told us you hit him. I'll get you for that' " (ibid.: 31).

Grandmother broke the tension by ordering Albert to return to his room and sober up. But suddenly Ethel appeared, brandishing a butcher knife at Gloria and shouting: " 'You don't belong here!' . . . 'Mom isn't your mother, you're just sponging on her, licking her boots to get her money. It isn't your home, its Mom's and ours, and we're not going to have you trying to worm your way in and get us all thrown out' " (ibid.: 31–2).

Gloria knew that there was a rifle stored in another uncle's room and ran to retrieve it to defend herself: "Albert and Ethel followed her, Ethel shouting: 'I'll kill you!' She raised the knife but Albert seized her arm and pushed her out of the room. The two went back to their own [room]" (ibid.: 32). Gloria heard Ethel screaming in the room next to hers: "I'm going to kill that girl if that's the only way we can get rid of her!" (ibid.: 32).

By now Gloria had moved quickly past Fear and Terror and was nearing a state of Panic. She loaded the gun, took it outside, and looked into Albert and Ethel's room, where she saw Ethel pick up the knife again and head for the door:

> Gloria's fear and fury merged into a tempestuous frenzy, and she raised her gun. But it was Albert who came out first. Gloria shot. When she saw her uncle crumple to the ground, she dropped the gun. The next instant Ethel rushed at the girl, screaming and waving her knife. Gloria turned to run out the gate and onto the road. She ran until the first car approached, signaled it, and breathlessly asked for a lift to the home of her grandmother's friend, a mile or so down the road.
>
> (ibid.: 32)

She was picked up by the police, later tried, found guilty, and sentenced to a long prison term.

After Gloria had been in jail for six years, the parole board requested a psychiatrist to perform a sodium amytal interview and Gloria agreed. These are the results of this procedure:

> The psychiatrist who interviewed Gloria under sodium amytal found her reconstruction of the offense consistent with what she had previously disclosed. However, Gloria was able to express much stronger feelings during the interview: "My stepfather, he was mean to me . . . He beat me, He hated us and I hated him . . . Mother doesn't love me" . . . Gloria then repeated the story of her crime, revealing great fear that her aunt was going to stab her.
>
> (ibid.: 37)

The psychiatrist's conclusion was that Gloria had "no overt psychiatric disorder" and that her behavior stemmed "largely from early conditioning, when she was made to feel unwanted and severely deprived" and that her homicidal act "was situational in character and ... occurred because of extreme provocation" (ibid.: 37–8).

I would say that "early conditioning" led to the formation of a monopolistic Fear–Terror–Panic complex, which was constellated at its highest level of intensity, Panic, on that hot, August Saturday. On the basis of this analysis, it was a Panic complex that drove Gloria to shoot when she perceived her own life to be in danger: she was not trying to kill Albert, she was attempting to protect herself.

Peter: a fury complex that leads to killing mother and sisters

When 18-year-old Peter returned home on furlough from the Navy, he fell into an old pattern and acceded to his mother's wish to hold some of his money for him. For the last night of his leave, Peter had planned an evening on the town with his girlfriend and needed his money. When his mother refused to return it to him, restricting his autonomy once more as she had done so many times in the past, Peter became furious and bludgeoned her to death with a hammer. When his 11-year-old twin sisters walked into the room where this had occurred, Peter, now in a panic state, killed them too. We have identified Restriction of Autonomy as the life stimulus for the crisis affect Anger–Rage–Fury. I believe the reader will be able to identify this life stimulus as a regular aspect of the behavior of Peter's mother toward her son.

Peter's mother, Vera, was born in a Baltic state that was annexed by the Soviet Union in 1940 and overrun by Hitler's army a year later. Some time during the next three years she married Peter's father, a German soldier who was killed when the Russians retook the country in 1945. Vera's brother was also killed in these battles, and her father also taken prisoner, which occasioned her mother's subsequent suicide. When the war ended, Vera's knowledge of German, French, English, and several Baltic languages led to her employment as an interpreter by the American army in western Germany: "Here she met a young lieutenant ... who married her, legally adopted her baby, Peter, and brought them to the United States" (ibid.: 4).

A son, Jimmy, was born when Peter was 4, and Karen and Kathy, the twin girls, arrived when he was 7. Peter always seemed to be a thorn in Vera's side, perhaps because he reminded her of her sufferings in Europe. She said of him: "Peter has never given me a day's joy ... He was born at the wrong time in the wrong place" (ibid.: 5).

Shortly after she gave birth to the twins, Vera received a letter informing her that her father, who had continued to live in Europe after his wife's death and his own release from prison, had also committed suicide. Vera immediately try to follow suit: she took an overdose of sleeping pills and left a note. On coming home from school, Peter found his mother and told a neighbor, who called the police. Vera was taken to a hospital where her life was saved, and she then spent several weeks on a psychiatric ward. After she returned home, her relations with her immediate family deteriorated: "Easily upset, she would argue with her husband, scold, and often beat her children, especially Peter" (ibid.: 7).

Peter was about 7 when his mother returned from the hospital. Despite the difficulties at home, the first four years at school were a happy time for him, as he did well in his studies and was well liked by his teachers and classmates. Peter and his brother Jimmy became close friends and his twin sisters adored him. It was during these same years, however, that Vera's irrational fear of poverty intensified, and one consequence was that she began to try and restrict Peter's spending. His father would sometimes give Peter some small change, and Peter would buy candy and little presents for his siblings: "[His mother] would fly into a rage. Where did he get the money? They couldn't afford it; they might all be starving next year if they didn't save" (ibid.: 7). When Peter was 10 years old, he took on a paper route and began to earn his own money. His mother insisted this money be kept in a separate account, to be used for college. Although Peter wanted spending money, he went along with his mother's holding his earnings in reserve – until Christmas came. When he asked his mother for ten dollars to buy gifts, she refused him. Peter was enraged and said he would bring the issue to his father's attention, adding, "He's not stingy like you" (ibid.: 8).

When Peter sought his father's mediation, his father sided with him: "Your mother's pinching pennies, God only knows why. But I'm your father and you are going to have the [ten dollars]" (ibid.: 8). At this, Vera erupted and screamed, "You're not his father! . . . He's only your stepfather, Peter. Your real father was killed in the war" (ibid.: 8). When Peter turned to his father in disbelief, his father said:

> "It's true that your first father was killed in the war. He never knew you. But I've been your second father since you were a year old, and I loved you so much and wanted you so much for my son that I adopted you. So I am your real father – just as much as I am Jimmy's or Kathy's or Karen's. Almost more, because you're my oldest son and you have my name."
>
> (ibid.: 8–9)

Peter began to cry and fled to his room.

From that day on, Peter changed. He withdrew more and more from his parents, especially his mother. By the time he was in junior high school, there was a decline in his grades and his social adaptation. Toward the end of the eighth grade, he and his mother had another argument over money. When Peter asked her for the amount he needed to pay for a field trip, she expressed her opinion that the trip was an extravagance and refused him the money.

Peter responded by inducing his brother to run away with him, taking funds he had been holding as treasurer of the science club at school. The two boys were picked up by the police and returned home the next day.

When Peter was in the ninth grade, the family moved. He seemed lost in his new high school and by the tenth grade was failing several subjects. A school counselor took an interest in him but she was unable to prevail upon his mother to find a therapist for him. Vera said: ". . . what Peter needs is to go into the army as soon as they will take him" (ibid.: 14). When Peter was 17 and in the eleventh grade, two important events occurred. He began to date a classmate and was accepted for active duty in the Navy.

When Peter obtained leave for Christmas, his return home began as a happy reunion:

> Karen and Kathy were overjoyed to see him; Jimmy looked at him with adoring eyes. Peter saw at once that his mother and father were proud of him. He arrived home on Christmas Eve, laden with presents for all the family. For once his mother made no objection to these extravagances, though there were a few uncomfortable moments when Peter felt she was having a hard time controlling herself.
>
> (ibid.: 15)

On the morning after Christmas, his mother asked him if he had his return ticket and Peter made a fatal mistake:

> When Peter replied that he did not as yet, but that he had the money for it, Mrs. Field suggested that she keep the money for him, lest he be tempted to spend it. A wave of anger passed over Peter that he should be treated as a child, but from old habit, and wishing to avoid a scene, he handed the money over to his mother. Besides, he had plenty in his pocket, and he had more in the bank.
>
> (ibid.: 15–16)

The money in his pocket went faster than he had expected and he found himself without funds for the evening on the town with Jennifer that he had planned for his last night at home. He decided, with considerable trepidation, to ask his mother for the money she was holding for his ticket:

> All morning Peter kept remembering the many humiliations he had suf- fered from his mother; and the anger he had so often choked down now came to the surface to aid him in his determination to get the sixty dollars. He was convinced his mother would refuse him, but this time he resolved to have his way. It seemed to him the decisive moment in his life; he must prove that he was a man. Nothing was going to stop him. In his mind, Peter rehearsed one approach after another, one argument after

another. None of them seemed satisfactory; he only knew that somehow or other he was going to win the battle.

(ibid.: 17)

Peter's anticipation of another restriction of his individuality by his mother had constellated the monopolistic Anger–Rage–Fury complex: "the anger he had so often choked down now came to the surface." That afternoon, his mother asked him to hang a picture for her. Glad to have a brief delay, Peter got wire, hooks, a hammer and hung the picture. Then Peter asked his mother for his money: "I want the flight money I gave you, Mother . . . It will just see me through my leave, and you can get the sixty dollars out of my savings tomorrow for my ticket" (ibid.: 17). Vera reacted true to form: "This was too much for Mrs. Field, and all her pent-up resentment at her son's extravagance – for Mrs. Field, the mortal sin – erupted" (ibid.: 18):

"What's the matter with you? What are you coming to? I thought you were growing up and could take some responsibility – and here you've been squandering all your earnings on wasteful nonsense, and now you want to throw away your savings too. Do you want to starve when you get older? Do you want to be on welfare when your father and I are gone and can't take care of you any more?"

(ibid.)

Peter attempted to reason with her: "Mother, you're just crazy on the subject of money. You and Dad aren't taking care of me. I'm earning my living and I have savings besides. It's *my* money" (ibid.: 18). Then he became somewhat threatening: "I guess I could go to court if I had to, But Dad'll make you give it to me" (ibid.: 18). Now Vera added another new and inflammatory dimension to her argument:

"He certainly won't!" screamed Mrs. Field. "He won't have you throwing your money away on that girl. That's all you've been doing your whole vacation, and I've stood enough. You gave me that money to keep for your flight back, and I'm keeping it for just that and nothing else. You won't get a penny of it for your spendthrift nonsense."

(ibid.: 18)

She was now threatening to block not only his autonomy, but also many other internal forces promoting his stage-appropriate development. Feeling her now to be a serious obstacle in the path of his self-realization, Peter no longer attempted to reason with his mother, but aggressively asserted his independence:

"It's my money and I'll do what I please with it. If you won't give it to me, I'm going to take it, I'll spend it the way I want. Then you can decide whether you want to take some of my savings out of the bank for me to get back to the post or not. If you don't want to, I don't care. I'll get back some other way, or I just won't go. But I'm going to have my money, here and now. I know where it is – it's in that empty coffee can, and if you won't give it to me I'll take it."

(ibid.: 18)

Vera, now beside herself, turned white with rage and clutched the coffee can: "You thief!" she cried. "You'd steal it, wouldn't you!" (ibid.: 18). It is at this moment, I believe, of being so characterized when he was simply demanding what was his, that Peter became possessed by the Anger–Rage–Fury complex. Later, Peter was to say that he did not know what came over him at this moment. But he had a hammer in his hand: "Blindly he struck at his mother, and with the first hammer-blow she fell to the floor. He struck her again on the head, and blood streamed out. At that moment Karen and Kathy, frightened at the noise, rushed into the kitchen. Peter turned his hammer first on one girl and then the other" (ibid.: 19). Later, it seemed to Peter that his attacks on his sisters was driven by his fear of discovery rather than any hatred of them.

When Peter fully realized he had killed his mother and two sisters, his panic mounted. He decided that to give himself a chance to escape he would need to kill both Jimmy and his father. He pocketed his father's revolver and waited in front of the house for Jimmy to return home from school. When Jimmy arrived home, smiled, and threw a snowball at him, everything changed: "Love for his brother and his father welled up in him, as well as remorse and horror at slaying his mother and sisters" (ibid.: 20). The life instinct had once again surfaced, and it illuminated his conscience. He told Jimmy what he had done and they walked together in silence to the police station. Peter was subsequently sentenced to from fifteen to thirty years imprisonment on each of the three murder counts, the terms to run concurrently.

Chapter 9

Little Father Time: homicides followed by suicide

Father Time is a child character in Thomas Hardy's 19th-century novel, *Jude the Obscure*, who, at the emotional nadir of his short life, hangs his two younger siblings and then himself.

Jude is the son of Arabella Donn and Jude Fawley. When the couple separated shortly after their marriage, Arabella did not let Jude know that she was pregnant. Instead, she left England to join her parents in Australia and, when she returned to England shortly after her child's birth, left the infant son with his maternal grandparents. The grandparents had given him the nickname, Father Time, because he looked so aged. They did not have him christened so they would be spared the expense of a Christian funeral if he died in damnation. When the child was "of an intelligent age," the grandparents sent him to his mother, but, as she was about to marry again, she sent him on to Jude and his new partner, who was Jude's cousin, Sue.

The Jungian analyst, Arlene TePaske Landau, understands Father Time as an ambivalent expression of the child archetype: "In *Jude the Obscure*, Little Father Time is the divine child and also the antithesis of the archetype of the divine child" (Landau 2003: 289). Seeing this "child" ultimately as the dark aspect of the divine child archetype, Landau is struck by the negativity of his affective life: "Little Father Time is filled with gloom and despair; he has no inner vision of joy or love, no experience of play and lightheartedness" (ibid.: 291). My more formal analysis of Father Time's emotional life, which will focus on the four necessary conditions for his lethal behaviors, will underline and amplify Landau's insight, for in my view she has captured the essence of his severely distorted affective development.

"Is it you who's my *real* mother at last?"

We are introduced to Father Time as he rides on the train to his new home. Hardy never tells us his exact age, but it seems that he is 7 or so years old at the time we first meet him, traveling alone on the train to join Jude and Sue. Father Time is pale, has large frightened eyes, speaks to no one, and has no interest in the countryside through which he is passing. When a woman who held a basket on her lap let a kitten out to play, he was the only passenger who did not laugh and seemed to be saying, "All laughing comes from misapprehension. Rightly looked at, there is no laughable thing under the sun" (Hardy 1895: 336). The life instinct is in abeyance, there is no interpersonal or personal Joy or Interest.

As he was not met at his destination, he walked to his new home: "The child fell into a steady, mechanical creep, which had in it an impersonal quality – the movement of the wave, or of the breeze, or of the cloud. He followed his directions literally, without an inquiring gaze at anything" (ibid.: 338). Shortly after he arrived and was met by Sue and Jude, Father Time asked Sue, "Is it you who's my *real* mother at last?" After her evasive answer, he asked, "Can I call you mother?" (ibid.: 339). Then a yearning look came over him, and he began to cry. Sue quickly said he could call her mother if he wished. This rather hopeful, emotional reaching out by Father Time did not, however, lead to a further breaking out of his isolation.

When Father Time would come home from school in the evening, he would repeat inquiries and remarks that had been made to him by the other boys concerning the fact that Jude and Sue were not married and this caused Sue and Jude considerable pain and sadness. Father Time's faulty social adaptation was now evident in his peer relations.

"All laughing comes from misapprehension"

As Father Time progressed into a lonely middle childhood, Sue and Jude often found him sitting silent, his "quaint and weird face set, and his eyes resting on things they did not see in the substantial world" (ibid.: 341). His face would remind Sue of the Muse of Tragedy, Melpomene.

When Father Time was 8 or so years old, he journeyed with Sue and Jude to an agricultural exhibition in a town miles from their own. They had taken Father Time "to try by every means of making him kindle and laugh like other boys . . ." (ibid.: 355). After she has expressed her delight in the roses that are on display, Sue says: "I feel that we have returned to Greek joyousness and have blinded ourselves to sickness and sorrow . . . There is one immediate shadow, however – only one" (ibid.: 362–3). She was looking at Father Time, "whom, though they had taken him to everything likely to attract a young intelligence, they had failed to interest" (ibid.: 263).

Father Time appeared to know what they were saying and thinking, and said: "I am very, very sorry, father and mother . . . but please don't mind. I can't help it. I should like the flowers very, very much, if I didn't keep on thinking they'd be all withered in a few days" (ibid.: 263). Father Time's capacity for enjoyment and interest is withering and dying because he is dissociated from the healthy emotional base of his personality. The life instinct that normally resides there has never been constellated for him.

"It do seem like Judgment Day"

As for so many of the individuals we have encountered in other chapters, the problem of unbearable affect really surfaces as the child begins to move toward adolescence. We go next to a time in the novel when three years have passed and Father Time, now 11 or so years old, is essentially unchanged. He has, however, two younger siblings, a boy and a girl, and Sue is pregnant for a third time. The family has arrived in a town where many years ago Jude failed miserably in his attempt to become a member of the university community. Although they arrived on a parade day, Remembrance Day, Jude is certain it would be his "Humiliation Day." When the sky grows overcast and thunder rumbles, Father Time shudders and whispers, "It do seem like Judgment Day" (ibid.: 395). "Judgment Day" becomes a suitable symbol for a level of unbearable affect, and there is more to come.

The family has considerable difficulty in finding lodgings and eventually is able to find an accommodation, but only for Sue and the children. Jude goes on to find a room for himself. Sue, under questioning from the landlady, foolishly tells her that she is not married. The landlady then says that since this is the case, she and the children can only stay the night. Sue goes out with Father Time to try and find other lodging, but fails to do so. Little Time says, "I ought not to be born, ought I?" (ibid.: 405). They return to their lodging for the one night, and Sue acknowledges that Jude has gone away so that the rest of them can have this room. Then the following conversation takes place between Sue and Little Father Time: He says, "It would be better to be out o' the world than in it, wouldn't it?" (ibid.: 406). Sue's reply is not a loving one: "It would almost, dear" (ibid.: 406). Father Time then asks, "if children make so much trouble, why do people have 'em?" (ibid.: 407). In her response, Sue avoids taking responsibility: "Oh, because it is a law of nature" (ibid.: 407). Father Time then laments: "And what makes it worse with me is that you are not my real mother, and you needn't have had me unless you liked. I oughtn't to have come to 'ee-that's the real truth! I troubled 'em in Australia, and I trouble folk here. I wish I hadn't been born" (ibid.: 407).

Sue's reply, "You couldn't help it, my dear" (ibid.: 407), partially exonerates him but in equal measure confirms that he is trouble. Father Time's next statement is in line with that view: "I think that whenever children be born that are not wanted they should be killed directly, before their souls come to'em, and not allowed to grow big and walk about!" (ibid.: 407). Again, Sue does not reply, suggesting she agrees with him.

She then introduces a new topic into their conversation: "There is going to be another baby" (ibid.: 407). Father Time jumps up wildly and said: "O God, mother, you've never a-sent for another; and such trouble with what you've got!" (ibid.: 407). Sue once again confirms that children are "trouble": "Yes, I have, I am sorry to say . . ." (ibid.: 407). Now, he is beside himself and weeping (the very picture of unbearable emotion):

"Oh, you don't care, you don't care!" he cried, in bitter reproach. "How ever could you, mother, be so wicked and cruel as this, you needn't have done it till we was better off, and well! To bring us all into *more* trouble! Nor us, and father a-forced to go away, and we turned out tomorrow; and yet you be going to have another . . . 'Tis done o' purpose-'tis-tis!" He walked up and down sobbing.

(ibid.: 407–8)

Sue asks for his forgiveness, saying it's not quite on purpose! Father Time responds: "I won't forgive you, ever, ever. I'll never believe you care, or father, or any of us any more!" (ibid.: 408). Identified now with his unbearable affect, he has cast the fatal die: his lethal behaviors will soon follow.

"Done because we are too menny"

Looking back from the vantage point of knowing about the killings that follow, this conversation with Sue was, I believe, the "last straw" for Father Time. It was immediately after this exchange that possession by homicidal and suicidal affects occurs. Father Time gets up, and goes away into the closet adjoining his mother's room in which a bed has been spread on the floor. Sue hears him say, "If we children was gone there'd be no trouble at all!" (ibid.: 408). She responds with a preemptory tone: "Don't think that dear . . . but go to sleep!" (ibid.: 408). It is by now impossible for Father Time to put the thought that it would be better for his parents without his siblings and himself out of his mind, for he is now under the sway of possession by the affect complex Rejection + Alienation–Shame–Humiliation.

The next morning, Sue joins Jude at his room for a quick breakfast and then they return to where she and the children are lodged. Sue goes into the children's room, shrieks, and then faints. Jude enters the room and looks about in bewilderment:

At the back of the door were fixed two hooks for hanging garments, and from these the forms of the two young children were suspended by a piece of box-cord round each of their necks, while from a nail a few yards off the body of little Jude was hanging in a similar manner. An over-turned chair was near the elder boy, and his glazed eyes were staring into the room; but those of the girl and the baby boy were closed.

(ibid.: 410)

A piece of paper was found upon the floor, on which was written in Father Time's hand, with the bit of lead-pencil that he carried: "*Done because we are too menny*" (ibid.: 411).

Ian Gregor has suggested that this is "the most terrible scene in Hardy's fiction, indeed it might reasonably be argued in English fiction . . ." (Gregor

1974: 224). It is true, this Hardy critic continues, that although the novel can hardly accommodate this brutal scene, "its animating purpose is rooted deep within the evolving structure of the novel." Later he observes: "The scene is obviously an attempt at the same kind of choric effect as that represented by Father Time himself, a reaching out beyond the particulars of the narrative to an impersonal tragic dimension, a dimension where Time ceases to be a child and becomes 'the whole tale of their situation'" (ibid.: 224). This enables the narrator to cite Hardy's description of Father Time's death mask:

> The boy's face expressed the whole tale of their situation. On that little shape had converged all the inauspiciousness and shadow which had darkened the first union of Jude, and all the accidents, mistakes, fears, errors, of the last. He was their nodal point, their focus, their expression in a single term. For the rashness of those parents he groaned, for their ill-assortment he had quaked, and for their misfortunes he had died.
>
> (ibid.: 224)

Father Time gives face to the intolerable state of possession by unbearable affect. As Hardy conveys, what is intolerable is having to carry the entire weight of a family's shadow – a not infrequent problem for children who are "disturbed."

Jung's discovery of the importance of the family atmosphere upon the growth of the child came when he found striking similarities between the profiles of word association tests of family members. He was led to conclude:

> It is not pious precepts nor the repetition of pedagogic truths that have a moulding influence on the character of the developing child; what most influences him are the unconscious personal affective states of his parents and teachers. Hidden conflicts between the parents, secret worries, repressed wishes, all these produce in the child an emotional state, with clearly recognizable signs, that slowly but surely, though unconscious, seeps into his mind, leading to the same attitudes and hence the same reactions to the environment.
>
> (Jung 1973a: 1007, 474)

Father Time's death mask makes it painfully clear that the emotional complexes that possessed him at the time of his homicidal and suicidal behaviors had been constellated and maintained in him by the "unconscious affective states" of his mother, his grandparents, and Sue and Jude. These hopelessly burdened the capacities of his innate affective system: They were just "too menny."

Chapter 10

Lethal conditions and psychological treatment

> I had always worked with the temperamental conviction that at bottom there are no insoluble problems, and experience justified me in so far as I have often seen patients simply outgrow a problem that had destroyed others. This "outgrowing," as I formerly called it, proved on further investigation to be a new level of consciousness.
>
> C. G. Jung, *Alchemical Studies*

Of the seven young people whose lethal outcomes we have so far analyzed in this book, only two – Gloria, and Peter – had received no therapy before their killings. The other five – Vivienne (Chapter 4), Kipland (Chapter 5), Eric and Dylan (Chapter 6), and Sinedu (Chapter 7) – had all received at least some form of treatment. First, we will look at the therapies of these young people who did progress to violent outcomes. Then, I will be discussing how I think psychological treatment of such individuals might unfold in the future, if focused throughout on the emergence of necessary conditions for life-destruction: social isolation, dissociation of the personality, unbearable emotion, and possession by affect.

Vivienne Loomis

In a letter to her former teacher, Mr May, written on 2 December 1973, nineteen days before she killed herself, Vivienne mentioned that the family was having weekly visits with a pastoral counselor. She wrote that the focus of the treatment was her father's questions about his future in the ministry. The therapy had originally been scheduled to start in September, but it was delayed to November because they had difficulty finding an appropriate counselor. This is all that Vivienne wrote about these sessions, but, after her death, her mother commented on them.

Mother said that the counseling was not especially oriented toward Vivienne as if hers were the main problems: "We felt that the thing was to focus on us as a group and try to work out all the relationships" (Mack and Hickler

1981: 110). Later, the parents had second thoughts and felt it would have been better for Vivienne to have had her own therapist:

> Vivienne resented the [family] sessions and thought they were stupid. She took a dislike to the counselor himself. According to Laurel, Vivienne would "close right up" in the meetings. Once when asked a question she got upset and cried and did not want to talk about anything. Mostly she sat silently and said nothing. Suicide was never mentioned.
>
> (ibid.: 110)

Mother described in greater detail the meeting in which Vivienne got upset and cried:

> She was physically there at every meeting . . . but she wouldn't talk. I remember one meeting, Vivienne suddenly started to cry. None of us could reach out and touch her. We all kind of looked at her. The therapist said, "You are really hurting," and asked her, "What would you like from the family?" And she said, "Understanding." "Which member of the family do you most want understanding from?" the therapist asked. And she said, "Daddy. I want Daddy to know me."
>
> (ibid.: 110)

When they got home that day, her mother said to Vivienne: "Honey, I would like to get to know you." Vivienne replied: "You wouldn't like it if you did know me" (ibid. 110). Later, her sister Laurel told their mother that "she meant I wouldn't like it if I knew she was planning to commit suicide" (ibid.: 110). In the 2 December letter to Mr May, Vivienne wrote that she was "probably the most destructive factor in the family," and then gave her reason for not immediately killing herself: "If I didn't have to worry about Mommy and Daddy, I wouldn't bother finishing this letter before I hung myself. But I have to stick with them. Sort of like one burden holding up another, which isn't too stable a thing to begin with" (ibid.: 111).

Three weeks later, she had given up on trying to hold her parents up.

Kipland Kinkel

On 20 January 1997, when he was in his last year of middle school, Kipland had the first of nine appointments with a psychologist. (The last visit occurred on 30 July 1997, in the middle of the summer before he entered high school, which was ten months before the killings he was to enact.) His mother was present during the first session, at which she told the psychologist that she was concerned about her son's temper and "his extreme interest in guns, knives, and explosives" (Kirk and Boyer 2000a: 4). She said at that time that she was afraid that Kipland might harm himself or others and that she was "deeply concerned with Kip's strained relationship with his father" (ibid.). (His father did not participate in the sessions.) At the same session, Kipland told the counselor that his mother thought "he was a good kid with some bad habits," whereas his father thought "he was a bad kid with bad habits" (ibid.). At the end of this first meeting, the counselor diagnosed Kipland as suffering from major depressive disorder. He saw no evidence of psychosis or thought disorder.

During the twenty-six day interval between the fourth and fifth counseling session, Kipland managed to get himself suspended from school twice, the first time for kicking a student in the head and the second time for throwing a pencil at a classmate. During their fifth meeting, Kipland's therapist referred him to his family physician who started Prozac four days later. The course of medication was continued for three months, the last two months occurring after the end of his psychological treatment.

In his notes covering the last three therapy sessions, the counselor wrote that Kipland had experienced a gradual lifting of his depression, a reduction of his anger, and was getting along better with his parents. Within a month after termination, however, Kipland had purchased another gun, a secret he kept from his parents.

Eric Harris and Dylan Klebold

On 30 January 1998, Dylan and Eric broke into a car and stole tools, other items, and caused substantial damage. After pleading guilty on 25 March 1988, they entered the District Attorney's juvenile diversion program, which they completed on 3 February 1999 (two months before their rampage). The program included individual counseling, an anger management course, and community service.

A termination report from the diversion program said that Dylan "Is intelligent enough to make any dream a reality" and "If he is able to tap his potential and become self-motivated he should do well in life" (Pankratz and Mitchell 1999). Eric's report said "Eric is a bright young man who is likely to succeed in life" and "He is intelligent enough to achieve lofty goals as long as he stays on task and remains motivated" (ibid.). Eric and Dylan were perfecting not only their assault plan but also their façade personalities.

In September 2000, Eric's parents stated that Eric was treated by a psychologist for obsessive compulsive disorder and depression (Abbott 2000). It appears that Eric had a first appointment with his therapist on 16 February 1998, shortly after his arrest in January 1998. No other information about his psychological treatment is available.

In a journal entry on 21 April 1998, Eric wrote: "My doctor wants to put me on medication to stop [me] thinking about so many things and to stop [my] getting angry" (*Columbine Report* 2006: 88). Peter Breggin (2001) has informed us that Eric had been placed on the antidepressant fluvoxamine a year before the attack on Columbine and that his autopsy revealed therapeutic blood levels of this medication. On 2 April 1999, the Marines contacted Eric in a routine recruiting call. Eric cleared two preliminary screenings, but his application was rejected on 15 April 1999, five days before his rampage, ostensibly because he was taking psychiatric medication.

Sinedu Tadesse

During her freshman year at Harvard, Sinedu Tadesse had begun seeing a counselor at the University Health Services. She continued these sessions through her sophomore and junior years. After her death, police investigators found among her papers a list of things she had written down to talk about with her therapist. For instance, "Sinedu writes that she is concerned that she is incapable of forgiveness. If people do anything that hurts her, she writes, forever afterward when she thinks about them her heart 'will go cold.' How does forgiveness work? is it that others express anger at the time, while she keeps it all inside her?" (Thernstrom 1997: 116).

Sinedu's anxiety about her incapacity for forgiveness was prescient, for it was after her roommate refused to continue to live with her during their senior years that her homicidal and suicidal plan took possession of her.

In 2005, I wrote to Sinedu's former therapist and asked if the content of his meetings with her was available. He said that he had declined to comment at the time of Sinedu's death because of the ethical restraints of his profession and must do so now because these restraints have no statute of limitations.

Necessary conditions and psychological treatment

Many therapists of quite diverse persuasions consider affects the core of therapy. The Jungian analyst James Hillman wrote, for instance: "Case histories, technical papers and the theoretical literature all show that emotion is the centre of every analysis and of every transformation in analysis" (Hillman 1992: 3). L. H. Stewart expressed a similar point of view when he said, "In analysis the affects can never be ignored. They are always present, whether openly expressed, or felt beneath the surface, or, if seemingly absent, then much in the consciousness of the analyst" (L. H. Stewart 1987b: 132). Hillman and Stewart both are pointing to a more general connection between affect and treatment. As Hillman adds: "To repeat, explanatory and therapeutic psychology in regard to emotion are enmeshed with each other. We offer that a unified theory of emotion is both a systematic explanation and a therapeutic method . . . namely, [emotional] *development*" (Hillman 1992: 287–8). Hillman suggests that development of emotion occurs through its affirmation by consciousness, admitting that the difficulty of such affirmation "lies in the healthy, natural tendency to avoid the numinous and demonic . . ." (ibid.: 288), which are intrinsic to the nature of emotion, being, in fact, emotion's archetypal aspect. As Jung said:

> On the one hand, emotion is the alchemical fire whose warmth brings everything into existence and whose heat burns all superfluities to ashes . . . But on the other hand, emotion is the moment when steel meets flint and a spark is struck forth, for emotion is the chief source of consciousness. There is no change from darkness to light or from inertia to movement without emotion.
>
> (Jung 1969a: 179, 96)

Emotion, therefore, signifies the possibility of development, and its purpose is to make change possible.

If we look again at Table 2.1 (see p. 40), we can see that an ideal treatment would return the pathological patterns in Column 2 to the optimal conditions in Column 1.

This effort to restore optimal conditions for the handling of affect will be much in our mind as we discuss psychological treatment when necessary conditions for lethal behaviors have been met. Let us look once more at the necessary conditions from this perspective.

Social isolation

Optimal emotional development requires affective dialogues with others framed by Interest and Joy. The emotional content of these dialogues may well consist of the crisis affects, which are frequently and inevitably constellated in all human interactions, but the dialogues themselves are both interesting and enjoyable. Individuals experiencing social isolation, however, undergo an increase in crisis affects at the same time that they are undergoing a decrease in activation of the life instinct, because dialogues with others have dried up and no longer bring either Interest or Joy. Psychological treatment aimed at reduction in the intensity of crisis emotions will have to focus on transference and countertransference, where they can be worked through. When therapy is aimed at increasing the activation of Interest and Joy, its focus will be on developing the human relationship between patient and therapist. The therapist can best keep these two aspects of treatment in mind by a kind of two-way thinking, focusing on one while not losing sight of the other.

Transference and countertransference

Hillman's view of the emotional nature of the transference, and its inevitable interpersonal character, highlights the notion I have been pressing:

> ... we can see why the *transference* has such a primary role in psycho-
> therapy. Affective contact is psychic contact ... The primary contact with
> the soul of another person is emotion ... In short, emotion is wholeness
> and the affective contact is the first level of healing, of making whole.
> Therefore the patient continually provokes the emotion of the therapist,
> involving him in anger, in love and desire, in hope and anxiety, in order to
> get a whole reaction. It is only this wholeness perhaps which works a cure.
>
> (Hillman 1992: 274–5)

Perhaps we should add to this passionate passage only one qualification,
that emotion moves toward wholeness. From his experience with patients,
Jung too learned that transference was, in its essence, emotional and
irreplaceable:

> Emotions are not detachable like ideas or thoughts, because they are iden-
> tical with certain physical conditions and are thus deeply rooted in the
> heavy matter of the body. Therefore the emotion of the projected contents
> always forms a link, a sort of dynamic relationship, between the subject
> and the object – and that is the transference. Naturally, this emotional link
> or bridge or elastic string can be positive or negative, as you know.
>
> (Jung 1977: 317, 138)

He would agree with Hillman, however, that even if the patient's transference
creates a distorted pattern of relationship, it is, nevertheless, an attempt by the
patient at some kind of effective interpersonal connection. As Jung wrote,
"Accordingly, I cannot regard the transference merely as a projection of
infantile-erotic fantasies. No doubt that is what it is from one standpoint, but I
also see in it ... a process of empathy and adaptation" (Jung 1961b: 662, 285).

I experienced what Jung meant when I worked with a challenging 12-year-
old boy, who would repeatedly make fun of me in a way that filled my consciousness with a surfeit of Shame. Usually, the only thing I could do to defend
myself was to hold to my seat and smile back weakly, in wan appreciation of
his deft ability to make me look stupid. After a year of this, the patient,
evidently much better, said: "Thank you for never taking me seriously!"

In a series of articles, a research group in the Department of Clinical
Psychology and Psychotherapy at the State University of Saarland, Saaur-
brucken, Germany, has shed new light on the affective aspects of such complicated transference and countertransference reactions and their bearing on
successful and unsuccessful treatment outcomes.

The research used facial affect as a measure in response to the increasing
focus in contemporary analyses of psychotherapy on interpersonal communication in the therapeutic relationship: "Considering the importance of
emotional expression in this process, the present study focused on facial
expressions of emotion and the interactant's response during the course of

treatment" (Merten, Anstadt, Ullrich, Krause, and Buchheim 1996: 199). The therapies studied consisted of eleven brief psychotherapies, each consisting of fifteen sessions. The use of a split-screen videotape allowed them to identify the facial affective expressions of both patient and therapist. The primary affects happiness, anger, contempt, fear, sadness, and surprise were identified both in the individual expressions of patients and therapists when not in directly dyadic interaction (i.e., when the therapist is watching the patient do something else beside talk to the therapist), and in the dyadic interactions between them when they were directly conversing. The researchers then attempted to determine which of the affects they observed most influenced the outcome of treatment.

All the therapists studied were experienced clinicians; in terms of orientation three of the therapists described themselves as cognitive-behavioral, four as psychoanalytic, two as client-centered, and two as "dynamic-intended," an East German version of insight, uncovering therapy. In line with the findings of many other psychotherapy researches, the theoretical perspective of the therapist was *not* predictive of treatment outcome. Nor did the facial affective behavior of the therapists exhibit any differences that could be related to a particular theoretical orientation. Also, one of the most successful treatments, Mr H., and one of the least successful cases, Ms A., were conducted by experienced psychoanalysts. Neither the dyadic or non-dyadic facial affective expressions of these two patients correlated with the outcomes of their treatment.

In initial interviews, the researchers identified two affective behaviors which proved to be determinative. The first was the *lead-affect* of the patient, which is a translation of a German term that is almost musical in its implications: "In the following, we call the affect with the highest proportion *leit-affekt* according to the metaphor of the leitmotiv" (Merten and Krause 2003: 116). The second emotional factor was a classification of the therapist's responses to the patient's lead-affect as (a) *reciprocal* or (b) *complementary/ compensatory*. In a reciprocal reaction, the therapist matched the patient's affect, either hedonically, positive–positive, or anhedonically, negative– negative. In a compensatory reaction, the therapist responded with an emotion other than the one presented by the patient. The first surprising finding was that when the therapist's response was fully reciprocal with the patient's, there was very little therapeutic movement. This result was consistent with Jung's observation of the difficulty a therapist can find moving within a psychological sphere that is similar in kind to the patient's, for then "nothing of fundamental therapeutic importance has happened." He was perhaps ahead of his time in realizing that a patient needs a compensatory affective response from a therapist:

> Once an unconscious content is constellated, it tends to break down the
> relationship of conscious trust between doctor and patient by creating,

through projection, an atmosphere of illusion which either leads to continual misinterpretations and misunderstandings, or else produces a most disconcerting impression of harmony. The latter is even more trying than the former, which at worst (though it is sometimes for the best) can only hamper the treatment, whereas in the other case a tremendous effort is needed to discover the points of difference.

(Jung 1966: 383, 187)

The second important discovery was that a compensatory response by the therapist to the patient's lead affect, in the *first interview*, was predictive of successful treatment outcomes. The authors offer their interpretation of this finding:

It is assumed that those therapists who are not submitting themselves unconsciously to the adaptation patterns the patients normally impose on their partners are successful. In doing so, the therapist stops a vicious circle by disproving the dreaded expectations of the patient. This can happen even if the therapist is not aware of doing so since these processes take place on the level of micromomentary nonverbal behavior . . .

(Merten and Krause 2003: 116)

We can ask if the compensatory responses of therapists are somehow expressions of the normal compensatory function of the unconscious, which, in the patients' psyche, has somehow been blocked from reaching consciousness. If so, the research may suggest that successful therapists' affects function like a healthy unconscious for the patient.

In their first sessions, Ms A., the unsuccessful case, exhibited 169 affective facial expressions, of which 104 were primary affects. Mr H., the successful case, showed 134 affective facial events, of which 61 were primary affects. The researchers did not stress this difference, but it is tempting to speculate that a greater amount of unmodulated archetypal affect is harder to modify than affects that have already been modified through previous effective interactions with others. The facial affective behaviors of the unsuccessful therapy patient and her therapist that were a measure of their dyadic interaction were quite similar:

Ms. A and her therapist were, from the first hour on, a typical reciprocal hedonic joy dyad. The patient also showed some sadness, fear, anger and contempt. There was an absence of surprise and disgust. Her therapist expressed the negative spectrum even less. His facial affect was completely dominated by expressions of happiness. We should keep in mind that massive anxiety attacks were being discussed.

(Krause and Merten 1999: 109)

It would also appear that mirroring is not sufficient to modify affect. In contrast to this dysfunctional pattern, the dyadic interaction between patient and therapist in the successful case was compensatory:

> Patient H's most frequent facial display was felt happiness, but many anger and disgust expressions also were observed. Therapist H's disgust reactions were even more frequent than that of his patient and were more frequent than his own happy expressions. The therapist showed no fear and no sadness but much surprise. In our terminology, this dyad began therapy with complementary affective reactions, with happiness as the patient's and disgust as the therapist's most frequently occurring affect.
>
> (Merten *et al.* 1996: 203)

The pattern of facial affectivity that was observed in the first sessions of therapy was also present during the course of treatment: "In therapy H we continued to observe a complementary [compensatory] dyad while the prot-agonists in therapy A were more reciprocal in the temporal organization of their facial affectivity" (ibid.: 204).

In the unsuccessful case, Ms A., the researchers were able to define the countertransference problem of the therapist, which fitted into the difficulty of the patient: "The internal problem was that the therapist could not tolerate his own aggressive feelings. This was implanted in expressing an abundance of mutual liking displayed in mutual smiling and much positive reciprocity" (Merten and Krause 2003: 118). In the successful treatment of Mr H., on the other hand, the therapist was able to show negative emotions even while the patient was smiling.

There was another notable difference between the therapists in the success-ful and unsuccessful cases: "Mr. H's therapist [successful in treating his patient] was seven times more often surprised than Ms. A's therapist [who was unsuccessful]" (Krause and Merten 1999: 109). Surprise was also augmented in the patients, along with anger and fear. The following comment was offered on these findings: "The augmented emotions fear and surprise can be interpreted as indicating the information processing of new and unexpected contents and as part of change processes in mental representations . . ." (Merten 2005: 329). In Chapter 13 of *The Symbolic Impetus* (2001), I reviewed the work of the psychoanalyst, Henry Smith, who discovered that during psychoanalysis his experience of Surprise was regularly followed by revelatory reflections on the therapeutic relationship or on the patient's or his own psychology (Smith 1995). In L. H. Stewart's archetypal affect system, Surprise is the innate (archetypal) affect which motivates development of self-reflective consciousness.

Another treatment outcome the German researchers noticed was *diversifi-cation* of emotional displays in patients whose psychotherapies had been successful. This, in turn, can be used as a way to identify that a treatment has succeeded:

> With regard to the results of the research project, Anstadt et al. (1996) point out that changes of a patient's behavior pattern in the course of a psychotherapy can be seen as an indication of structural changes and that these changes can be used to assess the success of a treatment. For example, in successful treatments, facial expression became more diversified.
>
> (Dreher, Mengele, and Krause 2001: 101)

Dreher and her colleagues further suggest that the therapists' dyadic interactions are such that they develop precisely those affects that the patient is unable to generate. I would add that structural transformations in the patient's complexes that permit more diversification of affect reflect a change in the type of affect-toned complexes available to the patient – from monopolistic, manifested by a single lead affect ("Johnny one note"), to a more pluralistic understanding of what affect itself should be:

> ... no single affect theory is permitted to dominate the personality monopolistically, to be suppressed or relegated to the mode of intrusion or permitted to oscillate in competition with alien affect theories. Instead, a modus vivendi is achieved in which there is mutual accommodation between the affects in the interests of a harmonious personality integration.
>
> (Tomkins 1963: 303)

It was thought that therapists who did not have a diversified expressive regulating system had difficulty in developing the affects the patient is unable to constellate: "What characterizes most successful therapists is the absence of a single, high-frequency leitaffekt [i.e. lead affect, implying a monopolistic theory of what affect should be]. From another perspective, we might say that therapeutic failure is related to a loss of variability in the therapist's expressive regulatory system" (Merten and Krause 2003: 120). As the therapist's response to the patient's lead affect is usually not a conscious one, researchers presented "a hierarchical scale of how one can fail within the sphere of this unconscious emotional answer" (Krause and Merten 1999: 112):

> On the lowest end, we find people, who are absolutely unable to perceive the unconscious affective relationship offer. It is not due to defences, but instead a more or less habitual affective blindness. This is more frequent than one would think.
>
> (ibid.: 112)

The therapist internally perceives the [patient's] affective relationship offer and reacts to this as an empathetic lay person, which means he or she behaves reciprocally to the patient's offer on the behavioural level as well as internally . . . In general, this is more of a guru type who completely and openly follows unconscious relationship offers, and declares his or her actions to be curative. This type [of therapist] differentiates itself from the first type in that he or she at least recognises the relationship offer.

(ibid.: 112)

The therapist internally perceives the relationship offer and reacts to it like an empathetic lay person, which means he or she behaves reciprocally to the patient's offer on the appropriate behavioural level but finds this to be inappropriate. However, he or she is unable to avoid responding in [the] way [invited by the patient]. This is the most frequent form of failure among well-trained therapists. We generally find here a disassociation between the internal experience [of the therapist] and the enactment [by the therapist in the therapy].

(ibid.: 113)

The therapist internally perceives the relationship offer as externally induced feelings, but keeps these feelings to him or her self, and gives a completely different answer than the one which is being forced upon him . . . It seems as if the therapist is displaying the affects which are missing in the episodes described by the patient, and which are also lost through his or her narrative.

(ibid.: 113)

The authors suggest that this hierarchy of emotional perceptiveness and responsive flexibility might be used as a guide in the training of prospective therapists.

Jung concluded an article that addressed the fundamental problems of modern psychotherapy with this statement: "The attitude of the psychotherapist is infinitely more important than the theories and methods of psychotherapy, and that is why I was particularly concerned to make this attitude known" (Jung 1970d: 537, 346). The research carried out by Krause and Merten indicates in addition that it is the therapist's capacity to generate an authentic emotional response to what the patient is saying that moves the therapy forward. It would seem that in encountering the affective system of another, a therapist is much more than someone affectively tuned to the patient's emotional frequency, and needs to be an individual who can also engage the patient in novel ways.

Human relationship

When Jung wrote: "We cannot fully understand the psychology of the child or that of the adult, if we regard it as the subjective concern of the individual alone, for almost more important than this is his relations to others" (Jung 1954: 80, 39). He indicated that he felt that any psychological state is highly dependent upon the quality of the person's emotional interactions with others. This is particularly important for therapy, which Jung conceives as an evolving relationship between therapist and patient, one fruit of which is the patient's maturing personality. As he put it, with each step in the resolution of the transference, the patient is able to move further on a road that "leads to a purely human relationship and to an intimacy based not on the existence of sexual or power factors but on the value of personality. That is the road to freedom which the analyst should show his patient" (Jung 1961b: 663, 286–7). Such intimacy in the therapeutic dialogue involves the constellation of the life instinct in both partners.

Krause and Merten studied affective interactions between dyads composed of healthy subjects and compared them with dyadic interactions they observed between disturbed individuals:

> The difference, between the structurally disturbed patients and healthy subjects, can be described in the following way. In the healthy subject the negative facial affect shown is related to the cognitive content in the discussion between two interaction-partners. Whereas the expression of happiness is related to the relationship as such. In the structural disturbances the [negative] facial affect is related directly to the self or to the partner.
>
> (Krause and Merten 1999: 112)

We might say that the healthy individuals were capable of emotional dialogues with others framed by the life instinct, while the disturbed subjects were not.

Another European research group, located in the Psychology Department of the University of Innsbruck in Austria, has thrown light on the development of the human relationship during therapy. One of their articles begins with this statement: "Therapeutic change always includes the change of affective processes" (Banninger-Huber and Widmer 1995: 43). Another paper starts this way: "Our contribution focuses on results from psychotherapy process research, which considers affective processes to be highly relevant in establishing and shaping the therapeutic relationship" (Benecke, Peham, and Banninger-Huber 2005: 81). The authors of both papers describe the primary affects that are involved as joy, fear, anger, and contempt. (They see Shame as an acquired emotion, and they do not address Sadness and Interest.)

In order to identify emotion, Banninger-Huber and Widmer studied selected sequences of videotaped psychoanalytic psychotherapies, which allowed microanalytic analyses of nonverbal cognitive-affective dyadic interactions. From the aspect of these interactions that expressed the Joy in the encounter and presumably provided much of its glue, they were able to identify prototypical affective microsequences, which they refer to by the acronym, PAMS:

> PAMs are mainly expressed nonverbally, and are characterized by frequent smiling and laughing [Joy] of both client and therapist (Banninger-Huber, 1992, 1996; Banninger-Huber, Moser & Steiner, 1990). They serve as a means of relationship regulation, and are a product of the regulatory activity of both persons involved in the interaction.
>
> (Banninger-Huber and Widmer 1999: 78)

Successful PAMs establish a resonant state with the therapist, which is a precondition for working on conflictive topics involving crisis affects. A resonant state between patient and therapist is, in my view, an interpersonal dialogue framed not only by Joy but also by the other affect of the life instinct, Interest. Therapy needs to be interesting as well as pleasant.

These researchers also attempted to understand productive therapeutic work in terms of "traps," attempts by the patient to seduce the therapist into enactments of the transference. In formulating the relative roles of traps and PAMs, the authors formulated what they call the "balance hypothesis":

> Basically, the therapist has to fulfill a double function. On the one hand, he or she has to provide a reliable working alliance to give the client a basic sense of security. This enables the client to explore his or her experiences and behaviors, and to accept and understand the therapist's interventions. On the other hand, the therapist has to maintain a certain level of conflictive tension by not taking over the client's role offers repeatedly. The maintenance of the tension is a prerequisite for recognizing and working on the client's problems.
>
> (ibid.: 80)

They conclude that therapists acquire essential information by falling into some trap or other, after which their subsequent interactive behavior needs to be guided by "an attitude of self-reflection . . ." (ibid.: 85).

I would add that to be able to bring this off, therapists need to be open to the dynamics of the innate affect Surprise, which is the motive force for the development of self-reflective consciousness. This, the reader will recall, was the conclusion of the Saarland group, which discovered that successful therapies are frequently guided by Surprise.

At this juncture, I want to apply the discovery of Krause and Merten regarding the relationship patterns of their healthy subjects, *interpersonal happiness with negative affects* as *content* of the interaction, to the patient–therapist relation. In order to do this without creating confusion, I will need to refer back to their case of Ms A., which I reviewed in the transference–countertransference section. This was an example of an unsuccessful case, in which the therapist's facial affect was completely dominated by expressions of happiness even when massive anxiety attacks were being discussed. The researchers were able to define the countertransference problem of the therapist, which fitted into the difficulty of the patient: "The internal problem was that the therapist could not tolerate his own aggressive feelings. This was implanted in expressing an abundance of mutual liking displayed in mutual smiling and much positive reciprocity" (Merten and Krause 2003: 118). How are we to know whether patient and therapist are expressing healthy Joy or are engaged in a transference–countertransference happiness trap?

I believe the results of a study by P. Ekman and W. V. Friesen, titled "Felt, false, and miserable smiles," will help us in making this important distinction. It is the felt and false smiles that require our attention. The authors used their own Facial Action Coding System, which measures all visible facial behavior, to distinguish among the various smiles. Felt smiles "include all smiles in which the person actually experiences, and would presumably report, a positive emotion" (Ekman and Friesen 1982: 242). False smiles "are deliberately made to convince another person that positive emotion is felt when it isn't" (ibid.: 244). I believe that when the patient and therapist are engaged in what Jung referred to in the citation at the beginning of this section as "a purely human relationship and an intimacy based . . . on the value of personality" their expressions of mutual Joy will be *felt* smiles. During a reciprocal transference–countertransference enactment, that is, a counterproductive one, both the patient's and the therapist's smiles will be *false* ones.

This brings us to the notable absence of any reference to the innate affect Interest in the Saarland or Innsbruck studies. Neither group of researchers included Interest in their classification of primary affects. When I wrote to Dr Krause, Director of Clinical Psychology at the University of Saarland, to ask about this, he replied that this particular emotion had not been systematically studied as yet but commented that "[Interest] is the only antitoxic expressive affect in countertransference reactions especially vis a vis borderline patients and perversions." One article by members of the Innsbruck group, from which only the abstract has been translated from the German, contains in that summary the following statement:

> Two clusters of facial affective behaviour of panic patients could be found. One, as hypothesised, with very intense attachment like behaviour and no fear, the other one with slightly more negative affects, but smiling as well. Interactive facial patterns of patients and their therapists are

rare and rather low. The missing of *interest* and anger is an indicator of boredom and a lack of seduction.

(Benecke, Krause, and Dammann, 2003, emphasis added)

Jung's case

Jung has presented a case that illustrates his own conviction about the importance of a human relationship that also affects the therapist to any truly healing therapeutic process:

> In psychotherapy, even if the doctor is entirely detached from the emotional contents of the patient, the very fact that the patient has emotions has an effect upon him. And it is a great mistake if the doctor thinks he can lift himself out of it. He cannot do more than become conscious of the fact that he is affected. If he does not see that, he is too aloof and then he talks beside the point. It is even his duty to accept the emotions of the patient and to mirror them.
>
> (Jung 1977: 319, 138–9)

The patient he was talking about on this occasion was a woman in her fifties, herself a doctor, who arrived in his office from America in such a state of confusion and "utter bewilderment" that Jung thought her "half crazy." He learned that she had been in treatment with a psychoanalyst whom Jung characterized as "a mystical cipher who was sitting behind her, occasionally saying a wise word out of the clouds and never showing an emotion" (ibid.: 320, 139). It was this experience that led her to get "quite lost in her own mists" (ibid.). Jung wrote that when he heard all that, "I naturally had an emotional reaction and swore, or something like that" (ibid.):

> Upon which she shot out of her chair and said reproachfully, "But you have an emotion!" I answered, "Why, of course I have an emotion." She said, "But you should not have an emotion." I replied, "Why not? I have a good right to an emotion." She objected, "But you are an analyst!" I said, "Yes, I am an analyst, and I have emotions. Do you think that I am an idiot or a catatonic?" "But analysts have no emotions." I remarked, "Well, your analyst apparently had no emotions, and, if I may say so, he was a fool!" That one moment cleared her up completely; she was absolutely different from then on. She said, "Thank heaven! Now I know where I am. I know there is a human being opposite me who has human emotions!"
>
> (ibid.)

Jung concluded: "My emotional reaction had given her orientation" (ibid.).

Dissociation of the personality

Andrew Moskowitz begins his article, "Dissociation and violence," by remarking: "The notion that people who appear to their neighbors or colleagues to be perfectly 'normal,' unremarkable, or even kind in disposition can, under some circumstances, commit heinous, violent crimes has long fascinated and repelled the public" (Moskowitz 2004: 21). He then goes on to present a case example of one such neighbor's unexpected homicides:

> On the morning of March 5, 2001, Charles "Andy" Williams, a 15 year old student, walked into Santana High School in California and shot 13 students and two staff. Two students were killed. As is often the case in adolescent murders, Andy was considered quiet and nice, and those who knew him were mystified that he could commit such an act.
>
> (ibid.: 21)

Indeed, Andy, who is now serving a sentence of fifty years to life, is considered a model prisoner. In an interview with Diane Sawyer of ABC that was aired in October 2002, he described his state of mind during the rampage: "I don't think crazy is the right word. It's like, an out-of-body experience – when I was in my body, I was out of my body at the same time . . . I didn't feel it was actually me doing it" (ibid.: 21–2). Andy didn't feel "it was actually me doing it," because in a real sense "he" wasn't doing it. A dissociated part of him enacted the murders. At the time of his rampage Andrew was, in my judgment, possessed by a monopolistic complex composed of one or more crisis affects that were responsible for the dissociation on the one hand and guiding his actions on the other. It must have taken years for a complex of this magnitude to form and split off and during this period it was unconscious. When constellated, however, it only took moments for it to overwhelm and displace Andrew's ego-consciousness and take command of his executive functions. The main clue that Andrew was without ego-consciousness was his reported sense of being out of his body – without ego-consciousness one is out of one's body.

Dissociation, lack of connection and communication between parts of the psyche, occurs in several forms, among which we might mention: (a) dissociation between parts of the ego-complex, which results in one-sidedness; (b) dissociation between ego-consciousness and the personal unconscious, which results in neurosis; (c) dissociation between ego-consciousness and the cultural unconscious, which results in writer's block; and (d) dissociation between ego-consciousness and the healthy affective basis of the personality, which is one of the necessary conditions for certain individuals to kill others, themselves, or both. In this section, our focus will be on the psychological treatment of dissociation type (d), the splitting of the ego from its original healthy affective base.

In all the many forms of dissociation, complex dynamics are at work. A pathological, monopolistic complex that is of sufficient magnitude and intensity to restrict an individual's capacity for emotional dialogues with others framed by Interest and Joy is also capable of blocking an individual's ability to engage in emotional dialogues with one's self in a way that involves the life instinct. Such a block – the basis for a split – is brought about in three main ways. First, the pathogenic complex interposes itself between consciousness and the unconscious, that is, causes psychic dissociation. Second, the resulting dissociation leads, through an arrest in development, to a marked reduction in symbol-formation. Without the symbol, the connection between the conscious and the unconscious breaks down, arresting development, for as Jung argued: "The unconscious can be reached and expressed only by symbols, and for this reason the process of individuation can never do without the symbol" (Jung 1968b: 44, 28). Third, the ratio of the positive affects of the life instinct to the crisis affects, which under optimal conditions for development should favor the positive, becomes under pathogenic conditions, tilted in favor of the negative. This further diminishes the capacity of the ego to integrate the crisis affects into developmental pathways. The unintegrated crisis affects further augment the magnitude and intensity of the pathological complex, and a vicious circle is established.

In these ways, the snowballing pathological complex decreases the quantity of libidinal warmth from Interest and Joy that will be accessible to the psyche for its process of subjective integration. This is a loss that retards the capacity for self-healing upon which all ongoing development depends in a regularly traumatogenic world. The compensatory function of the unconscious is now prevented from operating upon consciousness, so that restorative dreams filled with symbols of potential transformation are replaced by static fantasies that keep reiterating the pathological complex. The ego-complex and the pathological complex are now in direct competition for psychic energy. Under normal circumstances the ego has "a great power of attraction, like a magnet; it attracts contents from the unconscious, from that dark realm of which we know nothing; it also attracts impressions from the outside . . ." (Jung 1977: 18, 11). A pathological complex introduces a competing magnetic quality:

> Anything that does not suit the complex simply glances off, all other interests sink to nothing, there is a standstill and temporary atrophy of the personality. Only what suits the complex arouses affects and is assimilated by the psyche. All thoughts and actions tend in the direction of the complex; whatever cannot be constrained in this direction is repudiated, or is performed perfunctorily, without emotion and without care . . . The flow of objective thought is constantly interrupted by invasions from the complex . . .

> (Jung 1960: 102, 47–8)

The treatment of dissociation of the personality, which could be described as isolation with one complex from all the other richly populated complexity of the personality as a whole, is no different in principle than that of social isolation. The only difference is that the therapeutic focus is not on forming relations with others in the outer world so much as looking in dreams and fantasies for the manifestations of affect-toned complexes in addition to just the one preoccupying the patient. This focus seems to have the most potential for integrating the pathological complex, expanding the patient's emotional repertoire, and helping the patient re-establish contact with the healthy basis of the personality. But, what if the patient is unable to access the dreams and fantasies that bear witness to the creative activity of the psyche? When the dominating complex interferes with conscious awareness of spontaneously produced psychic images from other centers of the mind, and fantasy is generally curtailed, then another method than the analysis of spontaneously occurring fantasies and dreams must be found.

Jung pioneered such a method in his experiments with what he came to call active imagination, a technique for dialoging directly with the unconscious through a type of willed daydream. We can view active imagination from the perspective of the life instinct. The first step in active imagination is opening up to the unconscious and giving free rein to fantasy. Here, the dynamic Joy–fantasy/play takes the lead. The second step is maintaining an alert, attentive, active attitude toward the material that has emerged. Here, the dynamic Interest–curiosity/exploration takes the lead:

> The method of active imagination is really nothing more than a conscious engagement, as Jung says, in fantasy/play while at the same time expecting to be curiously interested in what occurs. Normal, innate individuation is an ongoing process that has as its aim the development of the individual. It is a manifestation of the life instinct which in the psyche takes the form of the dialectic of play and curiosity.
>
> (L. H. Stewart 1984)

In *Jung on Active Imagination*, Joan Chodorow has introduced key readings from Jung's writings on active imagination:

> Sometimes he names the expressive medium, for example bodily movement, painting, drawing, sculpting, weaving, writing. Sometimes he uses words like "dramatic," "dialectic," or "ritual," as if to describe the quality of an inner event. Then there are times when he seems to describe a typology of the senses, for example, "visual types" may expect to see fantasy pictures; "audio-verbal types" tend to hear an inner voice (1916/58, par. 170). Those with a "motor imagination" can take a mandala (or other motif) and make it into a beautiful dance (1928–30, p. 474).
>
> (Chodorow 1997: 8)

Here Jung is describing active imagination from many overlapping perspectives. As Jung had experienced the healing power of symbolic play, it is not surprising that he was instrumental in encouraging Dora Kalff to develop the therapeutic method that became known as sandplay (Bradway and McCoard 1997; Hill 1981; Kalff 1971).

Almost all child and many adult patients find sandplay as a way of staying in touch or reconnecting with the affective basis of their personalities:

> By playing again like a child, with all the seriousness of a child at play, the adult revives lost memories, releases unconscious fantasies, and in the course of time, constellates the images of reconciliation and wholeness of the individuation process. The effectiveness of the technique for the adult lies in Jung's profound insight that the fantasy world of childhood is not a world to be transcended; to the contrary, "the images are not lost, but come again in ripe manhood and should be fulfilled."
>
> (L. H. Stewart 1977: 11)

Winnicott: a case-history describing a primary dissociation

In a case history, Winnicott described a middle-aged woman who knew she had the potential for various kinds of artistic self-expression. She knew "enough about life and living and about her potential," he said, "to realize that in life terms she is missing the boat, and that she has always been missing the boat (at least, from near the beginning of her life)" (Winnicott 1971: 27–8). From my perspective, this suggests that innate affect complexes of dissociative magnitude had begun to structure themselves quite early in the patient's life.

Central to the understanding of this patient is the distinction Winnicott draws between fantasying and dreaming. Whereas "fantasying remains an isolated phenomenon, absorbing energy but not contributing-in either to dreaming or to living" (ibid.: 26), "Dream[ing] fits into object-relating in the real world, [just as] living in the real world fits into the dream-world in ways that are quite familiar, especially to psychoanalysts" (ibid.: 26). In his observations on the gifted child, Jung made a similar distinction, between "lively" and "aimless" fantasies:

> In the gifted child inattentiveness, absent-mindedness, and day-dreaming may prove to be a secondary defence against outside influences, in order that the interior fantasy processes may be pursued undisturbed. Admittedly the mere existence of lively fantasies or peculiar interests is no proof of special gifts, as the same predominance of aimless fantasies and abnormal interests may also be found in the previous history of neurotics and psychotics. What does reveal the gift, however, is the *nature* of these fantasies. For this one must be able to distinguish an

intelligent fantasy from a stupid one. A good criterion of judgment is the originality, consistency, intensity, and subtlety of the fantasy structure, as well as the latent possibility of realization. One must also consider how far the fantasy extends into the child's actual life, for instance in the form of hobbies systematically pursued and other interests. Another important indication is the degree and quality of his interest in general.

(Jung 1954: 237, 138)

The fantasying that has disturbed Winnicott's patient was established by the time she was 2 or 3, or even an earlier date, but it is not particularly creative or original. In her case, the fantasy activity, which has a static quality, originates, I believe, in the patient's pathological complexes, not in any imaginative activity of her psyche that might be attempting to transcend them.

Winnicott admitted that the case history showed an extremely complicated etiology, but it was quite clear that early on both parents had failed her, with these consequences for her present life: "Inevitably she is a disappointment to herself and to all those relations and friends who feel hopeful about her. She feels when people are hopeful about her that they are expecting something of her or from her, and this brings her up against her essential inadequacy" (Winnicott 1971: 28). This pattern of disappointing others who might want to see her thrive seems to me good evidence that the pathogenic complex developed as an accommodation to her parents' rejection of her development as a person, that is, as a reaction to their disappointment in her, and is, therefore, an attitude toward herself (Beebe 1988) that is composed primarily of Shame/Contempt. Winnicott suggests that she has the potential for enacting a lethal attack on herself and possibly others:

> All this is a matter for intense grief and resentment in the patient and there is plenty of evidence that without help she was in danger of suicide, which would simply have been the nearest that she could get to murder. If she gets near to murder she begins to protect her object so at that point she has the impulse to kill herself and in this way to end her difficulties by bringing about her own death and the cessation of the difficulties. Suicide brings no solution, only cessation of struggle.
>
> (Winnicott 1971: 28)

As Winnicott has pointed out in his article, "Death and murder in the adolescent process" (1986), it is a symbolic murder that is called for, the "murder" of the deprecating parental imagos.

In her earliest years, this woman's social play with her siblings and others was interfered with by fantasying, which in her case we have to understand as the dynamic activity of the disordered complex:

> From the point of view of my patient, as we now discover, while she was playing the other people's games she was *all the time engaged in fantasy-ing*. She really lived in this fantasying on the basis of a dissociated mental activity. This part of her which became thoroughly dissociated was never the whole of her, and over long periods her defence was to live here in this fantasying activity, and to watch herself playing the other children's games as if watching someone else in the nursery group.
>
> (Winnicott 1971: 29)

What I think is being described, from the standpoint of the patient's affective development, is a dissociation from the innate affect Joy, which is why both creative fantasy and play are so constricted. This pattern continued into her adolescence and adulthood.

By then, compulsive smoking and various boring and obsessive games had begun to be used to fill the gaps in her living. But her life remained essentially *joyless*. We can see that she has been cut off from the innate affect Joy and its dynamism for most of her life. Winnicott, working with her when she is around 50, nevertheless can envision the course that a successful treatment still might take:

> Inaccessibility of fantasying is associated with dissociation rather than with repression. Gradually, as this patient begins to become a whole person and begins to lose her rigidly organized dissociations, so she becomes aware of the vital importance that fantasying has always had for her. At the same time the fantasying is changing into imagination related to dream and reality.
>
> (ibid.: 26–7)

What he is describing, I believe, in this remarkably optimistic passage, is the development that can ensue following conscious awareness and integration of the pathological complex: re-establishment of contact with Interest and Joy and the release of unconscious imaginative fantasy.

Winnicott presents two of the patient's dreams. In the first dream, "she felt intense resentment against her mother (to whom she is potentially devoted) because, as it came in the dream, her mother had deprived her daughter, that is herself, of her own children" (ibid.: 30). She had these reactions to this unexpected direction of her thought about her own potential to be a mother:

> She felt it was queer that she had dreamed [about her feelings] in this way. She said: "The funny thing is that here I look as if I am wanting a child, whereas in my conscious thought I know that I only think of children as needing protection from being born." She added: "It is as if I have a sneaking feeling that some people do find life not too bad."
>
> (ibid.: 30–1)

My suggestion is that a symbol of a divine child (the one figure in the inner world that unquestionably does not find "life too bad") has been constellated, which indicates that Winnicott's patient has indeed re-established some degree of contact with the developmental potential that resides in the collective unconscious. The second dream, which occurred a week later, supports this view: "She was in a room with many people and she knew that she was engaged to be married to a slob. She described a man of a kind that she would not in fact like. She turned to her neighbour and said: 'That man is the father of my child' " (ibid.: 30). She and Winnicott arrived at the following conclusion regarding the unexpected denouement to this dream: "In this way, with my help, she informed herself at this late stage in her analysis that she has a child, and she was able to say that the child was about ten years old. In point of fact she has no child, yet she could see from this dream that she has had a child for many years and that the child is growing up" (ibid.: 30).

We could say that the "divine child" was the child of the "slob" in the same way that her newly released capacity for creative fantasy was the result of the years she had spent in analysis exploring her disappointment in herself. The progression Winnicott anticipated has occurred. In Jungian alchemical terms, there has been a *coniunctio*, signifying an active intercourse between masculine Interest and feminine Joy, the affective couple capable of generating the now 10-year-old and actively developing Divine Child.

The patient then made another significant advance in a subsequent two-hour session: "Before she went, at the end of two hours, she had experienced a wave of hate of her mother which had a new quality to it. It was much nearer to murder than to hate and also it felt to her that the hate was much nearer than it had previously been to a specific thing" (ibid.: 31). From the perspective of affect-toned complexes, Winnicott's patient has now begun to integrate the pathological mother complex, through carrying out, as we anticipated, a symbolic murder of the "mother," incorporating a capacity for contempt as opposed to merely internalizing a sense of other's disappointment in her. Access to the healthy creative basis of her own personality has expanded, as Winnicott tells us, linking these changes to the dream material that helped to precipitate them:

> These two dreams are given to show how material that had formerly been locked in the fixity of fantasying was now becoming released for both dreaming and living, two phenomena that are in many respects the same. In this way the difference between daydreaming and dreaming (which is living) was gradually becoming clearer to the patient, and the patient was gradually becoming able to make the distinction clear to the analyst. It will be observed that creative playing is allied to dreaming and to living but essentially does not belong to fantasying.
>
> (ibid.: 31)

The fixity of his patient's fantasy life up to the point of this breakthrough was due to its being a relatively static expression of the pathological complex. After the breakthrough, the patient and Winnicott were able to discuss the distinction between creative dreaming and obsessive fantasy. As he puts what he learned from the experience: "For me the work of this session had produced an important result. It had taught me that fantasying interferes with action and with life in the real or external world, but much more so it interferes with dream and with the personal or inner psychic reality, the living core of the individual personality" (ibid.: 31). I would add only that it is an affect-toned complex that interferes with dreaming and contact with emotional ground of the psyche, so that the work of releasing creative dreaming must involve integration of the complex and access to its emotional core.

There are two moments that Winnicott reports from the next session with his patient that also require our attention. Here is the first (in Winnicott's own words):

> She said that while I was talking she was fiddling with the zip of her bag: why was it this end? how awkward it was to do up! She could feel that this dissociated activity was more important to her sitting there than listening to what I was saying. We both tried to make an attack on the subject in hand and to relate fantasying to dreaming. Suddenly she had a little insight and said that the meaning of this fantasying was: "So that's what you think." She had taken my interpretation of the dream and she had tried to make it foolish.
>
> (ibid.: 32)

The innate affect Shame/Contempt, which we have already met as the content of her mother complex, and probably her father complex as well, has now been brought into the transference: "she had tried to make [her analyst] foolish." Winnicott continues with a second moment of affective significance:

> At the very end of the session she had a moment of intense feeling associated with the idea that there had been no one (from her point of view) in her childhood who had understood that she had to begin in formlessness. As she reached recognition of this she became very angry indeed. If any therapeutic result came from this session it would be chiefly derived from her having arrived at this intense anger, anger that was about something, not mad, but with logical motivation.
>
> (ibid.: 34)

The anger confirms that there has been a significant integration of Shame/Contempt, making it possible now for her to get in touch with her rage at her parents for failing to recognize and empathize with her initial condition of formlessness, which goes beyond her resentment at their failure to understand the difficulty she faced, early on, in producing formed, appropriate responses to their demands. "Formlessness," I believe, is also an image of her original, pristine, developmental potential, which they ignored in trying only to get her to conform to their standards of behavior (see Jung 1969b: 119–20, 96–7, on formlessness).

In the very next session, also two hours, there were three more affective moments that are noteworthy: "At the next visit, another two-hour session, the patient reported to me that since the last visit she had done a very great deal. She was of course alarmed to have to report what I might take as implying progress" (Winnicott 1971: 34). Winnicott was clear that his patient had *enjoyed* a great deal of what she had "done." This suggests that the restored access to the healthy affective basis of her personality had allowed her, for the first time in ever so long, to experience the primal affect of Joy.

As one dynamism of Joy is symbolic fantasy, the patient was able now, as a second step, to embark on a long-needed development of her symbolizing capacity. She began to reflect on the process of the therapy so far: "The patient went over the work that we had done with deeper recognition and understanding, especially feeling the symbolism in the dream which is absent in the limited area of fantasying" (ibid.: 35).

She enabled the therapy to take a third step forward when, according to Winnicott's report:

> She brought up the subject of playing patience [in the US this card game would be called solitaire], which she called a quagmire, and asked for help in regard to the understanding of it. Using what we had done together, I was able to say that patience is a form of fantasying, is a dead end, and cannot be used by me. If on the other hand she is telling me a dream – "I dreamt I was playing patience" – then I could use it, and indeed I could make an interpretation. I could say: "You are struggling with God or fate, sometimes winning and sometimes losing, the aim being to control the destinies of four royal families!" She was able to follow on from this without help and her comment afterwards was: "I have been playing patience for hours in my empty room and the room really is empty because while I am playing patience I do not exist." Here again she said: "So I might become interested in me."
>
> (ibid.: 36)

Their step toward sharing some of her experiences in a way that Winnicott could "use" suggests the further integration of a part of the innate affective system, this time Interest. She was more interesting because she could discuss her Interest, and her dissociation has been overcome to the degree that she is now capable of carrying out emotional dialogues with herself framed by Interest and Joy that then become coherent to her analyst and grist for the therapeutic mill.

Unbearable affect

As we have seen, a chronic state of unbearable affect can only develop if there is severe, protracted social isolation and dissociation of the personality, which can happen to a developing child very early. When isolation and dissociation operate to any significant extent, they function as elements in an escalating vicious circle. Then, the individual's diminished capacity to metabolize crisis affects quickly results in a build up of emotion to a level of intensity that we refer to as "unbearable." Any therapeutic success in reducing the isolation or dissociation, therefore, will help to forestall such affects reaching this insupportable level.

Elvin Semrad, one of the first psychiatrists to link unbearable affect with homicide, suicide and psychosis, arrived at a quite similar view in his treatment of patients struggling with toxic levels of the crisis affects. The therapist's first concern, he said, is "to develop and maintain a relationship which will meet the patient's fundamental needs of sustenance, support and gratification" (Semrad 1969: 31). He continued: "By providing the necessary support, the therapist permits the patient to bear the intolerable feelings" (ibid.: 18).

In an article, "Overview: a multidimensional approach to suicide," the suicidologist Edwin Shneidman (1989) reviewed all the approaches to suicide that have become traditional within western culture. He named them:

- literary and personal document approach;
- philosophical and theological approaches;
- demographic approach, sociocultural approach;
- sociological approach;
- dyadic, interpersonal, and familial approaches;
- psychodynamic approach;
- psychological approach;
- psychiatric, mental illness, and disease approach;
- legal and ethical approaches;
- prevention approach;
- systems theory approach;
- political, global, and supranational approaches.

While not minimizing the value of any of these approaches, Shneidman concluded that few of them really address the common proximate stimulus to suicide, which is intolerable psychological pain, "psychache," and few have focused on the fact that the common goal for all the different paths to suicide is cessation of consciousness. His clinical rule, therefore, for treatment of what he also called "metapain" was: "Reduce the level of suffering, often just a little bit, and the individual can choose to live" (ibid.: 17).

Shneidman encourages the therapist later to delicately and sympathetically *explore* the unbearable affect and help the patient to develop resolutions other than "cessation of consciousness." He and others have created level of pain scales that have been developed to quantify unbearable affect, which do have a degree of predictive value for suicidal behaviors (Holden, Mehta, Cunningham, and McLeod 2001; Shneidman 1999).

Jung, who could be a most practical psychotherapist, often pointed out that one thing that any therapist can do for a patient who is isolated with unmanageable emotion is to make available to the patient the full support of the therapist's personality. Speaking as a doctor who had often offered this kind of psychological care, he wrote:

> One can easily see what it means to the patient when he can confide his experience to an understanding and sympathetic doctor. His conscious mind finds in the doctor a moral support against the unmanageable affect of his traumatic complex. No longer does he stand alone in his battle with these elemental powers, but some one whom he trusts reaches out a hand, lending him moral strength to combat the tyranny of uncontrolled emotion. In this way the integrative powers of his conscious mind are reinforced until he is able once more to bring rebellious affect under control.
>
> (Jung 1966: 270, 132)

The operative phrase is "the integrative powers of [the] conscious mind." It is these, finally, that manage the affects. But it takes affective support, and particularly the affect of Interest from another person, to bring these powers into play. Buoyed by the interest of the therapist, the patient can begin to believe that it is possible to hold overwhelming affects and even be curious about them. As he takes up these possibilities, the life instinct of the patient comes into play, reducing the intensity of pain because now there is even enjoyment in exploring it. But in that endeavor, Jung reminds us, the support of the doctor continues to be crucial: "The rehearsal of the traumatic moment is able to reintegrate the neurotic dissociation only when the conscious personality of the patient is so far reinforced by his relationship to the doctor that he can consciously bring the autonomous complex under the control of his will" (ibid.: 271, 132–3).

James Hillman has come at the same problem from another angle by suggesting that the excess of emotion that produces the sense of intolerability may be understood as resulting from an imbalance between energy and form: "To put this another way, the dangerous excess of emotion . . . is due to the difference in degree between the energetic and formal aspects of the psyche" (Hillman 1992: 275). He points out that affect and psyche are not synonymous: "Emotion is the energetic aspect of psyche; psyche has a formal aspect as well" (ibid.). As the formal aspect, identified by Hillman as by Jung before him as an "image," is the container of the energy of emotion, therefore, "The disorder of emotional excess is due to the improper relation of these two aspects of the psyche" (ibid.). This perspective provides Hillman with a practical guide to the treatment of affective excess: "In therapy one must often go back to very early years to find a symbolic bridge between the energetic and formal aspects, and re-educate the patient by means of aesthetic, imaginative and social methods neglected in 'normal' education" (ibid.: 276). All of these civilizing methods increase the patient's ability to deploy meaningful, culturally comprehensible images that enable the emotions to be communicated in formal ways. Until the formal aspect of emotion has been developed, however, the goal of therapy has to be strengthening of ego-consciousness:

> Until the vessel is shaped, therapy of emotion may often require suppression or release of the energetic aspect for the sake of the container. Sometimes this alone can save a formless psyche from being destroyed by its emotion. Emotion is not always good nor always bad; it can either kill or cure, and it can only be "dosed" in respect to the quality of the formal organization of the psyche.
>
> (ibid.: 276)

Jung described how he became convinced of the value of the psychic image as a formal container for emotional energy. Beginning in the autumn 1913 and continuing through June 1914, Jung has a series of apocalyptic dreams and fantasies of world destruction. When he was unable to imagine a relation between his dreams and any events on the world horizon, he decided that he was menaced by a psychosis, which often does begin with the fantasy of world destruction. He wrote that when World War I broke out on August 14, his task became clear: "I had to try and understand what had happened and to what extent my own experience coincided with that of mankind in general" (Jung 1961a: 176). He dedicated himself to writing down his cataclysmic dreams and fantasies in order to try and understand them.

In was in this context that Jung discovered the integrative value of discovering the images that are concealed in threatening affects:

> To the extent that I managed to translate the emotions into images – that is to say, to find the images which were concealed in the emotions – I was inwardly calmed and reassured. Had I left those images hidden in the emotions, I might have been torn to pieces by them. There is a chance I might have succeeded in splitting them off; but in that case I would inexorably have fallen into a neurosis and so been ultimately destroyed by them anyhow. As a result of my experiment I learned how helpful it can be, from the therapeutic point of view, to find the particular images which lie behind emotions.
>
> (ibid.: 177)

Jung is pointing out, I believe, the value of achieving the proper balance between energy and form when dealing with the psyche.

If the build up of crisis affects continues unabated, then a point is reached when ego-consciousness is overwhelmed by the emotion, which simply pushes the ego aside in favor of archetypal affect. Jung speaks of this as an invasion by the archetypal psyche, and describes what ensues as a state of possession by the affect-toned complex. If the possession is complete, the patient moves from a state of problematic consciousness, in which it is still possible to question the feelings and the behaviors the complex is underwriting, to an unproblematic state of consciousness, in which one is sure one is right and simply says and does what the emotion wants, even if in its archetypal ruthlessness it disregards the usual limits of civility and care in dealing with others.

Possession by affect

The final condition for the emergence of lethal behavior is therefore possession by affect. If the four necessary conditions for lethal behaviors are viewed as a temporal sequence, then possession by affect does not occur unless social isolation, dissociation of the personality, and unbearable affect have already, in turn, reached critical levels. Any therapeutic amelioration of any of these conditions, therefore, makes possession by a monopolistic emotional complex and its inexorable archetypal affect far less likely. On the other hand, failure to intervene effectively at these earlier stages of a malignant emotional process can well-nigh ensure that the affect will come to possess the patient. We have defined emotion possession as the individual's unconscious identification with an affect-toned complex. Although the emotional complex that finally seizes the individual will have been developing over a long period of time, possession by this complex and the enactment of a lethal behavior on the basis of it can occur in as short time as a few seconds. It can of course be minutes, hours, days, weeks, or months before lethal behaviors are enacted on the basis of the possession, and it is best for the clinician to consider that, where there is evidence of possession, a chronic condition of risk is present. We saw this often in the background of the cases we discussed in Chapters 4–8.

One difficulty in providing treatment for the possessed individual is that, with possession, the person (having entered an "unproblematic" state of consciousness) is freed of the agonizing conflict, unbearable affect, and self-doubt that serve to motivate a person to seek psychotherapy. The significant others around the person can be lulled by the unproblematic consciousness to assume that treatment services are no longer needed. In fact the calm they are seeing in the patient is simply the eye of a hurricane.

Charles Whitman

In a notorious case that illustrates what we mean by possession, and why this does not seem too strong a word, on 1 August 1966, 25-year-old Charles Whitman went on a killing spree. First, he killed his mother in her apartment, apparently both strangling and bludgeoning her and then returned to his own home to kill his sleeping wife by stabbing her with a hunting knife. Later that same day, he barricaded himself atop the observation deck of the Tower at the University of Texas at Austin, and from this advantageous location shot and killed 14 people as well as wounding 26 others, before he was finally killed himself by police gunfire.

In a note he had left with his mother's body, he had given as his reason for killing her that it was the only way he "could see to relieve her sufferings . . ." (Lavergne 1977: 130). With his wife's body, he left another note that suggested the same complex had motivated his killing of her: "I don't know whether it is selfishness, or if I don't want her to have to face the *embarrassment* my actions would surely cause her. At this time, though, the prominent reason in my mind is that I truly do not consider this world worth living in, and am prepared to die, and I do not want to leave her to suffer it alone" (ibid.: 116, emphasis added). (In the note that Kipland Kinkel left after he killed his parents – Chapter 5 – he wrote that he killed his mother to protect her from the *embarrassment* his actions would surely cause her.) Whitman was, I believe, in a state of possession by affect throughout the entire day of the murders, but we will attempt to determine when exactly the eclipse of his ego-consciousness occurred.

Certainly there was a period of incubation that lasted at least several years. At the time that he was enrolled as a Marine scholar at the University of Texas, Austin (September 1961 to February 1963), Whitman was later reported to have said to a friend during a casual conversation "that he would like to go to the observation deck of the university's landmark tower and shoot people" (ibid.: 29). In a February 1964 diary entry, at a time when he was facing a court martial by the Marine corps, Whitman wrote: "My love for Kathy and my sense of responsibility to our unborn children is the only thing that keeps me from going berserk. At times it seems as if I am going to explode" (ibid.: 54).

His wife, moreover, was keenly aware of how depressed he could get and at times was afraid to leave him alone, in part because of the gun collection he kept at their home. On 29 March 1966, four months before the killings, when Whitman was a civilian student at the University of Texas, he met at the urging of his wife with a staff psychiatrist at the Student Health Center. In that interview, Whitman told the psychiatrist that something was happening to him and he didn't seem to be himself. He described a frequent fantasy "about going up on the Tower with a deer rifle and shooting people" (ibid.: 89). This is clear evidence that the affect-toned complex was continuing to generate the same fantasy that it had three years before when he had first voiced it to a fellow student.

An indication of the strength of the complex is that on 5 April 1966, instead of keeping his follow-up appointment with the psychiatrist, Whitman visited the tower and carefully inspected it. In late July 1966, a month before his rampage, he copied out a poem that he had written two years earlier when in the Marine brig (again suggesting the long-lived mind of the complex). The second stanza of the poem, which he had been carrying around in his head, contains the following lines:

> To burden others with your problems—are they
>   Problems—is not right.
> However, to carry them is akin to carrying a fused bomb.
> I wonder if the fuse can be doused.
> If it is doused, what will be gained?
>
> (ibid.: 107)

Assimilation of his ego-complex by the monopolistic complex is now picking up velocity and he is beginning to give in to it. "If it is doused, what will be gained?"

On 29 July 1966, Whitman finished his last day of classes and work. In the morning of 31 July he purchased the Bowie knife which he would use the following day to kill his wife. A couple who visited him in the evening of 31 July found him unusually calm. They had, unbeknownst to themselves, interrupted his typing of a letter in which he was writing about his decision to kill his wife. He had become free of conflict, again illustrating the dangers Jung assigned to the state of unproblematic consciousness, ". . . you have no conflict, because your are the conflict itself, you just flow like water or fire; you can be exploded in ten thousand pieces yet you are one with yourself because there is no center from which to judge . . ." (Jung 1976: 420). From there, it is hardly any step at all to frank enactment of whatever complex one has become identical with: in Whitman's case, the quality of the affect-toned complex that possessed him at the end is not clear, but it included a fantasy of saving people he loved, by killing them.

Mandalas *as protective circles*

The psychic container most frequently referred to by analytical psychologists is the *mandala*, the Sanskrit word meaning "magic circle." The analogous Greek term is *temenos*, the precincts of a temple or any isolated sacred place: "To do analysis, we need the safe container of the *temenos*, the magic enclosure that says: 'here we are safe, we can explore even the most violent fantasy' – so long as it remains fantasy. Once the boundaries between fantasy and reality are gone analysis becomes impossible" (Abramovitch 2006: 25).

The archetypal structure of the *mandala* is that of a circle squared or a square encircled. This geometric scheme appears both in the spontaneous fantasy and play productions of individuals and in traditional cultural forms, such as temple spaces or sporting arenas. As Jung notes, the mandala form

> . . . is not by any means a new invention, for it can be found in all epochs and in all places, always with the same meaning, and it reappears time and again, independently of tradition, in modern individuals as the "protective" or apotropaic circle, whether in the form of the prehistoric "sun wheel," or the magic circle, or the alchemical microcosm, or a modern symbol of *order*, which organizes and embraces the psychic totality.
>
> (Jung 1970c: 619, 325–6)

The *mandala* images that appear in the dreams and paintings of contemporary individuals (and not just when those individuals have been in Jungian analysis or have read Jung) seem to come up spontaneously as symbols of wholeness, order, and self-containment in times that are of disorder, disorientation, and fragmentation for the people who produced the *mandala* image. As Jung puts it:

> Experience shows that individual mandalas are symbols of *order*, and they occur in patients principally during times of psychic disorientation or re-orientation. As magic circles they bind and subdue the lawless powers [archetypal affects] belonging to the world of darkness, and depict or create an order that transforms the chaos into a cosmos.
>
> (Jung 1969b: 60, 31–2)

Jung comments on a series of pictures drawn by a 7-year-old boy, who was suffering from the problematic marriage of his parents and had great difficulty sleeping: "He had done a whole series of these drawings of circles and hung them up round his bed. He called them his 'loves' and would not go to sleep without them. This shows that the 'magical' pictures still functioned for him in their original sense, as a protective magic circle" (Jung 1969a: 687, 376).

Mandalas, he goes on to say, function to keep pathogenic intrusions from the external world at bay and pathological unconscious impulses from escaping into enactments:

> The symbol of the mandala has exactly this meaning of a holy place, a *temenos*, to protect the centre. And it is a symbol which is one of the most important motifs in the objectivation of unconscious images [and emotions]. It is a means of protecting the centre of the personality from being drawn out and from being influenced from outside.
>
> (Jung 1977: 410, 178–9)

In Chapter 2, we noted the beginning of mandala psychology as expressed in Kundalini yoga:

> But mandala psychology begins when one succeeds in forming the magic circle against the fires of passion; then one is in *anahata*. When you are able to say, "I am in a state of passion," you create the magic circle that saves you from the destructive effects of identifying with your emotion. For being merely emotional, without realizing what kind of condition you are in, destroys you as human being, you simply function as an animal.
>
> (Jung 1976: 349)

Among the impingements from the outside that are muted, we can expect to find disturbing life stimuli that might evoke the crisis affects, which are already at fever pitch. The magic circle also provides a container within which the innate affects composing the pathogenic complexes can be confronted. Jung described a case in which the patient had a *mandala* vision and then "experienced an agreeable relief . . . since he has succeeded in establishing a protected *temenos*, a taboo area where he will be able to meet the unconscious" (Jung 1968a: 63, 54).

What Jung discovered was that *mandala* forms are such especially potent symbols because they effectively function to prevent fragmentation of the ego-complex: "So we can understand why the figure of the protecting circle was seized upon. It is intended to prevent the 'outflowing' and to protect the unity of consciousness from being burst asunder by the unconscious" (Jung 1968b: 47, 29).

The dynamic consequence is the developmental use of unexpected affects visited upon the self by its contact with the world, rather than simply having to endure them as a traumatic overload that stops the process of development in its tracks. *Mandala* holds out not only the promise of self-healing but also the possibility of psychological growth: "In so far as the mandala encompasses, protects, and defends the psychic totality against outside influences and seeks to unite the inner opposites, it is at the same time a distinct *individuation symbol* . . ." (Jung 1970c: 621, 326).

Winnicott's notion of "holding" is akin to this function of the *mandala:* "The concept [of 'holding'] was applied by [Winnicott] to psychoanalysis proper, where it was the provision of a holding environment by the analyst that allowed analysis to extend backwards beyond the psychoneurosis to more fundamental elements in the personality" (Davis and Wallbridge 1981: 24). We would call these "fundamental elements" the healthy affective basis of the psyche. Winnicott attributes to what he calls "holding" both what we have termed subjective integration and what we have called objective relationship: "The establishment of integration and the development of ego-relatedness both rely upon good-enough holding" (ibid.: 100).

The Jungian way to talk about this internal and external relatedness is in terms of the union of opposites. At the center of *mandalas*, we often find a male–female pair, for instance, Shiva–Shakti or Father–Mother, embracing in continuous cohabitation. This pairing of energies is, I believe, a personification of the life instinct itself, with the male symbolizing the archetypal affect of Interest and the female the archetypal capacity to experience Joy. Their continuous cohabitation expresses the lifelong dialectical relationship between Interest and Joy, an essential configuration of the life instinct. Regaining contact with this dialogue between Interest and Joy is what permits an individual's commitment to life: "When the self finds expression . . . the unconscious reacts by enforcing an attitude of *devotion to life*" (Jung 1968b: 36, 24, emphasis added).

Vivienne, Kipland, Eric, Dylan, and Sinedu, the people in previous chapters of this book who went on to develop lethal behaviors, had lost their devotion to life, their zest for living, even though their psyches were still active. For such people, the saving experience would have to be a transference to a healing personality. Often for patients who are saved from tragic enactments, it is the constellation of a *mandala* in the personality of the therapist, or even in the office of the therapist, which offers the individual a magic, protective circle in which unbearable affect can be faced and transformed.

I can conclude that the optimal treatment program for a possessed individual on the verge of lethal behaviors would be physical holding in a hospital or residential center, medication holding when practical, and psychic containment in psychotherapy, or any combination of these measures.

Epilogue: the life instinct in historical perspective

The innate archetypal affects that constitute the emotional basis for both healthy and pathological developments of the kind we have been studying in this book are quintessentially human. These affects are not simply instincts that humans have inherited from other species. In refutation of Haeckel's recapitulation theory, that there is a repetition of evolutionarily ancestral adult stages in human embryological development, the Swiss zoologist, Adolf Portmann, wrote: ". . . the human system is present from the first in its full differentiation, sketched in all its parts, and developing its more definitive structures step by step . . . Human development reveals no stage at which a primate becomes a man" (Portmann 1990: 361–2). From the time humans first walked on this earth, their minds were rooted in the innate archetypal affects. Cultural expressions from time immemorial will reflect, therefore, the affects of the life instinct, Interest and Joy.

The life instinct in cultural perspective

Our ability to identify manifestations of the life instinct outside of our own consulting rooms would be extremely limited were it not for the natural tendency of the psyche to personify the affects:

> At the pre-psychological stage, and also in poetic language, which owes its power to its vital primitivity, emotions and affects are often personified as daemons. To be in love is to be "struck by Cupid's arrow," or "Eris has thrown the apple of discord," and so on. When we are "beside ourselves with rage" we are obviously no longer identical with ourselves, but are possessed by a daemon or spirit.
>
> (Jung 1970b: 627, 329)

One particularly expressive depiction of the life instinct that can readily be found in historical records from a variety of cultures is the image of the *syzygy*, that is, the conjunctive pairing of male and female figures, representing the dialectic of psychic energies – more specifically, the coming together of Interest (masculine) and Joy (feminine) to create an image of vitality, creativity, and potential psychic renewal. Jung pays a great deal of attention to the *syzygy* motif in his writings, seeing it as the signifier of the soul's emotional life:

> We encounter the anima historically above all in the divine syzygies, the male–female pair of deities. These reach down, on the one side, into the obscurities of primitive mythology, and up, on the other, into the philosophical speculations of Gnosticism and of classical Chinese philosophy, where the cosmogonic pair of concepts are designated *yang* (masculine) and *yin* (feminine). We can safely assert that these syzygies are as universal as the existence of man and woman. From this fact we may reasonably conclude that man's imagination is bound by this motif, so that he is largely compelled to project it again and again, at all times and in all places.
>
> (Jung 1969a: 120, 59–60)

Jung expanded on this theme of the universality of female-male pairs when he said: "The syzygy is immediately comprehensible as the psychic prototype of all divine couples" (Jung 1969b: 64, 34). Hillman concludes his work, *Anima: The Anatomy of a Personified Notion*, with this paragraph:

> Because of the anima–animus syzygy, psychology cannot omit spirit from its purview. The syzygy says that where soul goes there goes spirit too. Their syzygy illuminates imagination with intellect and refreshes intellect with fantasy. Ideas become psychological experiences, and experiences become psychological ideas. The job is to keep spirit and soul distinct (the spirit's demand) and to keep them attached (the demand of the soul).
>
> (Hillman 1985: 183)

As we have said, Logos (Interest) is discrimination and Eros (Joy) is relatedness.

In his theory of the archetypal affect system, L. H. Stewart found in the concept of the syzygy a sound basis for his definition of the emotions of the life instinct as paired opposites in dynamic relation: "The grounding place for me now-a-days in this realm of bewildering manifestations is the syzygy; understood as the archetypal affects of the libido, Joy and Interest, and their dynamisms, Play and Curiosity" (L. H. Stewart 1987b: 158).

From his developmental perspective, L. H. Stewart identified the Jungian anima and animus as the symbolic cultural attitudes which emerge from this perpetual, mutual fructification:

> The remaining two affects, joy and interest, are a pair of opposites that

flow into every aspect of life as the twin streams of the libido. These affects may be recognized as the root of the dynamics that Jung speaks of as mythical consciousness, personified in alchemy as Luna, and, logos consciousness, personified as Sol. The innate affects joy and interest . . . ultimately are culturally evolved as the syzygy, anima and animus: Eros and Logos.

(L. H. Stewart 1992: 95)

From this perspective, Joy and Interest become the psychic prototypes of all divine couples.

L. H. Stewart also contributed to our understanding of the universality of the cultural expressions of the life instinct when he conceived of Joy and Interest as two fundamental modes of life experience:

Here it is necessary to reflect on the two primary ways of experiencing life as expressed, for example, in the philosophical principles of Being and Becoming. Many efforts have been made to characterize these fundamental modes of life experience, as for example, the Tao as the interplay of Yin and Yang, the alchemical images Luna and Sol, or the cosmogonic principles of antiquity, Eros and Logos. All of these concepts and images seek to represent the alternation of life experience through two modes which nevertheless seem to be united within one whole. In so far as the archetypal affects of Joy and Interest may be considered prototypical forms of the expression of these life principles, they have presumably evolved, then, in relation to these two modes of experiencing life.

(L. H. Stewart 1987b: 136–7)

Subsequently, L. H. Stewart was able to the identify the affects of the life instinct in the "two dynamisms of the sephirotic tree of the Cabala, 'grace' and 'rigor' " (L. H. Stewart 1991) and in Jung's two kinds of thinking, fantasy/mythical thought and directive/logos thought. These are only a few examples of how Joy and Interest have been identified throughout western culture. We will now turn to another one, Milton's well-known 17th century poem, L'Allegro, in which there are numinous personifications of Interest and Joy and also of another innate affect, Surprise.

Milton's L'Allegro: Mirth, the Great Sun, the Lark

In 1631, John Milton composed the companion poems, L'Allegro and Il Penseroso. On 27 February 1740, the premiere of George Handel's L'Allegro, il Penseroso ed il Moderato was conducted by the composer himself. Between 1816 and 1820, William Blake painted twelve watercolors to illustrate L'Allegro and Il Penseroso. As an indication of the enduring vitality of the poems, on 23 November 1988, in Brussels, Belgium, the premiere performance was given of the dance *L'Allegro, il Penseroso ed il Moderato*, which was set to the music of Handel by the choreographer, Mark Morris. As Jeffrey Escoffier and Mathew Lore write in their Introduction to the book *Mark Morris' l'allegro, il penseroso ed il moderato: A celebration*: "Milton created, Handel elaborated, Blake illustrated, and then, three centuries later, Mark Morris came along and made something that was greater than the sum of its parts" (Escoffier and Lore 2001).

My focus will be on three images that appear both in Milton's poem *L'Allegro* and in Blake's illustrations of it: Mirth (Plate E.1), the Great Sun (Plate E.2), and the Lark (Plate E.3). The first two images are, I believe, numinous symbols of the paired opposites of the life instinct, Joy and Interest. The innate affect Joy is personified as the nymph "Mirth" and the innate affect Interest is personified as the "Great Sun." The "Lark," on the other hand, is an unexpected personification of an innate affect we have not considered up to now, Surprise–Startle–Astonishment.

Mirth

In *Images & Themes in Five Poems by Milton*, Rosemund Tuve has presented a close analysis of *L'Allegro* in which she has identified Mirth as the major image of this poem: ". . . she is a personification, that is, she is a way of talking about the absolutely not the contingently real" (Tuve 1957: 17). She questions the contingent reality of this symbol at both the personal and the cultural levels. First, Tuve argues against an exclusively personal interpretation of Mirth:

> For the subject of *L'Allegro* is every man's Mirth, our Mirth, the very Grace herself with all she can include. Therefore its images are not individualized. Milton does not describe a life, or a day, but through images causes us to recall, imagine, and savor the exact nature of joy when it is entirely free of that fetter, care, which ties down the joys we actually experience in an order of reality that does not present us with essences pure.
>
> (ibid.: 20)

Second, she suggests that, although Milton was aware of the long history of this image, he did not (as he might have done) introduce it into his poem for this reason:

> His power in the use of [traditional figures, such as Mirth] is not that he picks us up out of our own time to set us down in Homer's or Augustine's, a process which seems to change men very little and cause them straightway to refurnish an old time to their own ideas of comfort. It was not

Plate E.1 Mirth

1949.4:1 "Mirth" – Blake, William, 1757–1827. Copyright © The Pierpoint Morgan Library, New York.

[the] genesis [of these figures] in a vanished time but their power to outlive change that commended the figures to Milton.

(ibid.: 9–10)

From our standpoint, Mirth is an archetypal-image. In support of her thesis that this was the case, Tuve reviews the endurance of Mirth throughout the literary tradition that informed Milton, from her beginning as one of the Graces, through neo-Platonic philosophizing and symbol-making about her, into the long English literary tradition, beginning with Spenser in the 16th century. In Tuve's view (which is not unlike that of the contemporary archetypal psychologist James Hillman), the only threat to the vitality of Mirth, and similar symbolic figures, is their literalization, for then the creativity of the image, what Jung called the "play" of the archetype, will wither and die.

By emphasizing the overarching significance of Mirth, Milton succeeds in assigning to Mirth, after the habit of a goddess, the ability to *govern*. As Tuve points out, she rules the world of her poem, so that her "servants display the nature of [her] rule and its rewards, themselves constituting a praise of her they serve": "[She] is 'in' every action or place, sight or sound, in her poem (especially in the landscapes; often these have *only* the meaning of *expressing* – sometimes quite temporarily – the universal which the [goddess symbolizes]) . . ." (ibid.: 34).

Among Mirth's servants are Jest, Jollity, Wreathed Smiles, and Laughter. Jung considers this type of delineation as raising the attributes of an archetypal-image to a living figure: "The so-called Dionysian train (satyrs, tityrs, Sileni, Mimallones, etc.) consists of personifications of Dionysian attributes" (Jung 1961b: 106, 41). It is Tuve's view that structural excellence such as this guarantees the poem's permanent charm. We might say, a trans-personal and transcultural archetypal-image, Mirth orders the poem, organizing its numinosity from the energies inherent in the universal affect Joy.

Each of Blake's illustrations was accompanied by a separate sheet of paper bearing in Blake's writing on one side, the title, and on the other, Blake's selection of relevant text from the poem and his commentary. To accompany the watercolor of Mirth (Plate E.1), Blake transcribed these lines from *L'Allegro*:

Heart easing Mirth,

. . .

Haste thee Nymph & bring with thee
Jest & youthful jollity,
Quips & Cranks & Wanton Wiles,
Nods & Becks, & wreathed smiles,
Sport that wrinkled Care derides,
And Laughter holding both his Sides.

> Come & trip it as you go
> On the light phantastic toe,
> And in thy right hand lead with thee
> The Mountain Nymph Sweet Liberty;
> (Blake: 1816–20)

Below these Milton lines, Blake wrote: "These Personifications are all brought together in the First Design. Surrounding the Principal Figure which is Mirth herself" (ibid.). This characterization of the poem's strategy makes it evident that Mirth is a personification of the innate affect Joy and her "servants," as Tuve would say, are fantasy and play, personified as aspects of her attributes, which reveal themselves as dynamic forms.

The Great Sun

In a passage within his writings about the symbolism of the sun, Jung has identified its human personification, conceived as demon or hero, as the "finest of all symbols of the libido" (Jung 1967: 251, 171). Jung elaborates: "The psychic life-force, the libido, symbolizes itself in the sun or personifies itself in figures of heroes with solar attributes" (ibid.: 297, 202)

In a similar vein, Blake, to accompany his watercolor of the Great Sun (Plate E.2), which he called the Sun at His Eastern Gate, transcribed these lines from *L'Allegro*:

> Sometime walking not unseen
> By hedgerow Elms on Hillocks green,
> Right against the Eastern Gate
> Where the Great Sun begins his state,
> Robed in Flames & amber light,
> The Clouds in thousand Liveries dight,
> While the Plowman near at hand
> Whistles o'er the Furrowd Land,
> And the Milkmaid singeth blithe,
> And the Mower whets his Scythe,
> And every Shepherd tells his Tale
> Under the Hawthorn in the Dale.
> (Blake, 1816–20)

Below these lines, Blake wrote his own gloss:

The Great Sun is represented clothed in Flames Surrounded by the Clouds in their Liveries in their various Offices at the Eastern Gate. Beneath in Small Figures Milton walking by Elms on Hillocks green The

Plate E.2 The Great Sun

1949.4:3 "The Sun at his Eastern Gate" Blake, William, 1757–1827. Copyright © The Pierpoint Morgan Library, New York.

Plowman. The Milk-maid the Mower whetting his Scythe & the Shepherd & his Lass under a Hawthorne in the dale.

(ibid.)

I believe we are faced in this flaming Sun by a personification of the innate affect Interest. If we examine Milton's lines and Blake's illustration, we find not only the sun's mythical attendants from the classical world but also figures drawn from workaday technological reality at the dawn of the industrial age, such as people involved in activities of food production, material production, tool manufacture, and commerce. All the attendants of the sun personify the attributes and energies that attach to the affect Interest and its dynamisms, curiosity and exploration. In terms of the dialectic of the life instinct, the sun's daylight consciousness is cast as the paired opposite to the nocturnal consciousness that is moonlit Joy.

The Lark

In *L'Allegro*, Milton introduces us to the Lark with the following four lines, which are the ones Blake chose to transcribe in preparation for his illustration of this figure (Plate E.3):

To hear the Lark begin its flight,
And singing startle the dull Night,
From his Watch Tower in the Skies,
Till the dappled Dawn does rise
                    (ibid.)

The fact that the singing of the Lark *startles* the Night is our first indication that the Lark is a personification of the innate affect, Surprise. In the commentary to his illustration and in the illustration itself (Plate E. 3), Blake makes his own determination as to the Lark's identity and adds a figure, Earth, that is not mentioned in the poem: "The Lark is an Angel on the Wing dull Night starts from his Watch Tower on a cloud. The Dawn with her dappled Horses arises above the Earth The Earth beneath awakes at the Larks voice" (ibid.).

The Lark is presented as a Divine Child, with the dorsal aspect of his body and arms encased in feathers. Blake would have been familiar with the convention that birds, as aerial beings, can be used to signify spirits or angels. The figure Dawn is best construed as new consciousness, which regularly accompanies the constellation of the Divine Child. The image that does not appear in Milton but has been added by Blake is Earth. Night and Earth as a male–female divine *syzygy*, focus their gaze on the central figures, Lark and Dawn.

Two questions arise: Who are the "parents" of this symbolic Divine Child

Plate E.3 The Lark

1949.4:2 "The Lark" Blake, William, 1757–1827. Copyright © The Pierpoint Morgan Library, New York.

and what is its psychological significance? Blake's illustration suggests that it might be Earth Mother and Sky Father who are its parents. Jung offers this answer: ". . . the traditional alchemical view [is] that 'our infant,' the son of the Philosophers, is the child of the sun and moon" (Jung 1970e: 610, 424). In the alchemical literature the sun and the moon are frequently personified as Sol and Luna respectively. We can translate these perspectives into emotion terms and suggest that the affective parents of "our infant" are Interest and Joy. As I have demonstrated (*The Symbolic Impetus*, 2001), the dialectic relation between these components of the life instinct is indeed a fruitful one.

This brings us to a second question, concerning the psychic significance of the Divine Child. Jung writes: "As a matter of experience, we meet the child archetype in spontaneous and in therapeutically induced individuation processes" (Jung 1969a: 303, 180). It follows that one of the most common interpretations of the meaning of the child archetype is that it brings the promise of a new phase of psychological development:

> One of the essential features of the child motif is its futurity. The child is potential future. Hence the occurrence of the child motif in the psychology of the individual signifies as a rule an anticipation of future developments, even though at first sight it may seem like a retrospective configuration. Life is a flux, a flowing into the future, and not a stoppage or a backwash. It is therefore not surprising that so many of the mythological saviours are child gods. This agrees exactly with our experience of the psychology of the individual, which shows that the "child" paves the way for a future change of personality. In the individuation process, it anticipates the figure that comes from the synthesis of conscious and unconscious elements in the personality. It is therefore a symbol which unites the opposites; a mediator, bringer of healing, that is, one who makes whole.
>
> (Jung 1969a: 278, 164)

In Chapter 10, we reported that one difference between successful and unsuccessful psychotherapies is the increased occurrence of Surprise in the former as compared to the paucity of Surprise in the latter. We went on to explain this difference as based on the fact that the innate affect Surprise motivates the development of ego-consciousness and self-reflective consciousness. We can conclude that each advance of consciousness in the individuation process, which is itself propelled by the lifelong dialectic between the innate affects Interest and Joy, is marked by activation of the innate affect Surprise. In the language of Milton's poem, the Sun, entertaining Mirth invites the Lark. Dawn personifies new consciousness.

Bibliography

Abbott, K. (2000) "Harrises question therapist's care", *Rocky Mountain News*, Denver, CO, 19 September.

Abramovitch, H. (2006) "Analysis in the shadow of terror: securing the *temenos*, treating the 'enemy,' and surviving creatively", *The San Francisco Jung Institute Library Journal*, 25(1): 25–32.

Alvarez, A. (1971) *The Savage God: A Study of Suicide*. New York: W. W. Norton.

Armstrong-Perman, E. M. (1995) "Psychosis: the sacrifice that fails", in J. Ellwood (ed.) *Psychosis: Understanding and Treatment*. London: Jessica Kingsley.

Banninger-Huber, E. (1992) "Prototypical affective microsequences in psychotherapeutic interaction", *Psychotherapy Research*, 2: 291–306.

Banninger-Huber, E. and Widmer, C. (1995) "What can the psychology of emotion contribute to an understanding of psychoanalytic processes? A new approach to the investigation of guilt feelings and envy in psychotherapeutic interaction", in B. Boothe and R. B. Husigm (eds) *Perception, Evaluation, Interpretation*. Ashland, OH: Hogrefe & Huber.

Banninger-Huber, E. and Widmer, C. (1999) "Affective relationship patterns and psychotherapeutic change", *Psychotherapy Research*, 9: 74–87.

Beebe, J. (1988) "Primary ambivalence toward the self: its nature and treatment", in N. Schwartz-Salant and M. Stein (eds) *The Borderline Personality in Analysis*. Wilmette, IL: Chiron Publishers.

—— (1992) *Integrity in Depth*. New York: Fromm International Publishing Corporation, reprinted 1995.

Beebe, J., Cambray, J., and Kirsch, T. B. (2001) "What Freudians can learn from Jung", *Psychoanalytic Psychology*, 18: 213–42.

Benecke, C., Krause, R., and Dammann, G. (2003) "Affective dynamics in panic disorders and borderline personality disorders", *Personlichkeitsstorungen: Theorie and Therapie*, 7: 235–44.

Benecke, C., Peham, D. and Banninger-Huber, E. (2005) "Nonverbal relationship regulation in psychotherapy", *Psychotherapy Research*, 15: 81–90.

Blake, W. (c. 1816–20) Mirth, the Great Sun, the Lark, *Illustrations to Milton's L'Allegro and Il Penseroso and Descriptions of L'Allegro and Il Penseroso Designs*, 24 objects. New York: The Pierpont Morgan Library, photographic credit.

Bower, H. (1989) "Beethoven's creative illness", *Australian and New Zealand Journal of Psychiatry*, 23: 111–16.

Bradway, K. and McCoard, B. (1997) *Sandplay – Silent Workshop of the Psyche*. London: Routledge.

Breggin, P. (2001) "Fluvoxamine as a cause of stimulation of mania and aggression with a critical analysis of the FDA-approved label", *International Journal of Risk & Safety in Medicine*, 14: 71–86.

Briggs, B. and Blevins, J. (1999) "A boy with many sides", *Denver Post*, 2 May 1999.

Brooke, J. (1999) "Teacher of Colorado gunmen alerted parents", *New York Times*, 11 May.

Brown, B. and Merritt, R. (2002) *No Easy Answers: The Truth Behind Death at Columbine*. New York: Lantern Books.

Burton, R. (1621) *The Anatomy of Melancholy*, F. Dell and P. Jordan-Smith eds. New York: Farrar & Rinehart, 1927.

Carlson, R. (1995) "Silvan Tomkins's legacy: a grand theory of personality", *Exploring Affect: The Selected Writings of Silvan S. Tomkins*, E. V. Demos (ed.). New York: Cambridge University Press.

Cassirer, E. (1957) *The Philosophy of Symbolic Forms*, vol. 3: *The Phenomenology of Knowledge*. New Haven, CT: Yale University Press.

Chodorow, J. (1997) *Jung on Active Imagination*. London: Routledge.

Columbine Report (2000) "Glimpses of Klebold and Harris", Jefferson County Sheriff's Office (released 15 May 2000), http://www.cnn.com/SPECIALS/2000/columbine.cd/Pages/SUSPECTS_TEXT.htm (accessed 29 June 2006).

Columbine Report (2006) "Columbine documents", Jefferson County Sheriff's Office, "Columbine Documents", JC-001–025923 through JC-001–026859: 946 pages (released 6 July 2006), http://www.wcsh6.com/news/article.aspx?storyid=38029 (accessed 15 July 2006).

Crimmins, S. (1993) "Parricide vs. suicide: the dilemma of them or me", in A. V. Wilson (ed.) *Homicide The Victim/Offender Connection*. Cincinnati, OH: Anderson Publishing Company.

Davis, M. E. and Wallbridge, D. (1981) *Boundary and Space*. New York: Brunner/Mazel.

Demos, E. V. (1989a) "A prospective constructionist view of development", *Annual of Psychoanalysis*, 17: 287–309.

—— (1989b) "Resiliency in infancy", in T. F. Dugan and R. Coles (eds) *The Child in Our Times: Studies in the Development of Resiliency*. New York: Brunner/Mazel.

Demos, E. V. and Kaplan, S. (1986) "Motivation and affect reconsidered: affect biographies of two infants", *Psychoanalysis and Contemporary Thought*, 9: 147–221.

Dreher, M., Mengele, U., and Krause, R. (2001) "Affective indicators of the psychotherapeutic process; and empirical case study", *Psychotherapy Research*, 11: 99–117.

Ekman, P. (1994) "Strong evidence for universals in facial expressions: a reply to Russell's mistaken critique", *Psychological Bulletin*, 115: 268–87.

Ekman, P. and Friesen, W. V. (1982) "Felt, false, and miserable smiles", *Journal of Nonverbal Behavior*, 6(4): 238–52.

Eliot, G. (1861) *Silas Marner*. New York: Bantam Books, 1981.

Ellenberger, H. F. (1968) "The concept of creative illness", *Psychoanalytic Review*, 55: 442–56.

Erikson, E. H. (1959) "Identity and the life cycle", *Psychological Issues*, 1, Monograph 1. New York: International Universities Press.

Escoffier, J. and Lore, M. (eds) (2001) Mark Morris' *L'allegro, il penseroso ed il moderato: A Celebration*. New York: Marlowe & Company.

Fowler, J. C., Hilsenroth, M. J., and Piers, C. (2001) "An empirical study of seriously disturbed suicidal patients", *Journal of the American Psychoanalytic Association*, 49: 161–86.

Gardiner, M. (1985) *The Deadly Innocents: Portraits of Children Who Kill*. Preface by S. Spender, 1976. New Haven, CT: Yale University Press.

Garfield, D. A. S. (1995) *Unbearable Affect: A Guide to the Psychotherapy of Psychosis*. New York: Wiley.

Gibbs, N. and Roche, T. (1999) "The Columbine tapes", *Time*, 20 December.

Goldwert, M. (1992) *The Wounded Healers: Creative Illness in the Pioneers of Depth Psychology*. Lanham, MD: University Press of America.

Gould, S. J. (1977) *Ontogeny and Phylogeny*. Cambridge, MA: The Belknap Press of Harvard University Press.

—— (1981) *The Mismeasure of Man*. New York: W. W. Norton.

Graves, R. (1960) *The Greek Myths*, vol. 2, revised edition. New York: Penguin Books.

Gregor, I. (1974) *The Great Web: The Form of Hardy's Major Fiction*. London: Faber & Faber.

Guntrip, H. (1969) *Schizoid Phenomena: Object-relations and the Self*. New York: International Universities Press.

Hammer, J. (1998) "Kid is out of control" (alleged teenage killer Kip Kinkel), *Newsweek*, 131 (8 June): 32.

Hardy, T. (1895) *Jude the Obscure*. New York: The Modern Library.

Harper's Magazine (2002) "As you were" (last wishes) (excerpt from Columbine killer Eric Harris's journal), v. 304, 14 February.

Harris, E. (1997) Web page, 1997 documents, Jefferson County Sheriff's Office, Golden, CO, released 29 October 2003.

Harris, E. (1998) Web page, 1998 documents, Jefferson County Sheriff's Office, Golden, CO, released 29 October 2003.

Haviland, J. M. and Lelwica, M. (1987) "The induced affect response: 10-week-old infants' responses to three emotional expressions", *Developmental Psychology*, 23, 97–104.

Heide, K. M. (1993) "Adolescent parricide offenders: synthesis, illustration and future directions", in A. V. Wilson (ed.) *Homicide: The Victim/Offender Connection*. Cincinnati, OH: Anderson Publishing.

Henderson, J. L. (1984) *Cultural Attitudes in Psychological Perspective*. Toronto: Inner City Books.

Hill, G. (ed.) (1981) *Sandplay Studies: Origins, Theory and Practice*. San Francisco: C. G. Jung Institute of San Francisco.

Hillman, J. (1975) *Re-Visioning Psychology*. New York: Harper & Row.

—— (1985) *Anima: The Anatomy of a Personified Notion*. Dallas, TX: Spring Publications.

—— (1992) *Emotion: A Comprehensive Phenomenology of Theories and their Meanings for Therapy*. Evanston, IL: Northwestern University Press.

Holden, R. R., Mehta, K., Cunningham, E. J., and McLeod, L. D. (2001)

"Development and preliminary validation of a scale of psychache", *Canadian Journal of Behavioural Science*, 33: 224–32.

Hurvich, M., Benveniste, P., Howard, J., and Coonerty, S. (1993) "Assessment of annihilation anxiety from projective tests", *Perceptual and Motor Skills*, 77: 387–401.

Hussain, S. A. and Vandiver, T. (1984) *Suicide in Children and Adolescents*. New York: SP Medical & Scientific Books.

Izard, C. (1994) "Innate and universal facial expressions: evidence from developmental and cross-cultural research", *Psychological Bulletin*, 115: 288–99.

Jacobi, J. (1959) *Complex/Archetype/Symbol*. Princeton, NJ: Princeton University Press.

—— (1973) *The Psychology of C. G. Jung*, 8th edition. New Haven, CT: Yale University Press.

James, W. (1902) *The Varieties of Religious Experience*. New York: The Modern Library.

Jung, C. G. (1936–7) *Children's Dreams and Older Books on Dream Interpretation*, Prof. Dr. C. G. Jung at the Eidgenossiche Technische Hochshcule, H. H. Baumann, ed. Zurich.

—— (1938–9) *Psychological Interpretation of Children's Dreams*, notes on lectures given by Prof. Dr. C. G. Jung at the Eidgenossiche Technische Hochshcule, L. Frey and R. Scharf, eds. Zurich.

—— (1954) *The Development of Personality, Collected Works* 17, 3rd printing, with additional corrections. Princeton, NJ: Princeton University Press.

—— (1960) *The Psychogenesis of Mental Disease, Collected Works* 3, 2nd printing, with corrections and minor revisions. Princeton, NJ: Princeton University Press.

—— (1961a) *Memories, Dreams, Reflections*, A. Jaffe, ed. New York: Pantheon Books.

—— (1961b) *Freud and Psychoanalysis, Collected Works* 4, 2nd printing, with corrections. Princeton, NJ: Princeton University Press.

—— (1966) *The Practice of Psychotherapy, Collected Works* 16, 2nd edition, rev. and aug., 3rd printing, with corrections. Princeton, NJ: Princeton University Press.

—— (1967) *Symbols of Transformation, Collected Works* 5. Princeton, NJ: Princeton University Press.

—— (1968a) *Psychology and Alchemy, Collected Works* 12, 2nd edition, completely revised. Princeton, NJ: Princeton University Press.

—— (1968b) *Alchemical Studies, Collected Works* 13. Princeton, NJ: Princeton University Press.

—— (1969a) *The Archetypes of the Collective Unconscious, Collected Works* 9i, 2nd edition. Princeton, NJ: Princeton University Press.

—— (1969b) *Aion, Collected Works* 9ii, 2nd edition, with corrections and minor revisions. Princeton, NJ: Princeton University Press.

—— (1970a) *Psychiatric Studies, Collected Works* 1, 2nd edition. Princeton, NJ: Princeton University Press.

—— (1970b) *The Structure and Dynamics of the Psyche, Collected Works* 8, 2nd edition. Princeton, NJ: Princeton University Press

—— (1970c) *Civilization in Transition, Collected Works* 10. Princeton, NJ: Princeton University Press.

—— (1970d) *Psychology and Religion: West and East, Collected Works* 11, 2nd edition. Princeton, NJ: Princeton University Press.

—— (1970e) *Mysterium Coniunctionis, Collected Works* 14, 2nd edition. Princeton, NJ: Princeton University Press.

—— (1971) *Psychological Types, Collected Works* 6, 2nd printing. Princeton, NJ: Princeton University Press.

—— (1972) *Two Essays on Analytical Psychology, Collected Works* 7, 2nd edition, rev. and aug., paperback printing. Princeton, NJ: Princeton University Press.

—— (1973a) *Experimental Researches, Collected Works* 2. Princeton, NJ: Princeton University Press.

—— (1973b) *Letters*, vol. 1: 1906–1950, G. Adler, ed. Princeton, NJ: Princeton University Press.

—— (1975) *Letters*, vol. 2: 1951–1961, G. Adler, ed. Princeton, NJ: Princeton University Press.

—— (1976) *The Vision Seminars*, Book 2. Zurich: Spring Publications.

—— (1977) *The Symbolic Life, Collected Works* 18. Princeton, NJ: Princeton University Press.

—— (1984) *Dream Analysis Notes of the Seminars Given in 1928–1930*, W. McGuire, ed. Princeton, NJ: Princeton University Press.

—— (1988) Nietzsche's *Zarathustra*, notes on the seminar given in 1934–1939 by C. G. Jung, J. L. Jarrett, ed., vol. 2. Princeton, NJ: Princeton University Press.

Kalff, D. M. (1971) *Sandplay*. San Francisco: Browser Press.

Kienhorst, I. C. W. M., De Wilde, E. J., Diekstra, R. F., and Wolters, W. H. G. (1995) "Adolescents' image of their suicide attempt", *Journal of the American Academy of Child and Adolescent Psychiatry*, 34, 623–28.

King, P. and Murr, A. (1998) "A son who spun out of control (teenager Kip Kinkel, kills his parents and classmates in Springfield, Oregon)", *Newsweek*: 131, 1 June: 32.

Kirk, M. and Boyer, P. J. (2000a) "The killer at Thurston High", *Frontline (PBS), WGBH, Educational Television*, Boston, MA (aired 18 January 2000).

—— (2000a) "Transcript", 1–40, http://www.pbs.org/wgbh/pages/frontline/shows/kinkel/etc/tapes.html (accessed 30 June 2006).

—— (2000b) "Chronology", 1–17, http://www.pbs.org/wgbh/pages/frontline/shows/kinkel/kip/cron.html (accessed 30 June 2006).

—— (2000c) "Transcript of Kip Kinkel's confession", 1–22, http://www.pbs.org/wgbh/pages/frontline/shows/kinkel/etc/confesst.html (accessed 30 June 2006).

—— (2000d) "Kip's writings and statements", 1–6, http://www.pbs.org/wgbh/pages/frontline/shows/kinkel/kip/writings.html (accessed 30 June 2006).

—— (2000e) "Interview with Kristin Kinkel", 1–17, http://www.pbs.org/wgbh/pages/frontline/shows/kinkel/kip/kristin.html (accessed 30 June 2006).

—— (2000f) "Dr. Hick's Treatment Notes on Kip Kinkel", 1–8, http://www.pbs.org/wgbh/pages/frontline/shows/kinkel/trial/hnotes.html (accessed 30 June 2006).

—— (2000g) "Dr. Orin Bolstad's testimony", 1–48, http://www.pbs.org/wgbh/pages/frontline/shows/kinkel/trial/bolstad.html (accessed 30 June 2006).

Kohut, H. (1977) *The Restoration of the Self*. New York: International Universities Press.

Krause, R. and Merten, J. (1999) "Affects, regulation of relationship, transference and countertransference", *International Forum of Psychoanalysis*, 8: 103–14.

Laing, R. D. (1969) *Self and Others*, 2nd edition. London: Tavistock Publications.

Landau, A.T. (2003) "The impulse to destroy in Thomas Hardy's *Jude the Obscure*", in J. Beebe (ed.) *Terror, Violence and the Impulse to Destroy: Perspectives from Analytical Psychology*, papers from the 2002 North American Conference of Jungian Analysts and Candidates. Daimon Verlag.

Lavergne, G. M. (1977) *A Sniper in the Tower*. New York: Bantam Books.

Leenaars, A. A., Lester, D., and Heim, N. (1996) "Menninger's motives for suicide notes from Germany and the USA", *Crisis: The Journal of Crisis Intervention and Suicide Prevention*, 17: 87.

Lester, D. (1997) "Menninger's motives for suicide in suicide notes from America and Germany", *Perceptual and Motor Skills*, 85: 1194.

Lorenz, K. (1976) "Psychology and phylogeny", in J. S. Bruner, A. Jolly, and K. Sylva (eds) *Play: Its Role in Development and Evolution*. New York: Basic Books.

Lowe, P. (1999a) "Killers' hatred shows in vitriolic 'film festival' ", *Denver Post*, 14 December.

Lowe, P. (1999b) "Suicide tapes transcript", *Denver Post*, 21 December 1999.

Lynd, H. M. (1958) *On Shame and the Search for Identity*. New York: Harcourt, Brace & World.

McCully, R. S. (1978) "The laugh of Satan: a study of a familial murderer", *Journal of Personality Assessment*, 14: 81–91.

McGuire, D. (1982) "The problem of children's suicide: ages 5–14", *International Journal of Offender Therapy and Comparative Criminology*, 26: 10–17.

Mack, J. E. and Hickler, H. (1981) *Vivienne: The Life and Suicide of an Adolescent Girl*. Boston, MA: Little, Brown & Company.

MacLean, P. D. (1993) "Cerebral Evolution of Emotion", in M. Lewis and J. Haviland (eds) *Handbook of Emotions*. New York: The Guilford Press.

Malatesta, C. Z. (1985) "Developmental course of emotion expression in the human infant", in G. Zivin (ed.) *The Development of Expressive Behavior: Biology, Environment, Interaction*. New York: Academic Press.

Malatesta, C. Z. and Haviland, J. M. (1982) "Learning display rules: the socialization of emotion expression in infancy", *Child Development*, 53: 991–1003.

Maltsberger, J. T. (2004) "The descent into suicide", *International Journal of Psychoanalysis*, 85: 653–68.

Mastropieri, D. and Turkewitz, G. (1999) "Prenatal experience and neonatal responsiveness to vocal expressions of emotion", *Developmental Psychobiology*, 35: 204–14.

Merten, J. (2005) "Facial microbehavior and the emotional quality of the therapeutic relationship", *Psychotherapy Research*, 15(3): 325–33.

Merten, J. and Krause, R. (2003) "What makes good therapists fail?", in P. Philippott (ed.) *Nonverbal Behavior in Clinical Settings*. London: Oxford University Press.

Merten, J., Anstadt, Th., Ullrich, B., Krause, R., and Buchheim, P. (1996) "Emotional experience and facial behavior during the psychotherapeutic process and its relation to treatment outcome: a pilot study", *Psychotherapy Research*, 6: 198–212.

Mill, J. S. (1924) *Autobiography of John Stuart Mill*. New York: Columbia University Press, 1960.

Milton, J. (1971) *The Complete Poetry of John Milton*, by John T. Shawcross, revised edition. Garden City, New York: Anchor Books/Doubleday.

Moskowitz, A. (2004) "Dissociation and violence: A review of the literature", *Trauma, Violence, & Abuse*, 5: 21–46.

Muchielli, R. (1970) *Introduction to Structural Psychology*. New York: Funk & Wagnalls.

Neumann, E. (1990) *The Child*. Boston, MA: Shambhala Publications.

Obmascik, M., Simpson, K., and Oulton, S. (2000) "Parents blindsided by plot", *Denver Post*, 22 November.

Orbach, I. (2003) "Mental pain and suicide", *Israel Journal of Psychiatry and Related Science*, 40: 191–201.

Otto, R. (1923) *The Idea of the Holy: An Inquiry into the Non-rational Factor in the Idea of the Divine and its Relation to the Rational*. New York: A Galaxy Book, Oxford University Press, 1958.

Pankratz, H. and Mitchell, K. (1999) "Pair got glowing DA report", *Denver Post*, 23 April.

Panksepp, J. (1998) "Attention deficit hyperactivity disorders, psychostimulants, and intolerance of childhood play", *Current Directions in Psychological Science*, 7: 91–7.

—— (2000) "Affective consciousness and the instinctual motor system: the neural sources of sadness and joy", in R. D. Ellis and N. Newton (eds) *The Caldron of Consciousness: Motivation, Affect and Self-organization – An Anthology*, Amsterdam. Netherlands: John Benjamins.

—— (2002) "On the animalian values of the human spirit: the foundational role of affect in psychotherapy and the evolution of consciousness", *European Journal of Psychotherapy, Counseling & Health*, 5: 225–45.

Papousek, M. and Papousek, H. (1981) "Musical elements in the infant's vocalization: their significance for communication, cognition, and creativity", in L. P. Lipsitt and C. K. Rovee-Collier (eds) *Advances in Infancy Research*, vol. 1, Norwood, NJ: Ablex.

Perry, J. W. (1986) "Spiritual emergence and renewal", *ReVISION*, 8:33–8, special issue: The psychotic experience: disease or evolutionary crisis?

Pfeffer, C. (1986) *The Suicidal Child*. New York: The Guilford Press.

Piaget, J. (1927) "The first year of life", in H. E. Gruber and J. J. Voneche (eds) *The Essential Piaget*. New York: Basic Books, 1977.

—— (1952) *The Origins of Intelligence in Children*. New York: International Universities Press.

—— (1954) *Construction of Reality in the Child*. New York: Basic Books.

—— (1962) *Play, Dreams and Imitation in Childhood*. New York: W.W. Norton.

—— (1967) *Six Psychological Studies*. New York: Random House.

—— (1971) *Biology and Knowledge: An Essay on the Relations between Organic Regulations and Cognitive Processes*. Chicago: University of Chicago Press.

—— (1978) *Behavior and Evolution*. New York: Pantheon Books.

—— (1980) *Adaptation and Intelligence, Organic Selection and Phenocopy*. Chicago: University of Chicago Press.

Portmann, A. (1954) "Biology and the phenomenon of the spiritual", in J. Campbell (ed.) *Spirit and Nature: Papers from the Eranos Yearbooks*, vol. 1. Princeton, NJ: Princeton University Press.

—— (1990) *A Zoologist Looks at Humankind*. New York: Columbia University Press.

Provence, S. and Lipton, R. C. (1962) *Infants in Institutions: A Comparison of their Development with Family-reared Infants During the First Year of Life*. New York: International Universities Press.

Reichard, S. and Tillman, C. (1950) "Murder and suicide as defenses against schizo-phrenic psychosis", *Journal of Clinical Psychopathology*, 11: 149–63.

Reynolds, P. C. (1976) "Play, language and human evolution", in J. Bruner, A. Jolly and K. Sylva (eds) *Play: Its Role in Development and Evolution*. New York: Basic Books.

—— (1981) *On the Evolution of Human Behavior: The Argument from Animals to Man*. Berkeley, CA: University of California Press.

Rogers, P. (1998) "Mortal lessons (Oregon student Kris (*sic*) Kinkel, who allegedly killed classmates and parents)", *People Weekly*, 49 (June 8): 64.

Roth, P. (2005) " 'I Got a Scheme!" The words of Saul Bellow, *The New Yorker*, 81(10), 25 April: 72–85.

Samuels, A., Shorter, B., and Plaut, F. (1986) *A Critical Dictionary of Jungian Analy-sis*. London: Routledge & Kegan Paul.

Seibert, T. (1999) "Harris, Klebold tapes chilling", *Denver Post*, 13 December 1999.

Semrad, E. (1969) "A clinical formulation of the psychoses", in E. Semrad and D. Van Buskirk (eds) *Teaching Psychotherapy of Psychotic Patients*. New York: Grune & Stratton.

Shapiro, V., Fraiberg, S., and Adelson, E. (1980) "Billy: infant-parent psychotherapy on behalf of a child in a critical nutritional state", in S. Fraiberg (ed.) *Clinical Studies in Infant Mental Health*. New York: Basic Books.

Shneidman, E. (1989) "Overview: a multidimensional approach to suicide", in D. Jacobs and H. N. Brown (eds) *Suicide: Understanding and Responding*. Madison, CT: International Universities Press.

—— (1993) *Suicide as Psychache: A Clinical Approach to Suicidal Behaviour*. North-vale, NJ: Jason Aronson.

—— (1999) "The psychological pain assessment scale", *Suicide and Life-Threatening Behavior*, 29(4): 287–94.

Simpson, K. and Blevins, J. (1999) "They killed 12 students and one teacher and wounded 23 before killing themselves", *Denver Post*, 23 April.

Singer, T and Kimbles, S. L. (2004) *The Cultural Complex: Contemporary Jungian Perspectives on Psyche and Society*. New York: Brunner-Routledge.

Slaby, A. E. and Garfinkel, L. F. (1994) *No One Saw My Pain: Why Teens Kill Them-selves*. New York: W.W. Norton & Company.

Smith, H. (1995) "Analytic listening and the experience of surprise", *International Journal of Psycho-Analysis*, 76: 67–78.

Snyder, F. (1966) "Toward an evolutionary theory of dreaming", *American Journal of Psychiatry*, 123: 121–36.

Sophocles (442–1 BC) "Ajax", in D. Grene and R. Lattimore (eds) *The Complete Greek Tragedies*, vol. II. Chicago: University of Chicago Press.

Spitz, R. (1946a) "Hospitalism: a follow-up report", *The Psychoanalytic Study of the Child*, II: 113–17.

—— (1946b) "Anaclitic depression", *The Psychoanalytic Study of the Child*, II: 313–42.

—— (1951) "The psychogenic diseases of infancy: an attempt at their etiologic clas-sification", *The Psychoanalytic Study of the Child*, VI: 255–75.

—— (1965) *The First Year of Life: A Psychoanalytic Study of Normal and Deviant Development of Object Relations*. New York: International Universities Press.

Stern, D. (1977) *The First Relationship*. Cambridge, MA: Harvard University Press.

Stewart, C. T. (2001) *The Symbolic Impetus: How Creative Fantasy Motivates Development*. London: Free Association Books.

Stewart, L. H. (1977) "Sand play therapy: Jungian technique", in B. Wolman (ed.) *International Encyclopedia of Psychiatry, Psychology, Psychoanalysis and Neurology*. New York: Aesculapius Publishers.

—— (1981) "The play-dream continuum and the categories of the imagination", presented at the seventh annual conference of The Association for the Anthropological Study of Play (TAASP), Fort Worth, April 1981.

—— (1984) "The dialectic of play and curiosity", *Affects and Archetypes I and II*, paper presented at active imagination seminar in Geneva, Switzerland, August 1984.

—— (1987a) "A brief report: affect and archetype", *Journal of Analytical Psychology*, 32: 35–46.

—— (1987b) "Affect and archetype in analysis", in N. Schwart-Salant and M. Stein (eds) *Archetypal Processes in Psychotherapy*. Wilmette, IL: Chiron Publications.

—— (1988) "Jealousy and envy: complex family emotions", in L. H. Stewart and J. Chodorow (eds) *The Family: Personal, Cultural and Archetypal Dimensions*. Boston, MA: Sigo Press.

—— (1991) "Individuation", unpublished manuscript.

—— (1992) *Changemakers: A Jungian Perspective on Sibling Position and the Family Atmosphere*. New York: Routledge.

Stewart, L. H. and Stewart, C. T. (1981) "Play, games and affects: a contribution toward a comprehensive theory of play", in A. T. Cheska (ed.) *Play as Context*. West Point, New York: Leisure Press.

Styron, W. (1990) *Darkness Visible*. New York: Random House.

Thernstrom, M. (1997) *Halfway Heaven: Diary of a Harvard Murder*, New York: Doubleday.

Tomkins, S. S. (1962) *Affect Imagery Consciousness*, vol. I, *The Positive Affects*. New York: Springer.

—— (1963) *Affect Imagery Consciousness*, vol. II, *The Negative Affects*. New York: Springer.

—— (1991) *Affect Imagery Consciousness*, vol. III, *The Negative Affects Anger and Fear*. New York: Springer.

—— (1995a) "The socialization of affect and the resultant ideo-affective postures which evoke resonance to the ideological polarity", in E. V. Demos (ed.) *Exploring Affect: The Selected Writings of Silvan S. Tomkins*. New York: Cambridge University Press.

—— (1995b) "Script theory", in E. V. Demos (ed.) *Exploring Affect: The Selected Writings of Silvan S. Tomkins*. New York: Cambridge University Press.

Tuve, R. (1957) *Images & Themes in Five Poems by Milton*. Cambridge, MA: Harvard University.

Verlinden, S., Hersen, M., and Thomas, J. (2000) "Risk factors in school shootings", *Clinical Psychology Review*, 20: 3–56.

Vaughan, K. and Kass, J. (2003) "Police release more Columbine writings", *Scripps-McClatchy Western Service*, 9 January.

Wanamaker, M. (1999) "William Styron and the literature of early maternal loss", *Psychoanalytic Review*, 86: 403–32.

Werner, H. (1957) *Comparative Psychology of Mental Development*, rev. edition. New York: International Universities Press.

Williams, A. H. (1995) "Murderousness in relationship to psychotic breakdown (madness)", in J. Ellwood (ed.) *Psychosis: Understanding and Treatment*. London: Jessica Kingsley.

Wilson, A. (1986) "Archaic transference and anaclitic depression: psychoanalytic perspectives on the treatment of severely disturbed patients", *Psychoanalytic Psychology*, 3: 237–56.

Winnicott, D. W. (1971) *Playing & Reality*. New York: Routledge.

—— (1977) *The Piggle*. New York: International Universities Press.

—— (1986) "Death and murder in the adolescent process", in C. Winnicott, R. Shepherd, and M. Davis (eds) *Home Is Where We Start From*. New York: W.W. Norton.

Index